Policy Agendas in British Politics

Comparative Studies of Political Agendas Series

Series editors
Frank R. Baumgartner is the Richard J. Richardson Distinguished Professor of Political Science at the University of North Carolina at Chapel Hill, USA
Laura Chaques, Associate Professor of Political Science, University of Barcelona and research fellow at the Institut Barcelona d'Estudis Internacionals (IBEI), Spain
Christoffer Green-Pedersen, Professor, Aarhus University, Denmark
Arco Timmermans, Research Director, Montesquieu Institute, The Hague, and Associate Professor of Comparative Public Policy, Institute of Public Administration, Leiden University, Belgium
Frederic Varone, Professor of Political Science, University of Geneva, Switzerland

The series publishes books on policy agenda-setting dynamics broadly understood. This includes, for instance, books dealing with the policy effects of agenda dynamics, the relationship between the political agenda, public opinion and the media agenda, and agenda dynamics in relation to particular issues. The series publishes both comparative books and books dealing with single countries if these single countries are placed in a comparative context. The books can be either monographs or edited volumes.

Titles include:

Isabelle Engeli, Christoffer Green-Pedersen and Lars Thorup Larsen (*editors*)
MORALITY POLITICS IN WESTERN EUROPE
Parties, Agendas and Policy Choices

Peter John, Anthony Bertelli, Will Jennings and Shaun Bevan
POLICY AGENDAS IN BRITISH POLITICS

Comparative Studies of Political Agendas Series
Series Standing Order ISBN 978–0–230–35977–2 (Hardback)
978–0–230–35978–9 (Paperback)
(*outside North America only*)

You can receive future titles in this series as they are published by placing a standing order. Please contact your bookseller or, in case of difficulty, write to us at the address below with your name and address, the title of the series and the ISBNs quoted above.

Customer Services Department, Macmillan Distribution Ltd, Houndmills, Basingstoke, Hampshire RG21 6XS, England

Policy Agendas in British Politics

Peter John
*Professor of Political Science and Public Policy,
School of Public Policy, University College London, UK*

Anthony Bertelli
Professor of Public Policy, Political Science and Law and C.C. Crawford Chair in Management and Performance at the University of Southern California. He is also Professor of Public Policy Analysis at the University of Birmingham

Will Jennings
Reader in Politics, University of Southampton, UK and Research Associate, Centre for Analysis of Risk and Regulation, London School of Economics, UK

Shaun Bevan
Research Fellow at the Mannheim Centre for European Social Research (MZES), University of Mannheim, Germany

palgrave
macmillan

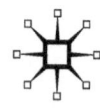

© Peter John, Anthony Bertelli, Will Jennings and Shaun Bevan 2013

All rights reserved. No reproduction, copy or transmission of this publication may be made without written permission.

No portion of this publication may be reproduced, copied or transmitted save with written permission or in accordance with the provisions of the Copyright, Designs and Patents Act 1988, or under the terms of any licence permitting limited copying issued by the Copyright Licensing Agency, Saffron House, 6–10 Kirby Street, London EC1N 8TS.

Any person who does any unauthorized act in relation to this publication may be liable to criminal prosecution and civil claims for damages.

The authors have asserted their rights to be identified as the authors of this work in accordance with the Copyright, Designs and Patents Act 1988.

First published 2013 by
PALGRAVE MACMILLAN

Palgrave Macmillan in the UK is an imprint of Macmillan Publishers Limited, registered in England, company number 785998, of Houndmills, Basingstoke, Hampshire RG21 6XS.

Palgrave Macmillan in the US is a division of St Martin's Press LLC, 175 Fifth Avenue, New York, NY 10010.

Palgrave Macmillan is the global academic imprint of the above companies and has companies and representatives throughout the world.

Palgrave® and Macmillan® are registered trademarks in the United States, the United Kingdom, Europe and other countries.

ISBN 978–0–230–39039–3 hardback
ISBN 978–0–230–39042–3 paperback

This book is printed on paper suitable for recycling and made from fully managed and sustained forest sources. Logging, pulping and manufacturing processes are expected to conform to the environmental regulations of the country of origin.

A catalogue record for this book is available from the British Library.

A catalog record for this book is available from the Library of Congress.

Contents

List of Figures and Tables vi

Preface and Acknowledgements x

1 The Policy Agenda and British Politics 1
2 Policy-Making and British Politics 23
3 Measuring the Policy Agenda: Policy, Public and Media in Britain 41
4 Change and Stability in Executive and Legislative Agendas 55
5 Policy Punctuations 94
6 Structural Shifts in British Political Attention 114
7 Public Opinion and the Policy Agenda 130
8 The Media 153
9 Budgets and Policy Implementation 168
10 Conclusion 199

Notes 209
References 215
Author Index 231
Subject Index 235

Figures and Tables

Figures

3.1	Number of sentences in the Speech from the Throne	47
3.2	Number of Acts of the UK Parliament	49
4.1	Incrementalism in macroeconomy in speeches and laws, 1945–2008	58
4.2	Focused adaptation in international affairs and foreign aid in speeches and laws, 1945–2008	61
4.3	Punctuations and focused adaptation in attention to defence in speeches and laws, 1945–2008	63
4.4	Punctuation, focused adaptation and issue attention cycle in government operations in speeches and laws, 1945–2008	66
4.5	Focused adaptation and issue attention cycles in attention to law, crime and the family in speeches and laws, 1945–2008	68
4.6	Focused adaptation in attention to health in speeches and laws, 1945–2008	70
4.7	Issue attention cycles in attention to education in speeches and laws, 1945–2008	72
4.8	Issue attention cycles and focused adaptation in attention to social welfare in speeches and laws, 1945–2008	74
4.9	Incrementalism in attention to housing and community development in speeches and laws, 1945–2008	76
4.10	Issue attention cycles and incrementalism in attention to transport in speeches and laws, 1945–2008	78
4.11	Issue attention cycles in attention to the environment in speeches and laws, 1945–2008	80
4.12	Focused adaptation in attention to public lands (territorial issues) in speeches and laws, 1945–2008	81
4.13	Focused adaptation in attention to agriculture in speeches and laws, 1945–2008	83
4.14	Incrementalism in attention to energy in speeches and laws, 1945–2008	85

List of Figures and Tables vii

4.15	Issue attention cycles in attention to civil rights, minority issues, immigration and civil liberties in speeches and laws, 1945–2008	86
4.16	Incrementalism in labour and employment in speeches and laws, 1945–2008	88
4.17	Issue attention cycles in attention to banking in speeches and laws, 1945–2008	89
4.18	Incrementalism in attention to science in speeches and laws, 1945–2008	90
4.19	Focused adaptation in attention to foreign trade in speeches and laws, 1945–2008	91
5.1	Frequency distribution of annual percentage change in the Speech from the Throne	98
5.2	Frequency distribution of annual percentage change in Acts of Parliament	98
6.1	Likely change points, Speeches from the Throne, 1946–2008	117
6.2	Likely change points in Acts of Parliament	122
6.A1	Scatter plot of macroeconomic topics in Acts of Parliament	128
6.A2	The posterior mean and probabilities of a change point	129
7.1	The public agenda and problem recognition: defence	132
7.2	The public agenda and problem recognition: international affairs	133
7.3	The public agenda and problem recognition: macroeconomics	134
7.4	Long-term change and the public agenda: crime	135
7.5	Long-term change and the public agenda: health	136
7.6	Long-term change and the public agenda: education	136
7.7	Long-term change and the public agenda: immigration	137
7.8	Patterns in the public agenda: labour and employment	138
7.9	Patterns in the public agenda: environment	139
7.10	Patterns in the public agenda: energy	139
7.11	Mean levels of issue importance between 1960 and 2008	141
7.12	The policy–opinion link: macroeconomics	142
7.13	The policy–opinion link: defence	143
7.14	The policy–opinion link: international affairs	143
7.15	The policy–opinion link: health	144
7.16	The policy–opinion link: education	144
7.17	The policy–opinion link: welfare	145
7.18	The policy–opinion link: housing	145

viii List of Figures and Tables

7.19	The policy–opinion link: immigration	146
7.20	The policy–opinion link: law and crime	147
7.21	Average MIP-topic correlations, by policy-making arena (1960–2008)	149
7.22	Likely change points in public opinion	150
8.1	Quarterly *The Times* domestic and international headlines	155
8.2	Quarterly *The Times* policy and non-policy headlines	156
8.3	Quarterly *The Times* headlines by policy area	158
8.4	Yearly economic attention, media, Speech from the Throne and Acts of Parliament, 1960–2008	161
8.5	Yearly defence attention: media, Speech from the Throne and Acts of Parliament, 1960–2008	162
8.6	Likely change points for the media, 1960–2008	164
9.1	Percentage of public expenditure and the Speech from the Throne on the macroeconomy, 1951–2007	172
9.2	Percentage of public expenditure and the Speech from the Throne on defence	173
9.3	Percentage of public expenditure and the Speech from the Throne on law and crime	175
9.4	Percentage of public expenditure and the Speech from the Throne on health	175
9.5	Percentage of public expenditure and the Speech from the Throne on education	176
9.6	Percentage of public expenditure and the Speech from the Throne on social welfare	178
9.7	Percentage of public expenditure and the Speech from the Throne on community development, planning and housing issues	179
9.8	Percentage of public expenditure and the Speech from the Throne on transport, 1951–1989	180
9.9	Percentage of public expenditure and the Speech from the Throne on agriculture, 1951–1989	181
9.10	Policy agendas for the macroeconomy, 1951–2007	182
9.11	Policy agendas for defence, 1951–2007	183
9.12	Policy agendas for the law and crime, 1951–2007	184
9.13	Policy agendas for health, 1951–2007	185
9.14	Policy agendas for education, 1951–2007	186
9.15	Policy agendas for social welfare, 1951–2007	187
9.16	Policy agendas for community development, planning and housing issues, 1951–2007	188

9.17	Policy agendas for transport, 1951–2007	188
9.18	Policy agendas for agriculture, 1951–2007	189
9.19	Frequency distribution of annual percentage changes in the Speech from the Throne and Acts of Parliament	190
9.20	Likely change points in budgetary expenditure	192

Tables

2.1	Summary of accounts of British policy-making	37
2.2	Instability and stability of attention and institutions—accounts of British politics	37
2.3	Instability and stability of attention and institutions—possible expectations of models of decision-making	38
3.1	UK policy agendas major topic codes and abbreviations	42
3.2	Summary of UK Policy Agendas Project datasets	46
4.1	Summary statistics of speech policy topic attention by year, 1945–2008	57
4.2	Summary statistics of acts policy topic attention by year, 1945–2008	57
5.1	Change in percentage attention to speeches and laws	99
5.2	Policy punctuations in the Speech from the Throne, 1945–2008	100
5.3	Policy punctuations in Acts of UK Parliament, 1945–2008	103
5.4	Types of punctuations	106
5.5	List of identified act punctuations by issue, 1945–2008	107
5.6	High-salience punctuations in acts	110
7.1	Summary statistics of public opinion policy topic percentage by year, 1960–2008	141
8.1	Summary statistics of media policy topic attention by quarter, 1960–2008	160
8.A1	UK Policy Agendas Project media dataset major topic codes	167
9.1	Summary statistics of budgetary expenditure in billions by policy topic, 1951–2007	171
9.2	Policy punctuations in UK budgets, 1951–2007	191

Preface and Acknowledgements

In his speech to the 1996 Labour Party Conference, the leader of the Opposition, Tony Blair, declared, 'Ask me my three main priorities for government, and I tell you: education, education, education.'[1] This sound bite became famous in subsequent years for representing the 'New Labour' brand of that time. Blair's slogan signalled that the Labour Party had decided to focus on this key issue—and on other public services, such as the National Health Service—for debate in the upcoming 1997 election. Proposals to reform education and health were key elements of the Labour Party's manifesto in 1997 and became important policies for the newly elected government. Blair's bold statement showed that the revitalised Labour Party had seized the current policy agenda.

There was a wider context to New Labour's policy initiatives. The long wave of economic problems that had affected post-war Britain had subsided by the mid-1990s, creating an opportunity to emphasise social policy and the quality of public services. Not that the previous Conservative government was idle in these respects, as non-foreign policy items, such as criminal justice, had already started to become prominent in its policy programmes since 1993. In this book, we show that the mid-1990s was indeed the point of time when the British public policy attention shifted and the distinct period of the late 1990s and 2000s had begun. The dynamics of the policy agenda—the configuration of issues to which government attends at any point in time—are crucial to understanding national politics and policy. Attention to certain issues can define a period of office of a government and distinguish it from another. It can highlight differences in the priorities of political parties and reveal the sorts of problems facing government.

Such shifts in policy emphasis are what this book is about. We seek to understand why British government concentrated on particular issues on the policy agenda for more than half a century from 1945 to 2008. In so doing, we aim to uncover much about the nature of policy-making: whether it shifts dramatically or gradually, and if changes are sustained over time. In particular, we are interested in the critical junctures and key periods of reform that illustrate and help to comprehend the strategies of decision-makers as they endeavour to manage the interests that keep policy priorities in place, but also in how they meet new challenges and take advantage of them. All political systems experience this tension between continuity and change, and we provide a novel account of it for Britain.

The ideas in the book reflect the interests of the authors as they engage with approaches in political science and bring to bear their own experiences and intellectual sensibilities. Peter John has been interested in stability and change in public decision-making since teaching public policy in the early 1990s. He has researched agenda setting in two projects: the first was on budgets (John and Margetts 2003); and the second concerned urban policy (John 2006a). However, he only started studying policy agendas in earnest after receiving a small grant from the British Academy with 'The policy priority of UK governments: a content analysis of King's and Queen's speeches, 1945–2005' (reference SG42076), which coded this annual measure of the official policy of the UK government according to the coding system of the Policy Agendas Project. These data became the basis of the collaboration with Will Jennings, exploring change and stability in British politics, and public opinion and the policy agenda (Jennings and John 2009; John and Jennings 2010). This led them to start to explore possibilities for coding the policy agenda of other institutional venues in British politics. With these projects completed, Peter John became the natural choice as the principal investigator for the UK franchise of the Comparative Agendas Project, which received funding from the UK Economic and Social Research Council: 'Legislative Policy Agendas in the UK' (reference R105938). This was part of the European Science Foundation (ESF): a EUROCORES ECRP 2007 collaboration called 'The Politics of Attention: West European Politics in Times of Change', led by Stefaan Walgrave, Department of Political Science, University of Antwerp. It is this project that supplied much of the data for this book. The project extended the collaboration with Will Jennings and employed Shaun Bevan as a researcher in 2008–2011. Tony Bertelli also joined the project in 2008, working with Peter John on a new approach to the study of political prioritisation, public policy investment (Bertelli and John 2013), which is investigated in a separate book with Oxford University Press (Bertelli and John n.d.).

Any book project collects a number of intellectual and practical debts along the way. We first thank our funders, the British Academy and the UK Economic and Social Research Council, without which the work could not have taken place. We received additional support from the University of Manchester (from its Hallsworth fund), from the London School of Economics and Political Science, and from the University of

Southern California. We thank Darren Halpin for collaborating with us on policy agendas in Scotland. We would like to thank the many coders who worked on the project, such as Hanhua Liu and Albert Sabater, who worked on the first Queen's Speech project, and Helen Chester, Robin Pettitt, Kate McCormick, Wasel bin Sadat, Kaylee Binding, Paul Copeland, Christopher Hughes, Rebecca Reilly-Cooper, Thomas Purcell and Katy Allison, who worked on the later part. We thank Yadi Zhong for excellent research assistance in preparing Chapter 6. Peter John would like to thank Adam Pile of the Economic and Domestic Affairs Secretariat (Legislation) Cabinet Office for patiently explaining the procedures for drafting the Queen's Speech, in an interview carried out on 27 July 2012.

We have had many opportunities to present our work during the lifetime of the project, such as to conferences of the American Political Science Association, the UK Political Studies Association and the European Consortium of Political Research, and we greatly appreciate the comments of participants made at these events. Peter John also gives special thanks to the members of the Department of Government at the University of Essex, who heard him present the outline of the book on 6 March 2012, as well as to participants at the Public Administration Panel 3: Policy Sciences, Success, Inaction and Agendas at the Political Studies Association Annual Conference, Belfast, 3 April 2012. We are also very grateful to the editors of the *Comparative Studies of Political Agendas* book series—Christopher Green-Pederson, Laura Chaqués Bonafont, Arco Timmermans, Frédéric Varone and Frank Baumgartner— who encouraged us to submit a proposal to Palgrave and for their feedback during the project. We received some very perceptive and thought-provoking comments from academics and friends who read the first version of the manuscript: we thank Perri 6, Jonathan Bradbury, Paul Cairney, Wyn Grant, David Judge and Joni Lovenduski, and we believe our responses—as far as our abilities allowed—improved the quality of the manuscript considerably. We also appreciate the support and encouragement of the staff at Palgrave, especially Amber Stone-Galilee and Andrew Baird. Dyana Mason patiently went through the typescript when it was close to completion, finding and rectifying those troublesome infelicities of style that authors find so hard to spot.

1
The Policy Agenda and British Politics

The policy agenda is the range of salient issues that the government and other key decision-makers concentrate on at any one point in time (Kingdon 1995, p. 3). Such topics can include the economy, health, education and foreign policy, and the content of the agenda can change according to shifts in priorities. While there is much in politics that is relatively stable, such as institutional rules or constitutions, the policy agenda is intended to reflect the set of problems a society faces at a particular moment in time and reveals how government directs action to areas where it thinks it is needed. The policy agenda is also distinct from the day-to-day tumble of political argument, scandals, leadership rivalries and exchanges between the political parties, which is about how politicians react to the pressure of events and to the controversies that are highlighted by the media—even if those events do often press upon policy. The agenda reflects strategic choices by elected politicians and other decisions-makers in and around government about which issues to attend to and to act upon—or at least give the appearance of acting upon—using the powers and authority of the state or executive under their control. The policy agenda often involves pre-commitment, that is, it is signalled some time in advance as a programme for government to implement. The idea is that a government should try to carry out its plan of action and as a result gain approval from the electorate at the end of its term in office.

Public policy is the substance of politics. Any government must attend to many general concerns, including managing a political party, keeping ministers in office, outmanoeuvring opponents, managing the civil service or more generally maintaining confidence in government. Yet a government or executive's main job is to make concrete decisions about what to do about problems in society, and this is what most other elite participants in the political process—from interest groups to media organisations—are also engaged with. These issues fall into a number of categories depending on the problems to hand, whether it is regulating firms and markets, managing relations with foreign states, delivering the services of the welfare state, building infrastructure or responding to public disorder and crime, and so on. These are fundamental activities of the modern democratic state and concern different aspects of collective human experience as presented to policy-makers, which range from the need for housing, education and safety to the promotion of good health, for example. Government policies also shape the relationship of the institutions of the state to other actors, such as with its citizens or to other nation states, or concern the internal management or structure of public institutions.

Even though some aspects of these activities overlap, for instance, foreign affairs relates to economic policy in trade agreements, the distinctions are usually clear. Broad classes of topics encapsulate a diverse array of more narrowly and technically defined issues or problems. For example, economic policy incorporates issues relating to inflation, unemployment, the national debt, taxation, exchange rates and interest rates, and education policy covers the school curriculum, vocational training and universities. While much is said about the need to integrate policy across domains, a lot of the activity of modern states is specialised; and this creates a separate set of interactions and relationships between the participants and power holders within each sector. This is a basic claim of students of public policy, such as those who argue for a sub-government approach whereby many decisions are delegated to semi-independent policy communities (e.g. Freeman 1955; Richardson and Jordan 1979) or to policy networks of key organisations and groups (Marsh and Rhodes 1992b; Rhodes 1988; Richards and Smith 2002).

Actors in policy subsystems are usually preoccupied with routine issues, but to secure major reform they need the involvement of key decision-makers in the centre of government. While participants in the world of sub-governments spend the bulk of their time on their topic of specialisation—whether it is energy or agriculture, for example—peak or core decision-makers have the task of managing the national policy agenda. Their time and resources are scarce, and their attention cannot be guaranteed. The Prime Minister, Chancellor of the Exchequer or Cabinet Secretary cannot solely focus on the economy or foreign policy, though sometimes they might wish to do so during a period of crisis. These decision-makers must balance their time between issues and adjust their attention according to their perception of their relative levels of importance. In a foreign policy crisis, such as in 1982 when the UK's Falkland Islands were occupied by Argentina, the decision-makers at the centre of government may well focus on a single topic, but they will not totally neglect others as that would create a backlog of policy-making. Moreover, acting on just one issue can make a government appear anxious rather than responsible. So within a legislative year, attention will be spread across many domains.

The reason the agenda is distinctive for each government—and for each year it is in office—is that it reflects priority of a given set of issues over another. It is often contended that this is due to practical limits to the number of matters politicians can attend to at any moment in time (Baumgartner and Jones 1993; Jones 1995, 1999, 2009; Jones and Baumgartner 2005a, 2005b). Only so many bits of paper can land on a minister's desk—or e-mails cross a screen—in a given day, week or month, and constraints on her or his attention entail a focus on a smaller number of issues than the total possible. We should be cautious using this argument, however, as a considerable apparatus is in place to process information for the consumption of elected officials. It is the job of the civil service and a cadre of special advisers—and other experts—to screen, process and prioritise information before it reaches the minister or other political decision-maker. To a certain extent, all decision-makers operate with limited information. Yet we would be quite surprised should they behave like lemmings when momentum builds to shift attention across the domains of public policy. We think it necessary to look elsewhere to explain shifts in attention rather than to extend a model of individual decision-making. Any mechanism behind policy agenda change must account for the capacity of organisations and the processing of information at the aggregate level.

The second reason for the limited space of the policy agenda is the degree of institutional capacity to respond to problems and concerns. Practical constraints in the legislative timetable restrict the range of topics that can be discussed, especially when gatekeepers and agenda setters exercise their preferences (Bräuninger and Debus 2009; Shepsle 1979). There are limits to the numbers of laws that can emerge from the legislature in a session, so the government sometimes has to choose, say, between a bill that will reform criminal prosecutions with one that reshapes the health service on the basis of what is politically, quite apart from cognitively, feasible. Further, there are limits to the finances available to fund these schemes as there are often spending ceilings the government cannot exceed. Since most laws cost public money to implement, a government needs to focus on what they can do within their spending targets, postponing legislation that is too expensive if need be. Effective constraints on the size of the agenda mean there is competition for space. Policy-makers need to choose to attend to one issue or another, which may have to do with its urgency or the priorities of decision-makers. It is unlikely that policy-makers would allocate an equal amount of attention to each issue or for initial allocations to remain set in the face of changing social, economic and political conditions.

There are also demands in the political system to respond to one or two pressing public problems rather than to the whole spectrum (Birkland 1997). This might relate to the cycling of issues as government addresses one issue or when the problems associated with it diminish (Downs 1972), whereas the pressing nature of a new problem demands a new set of activities, public statements, commissioning of research, which generate interest and feedback to all public decision-makers and those who work in the media. Crises have a habit of appearing, almost by accident—flooding, oil spills, large administrative errors or wars—and often require instant attention by ministers. Moreover, efforts to reform the system may bubble up from below for or come from international bodies, such as the European Union (EU). These may require a government to reform one sector followed by proximate areas impacted by the original reforms. In the US, the work of Adler and Wilkinson (2013) shows how measures to reform one issue often require a set of related changes. Many of these changes may happen away from the public eye in meetings of regulators and others responsible for the legal control of public activities (Page 2001), and which have further consequences for the larger policy agenda.

In any case, prioritising public policies is essential to the conduct of government. A lack of focus would almost certainly diminish a government's effectiveness. It needs to create a successful set of policies upon which to base its re-election campaign. There has to be an active choice to prioritise, while at the same time acting responsibly by attending to the range of policy problems that confront citizens. Bertelli and John (forthcoming) relate the task of the government in choosing priorities to that faced by a fund manager in choosing financial assets. When allocating attention to policies, the government considers the return from conditional responsiveness to public priorities, the risk owing to variability in those returns and the uncertainty arising because the public has difficulty in articulating its priorities. Taking more risks in such conditional responsiveness in times when the public does not express clear priorities appears to be part of responsible government as it can help win elections (Bertelli and John forthcoming). The machinery of the state thus can be targeted toward some problems, while at the same time moving away from others when they have been addressed. Partly for these reasons, it is reasonable to expect relative attention to issues to change in response to emerging issues and the priorities of political leaders and parties. Moreover, scholars have argued that policy entrepreneurs seek to realise opportunities so that certain issues rise to the top of the political agenda (Kingdon 1995; Mintrom and Norman 2009; Walker 1977), while the outcome of elections provide opportunities for political parties to carry out their manifesto promises (e.g. Hofferbert and Budge 1992; McDonald and Budge 2005), or when in government parties seek to make a difference when compared with parties of the opposing stripe (e.g. Alesina et al. 1997; Castles 1982; Garrett 1998; Imbeau et al. 2001; Keman 2006; McDonald and Budge 2005; Midtbø 1999; Robertson 1976; Schmidt 1996; Swank 2002).

Accounts of the policy agenda

To represent how the policy agenda changes over time, scholars have developed a number of approaches that draw on the foregoing insights. There is a large literature on agenda setting: some of it focused on the character (Cobb and Elder 1983) and the extent of bias in the agenda (Schattschneider 1960), while other works consider the causal mechanisms participants ascribe to represent their interests (Button 1978; Majone 1989; Stone 1989). Here we set out three approaches that are particularly concerned with the amount of attention given to specific policy arenas and how it changes, a question that has preoccupied some of the most influential students of public policy. Then we offer our own approach.

Incrementalism

The first approach is incrementalism, which was developed early in the intellectual history of public policy studies (see Braybrooke and Lindblom 1963; Dahl and Lindblom 1953; Davis et al. 1966, 1974; Lindblom 1959, 1975; Wildavsky 1984). This approach claims policy change occurs through a series of small-scale adjustments or non-radical changes. Groups both within and without the bureaucracy negotiate public decisions; policies emerge in gradual steps rather than in dramatic initiatives; policy-makers almost never review all available policy options; decision-makers take the previous time period as the base or benchmark from which to make adjustments to public spending; and politicians and bureaucrats apply norms or rules of thumb to arrive at decisions. The content of policy outputs rarely departs from a limited range of what decision-makers consider to be a fair distribution. Moreover, the political system is able to resist or limit the impact of major shifts in public opinion, and disagreements among competing interests may lead to little or no policy change as policy proposals are vetoed by powerful actors who occupy semi-autonomous fiefdoms amid fragmented political institutions.

Incrementalism has received much criticism from students of public policy. Many scholars question the claim that policy proceeds smoothly. Empirically, there are critical junctures when the agenda of the political system shifts, for instance, when parties have an influence on policy outcomes (Castles 1982; Hofferbert and Budge 1992) or when the indivisibility of a new programme like space exploration demands a large-scale policy change (Schulman 1975, 1980). The advocacy coalition approach to long-term policy change suggests key external shocks rarely happen, but when they do they disrupt the consensus about public policy, alter the membership of the coalitions and create large policy changes (Sabatier and Jenkins-Smith 1993).

There has also been a debate about whether confirmation or rejection of the incrementalist model depends on the measures and the data sources that studies use (Gist 1982; Natchez and Bupp 1973). There has been a lack of agreement on what is the definition of an increment, which can seem to incorporate any policy change, however large (Bailey and O'Connor 1975). Berry's (1990) review of empirical studies observes the variations even in definitions of incrementalism, which makes comparison across the studies and data sources very hard to achieve. He doubts whether scholars measure the same thing and argues it is not possible to have a coherent definition of incrementalism. As a result of a sustained and virulent attack (e.g. Goodin 1982), the conclusion of many scholars is that incrementalism had been 'thoroughly routed' (Jones 2001, p. 142).

In spite of a plurality of critiques, it is possible to identify what Lindblom (1979, p. 517) calls a 'core meaning' to the term, which is a political pattern in which policy change only occurs at the margins, that is, 'what will be the case tomorrow will not differ radically from what exists today'. When defined in this way, few scholars would claim that the model provides an inaccurate account of at least some periods of decision-making, such as the US in the interwar years, even if it is possible to find other periods when large changes did occur. At certain stages of decision-making, bureaucrats and politicians can evaluate the full range of options and take decisions that reflect the preferences of policy-makers. At other phases, notably implementation, a more incremental style would prevail (Etzioni 1967). It is important not to underestimate the incremental model of decision-making as it corresponds with much of the routine of policy-making, and represents how decision-makers seek predictability and order in the policy process, such as when putting laws and budgets into place.

The issue attention cycle

A second account that has received some attention, especially in the textbooks (e.g. Parsons 1995, p. 115), is the issue attention cycle (Downs 1972), though it has recently—and unjustly—receded from view. This is the idea that problems hit the policy agenda because of a crisis. Publics and elites get focused on them, but after a while the interest declines. Downs (1972, p. 39) writes, 'public attention rarely remains sharply focused upon any one domestic issue for very long—even if it involves a continuing problem of crucial importance to society... Public perception of most "crises"... does not reflect changes in real conditions as much as it reflects the operation of a systematic cycle of heightening public interest and then increasing boredom with major issues'. Stages of the issue attention cycle are as follows:

1. Pre-problem: some undesirable concern exists but has not been addressed, and may be even worse than when it is ultimately discovered.
2. Alarmed discovery and euphoric enthusiasm: an external event, like a riot in a city, leads to a call to do something.
3. Realising the cost of significant progress: costs come to light that may be significant, such as large public expenditures, substantial changes in lifestyles or technological difficulties.
4. Gradual decline of public interest: overall interest fades in the absence of a solution to the problem.
5. Post-problem: attention fades even though many policies and new institutions may have been introduced to deal with the problem.

Issues that have been through the cycle do get, on average, more attention than those that have not, so pre-problem conditions are not reintroduced, which is a common misperception of the model. Downs does not claim that all issues are capable of such a cycle, meaning that his is not a general theory of agenda setting. These kinds of issues usually affect a minority of the population, and solving them would incur high costs. So they tend to be issues that are on the outside the core agenda, which attract interest but then in time get relegated to the periphery once again. The issue attention claim has not been tested systematically (but see Peters and Hogwood 1985), and also attracts critics who believe that major agenda shifts do have the potential to stay in place (Baumgartner and Jones 2009, pp. 86–89, 101–102). Nonetheless, the model remains plausible and there is good reason to expect some issue attention cycles to appear in data on the priorities of policy-makers.

Punctuated equilibrium

The third approach is the punctuated equilibrium model, which posits long periods of stability in decision-making interspersed with periods of rapid change. In this, stable groups of policy actors, often protected by separated political institutions as in the US context, keep policy change to a minimum during long periods of equilibrium. However, political systems can at times undergo rapid changes that are in contrast to gradual adjustments to previous decisions. Periods of equilibrium can be punctuated by a large change in the priorities of the decision-making agenda, such as due to a change in partisan control, a decline in private sector profits or from a shift in public opinion (Jones et al. 2002, pp. 13–15). Issues gather momentum because interested participants, like those in the media, gravitate toward them. Once issues have enough impetus to change, they move rapidly from stasis to innovation in what Baumgartner and Jones (1993, p. 125) call positive feedback. It is important to note that punctuated equilibrium is not a theory of decision-making as such, but a claim about how focusing events affect decision-making processes (Kingdon 1995).

This claim has roots in the theory of organisations. Serial processing—when the results of one action are effectively required before another is considered—buttresses status quo policies in times of stability, but compels policy-makers to focus on new issues to the exclusion of others once the agenda shifts. The result is that 'some problems gain disproportionate attention from many policy venues' (Baumgartner and Jones 1993, p. 250). More policy-makers become involved because 'the diffuse jurisdictional boundaries that separate the various overlapping institutions of government can allow many governmental actors to become involved in a new policy area' (True et al. 1999, p. 99). In the language of Jones and Baumgartner, issue monopolies that govern policy sectors, like urban policy or nuclear power, break down and become re-established later, but at a new equilibrium point, when a new constellation of interest groups and institutional rules cement a set of policy proposals into place until the next punctuation.[1] In this account, 'punctuations are a regular and important feature of US budget making and US policymaking' (True et al., p. 111). US policy researchers pay tribute to the seminal work of Padgett (1980, 1981) who developed a serial judgement model of the budget process that implies 'the occasional occurrence of very radical changes' (Padgett 1980, p. 366; True et al. 1999, p. 107). Carpenter's (1996) model of adaptive signal processing has some similarities with a model of bounded rationality subject to the incidence of cascades (see the discussion below). Current work seeks to integrate punctuated equilibrium into a general theory of information processing (Workman et al. 2009).

The existence of punctuations may simply limit the applicability of the incrementalist model, rather than supersede it. Even incrementalist writers, such as Davis et al. (1966), who investigate policy changes over a long time period, find that stable periods of decision-making could be disrupted by exogenous factors they denote as 'random shocks to an otherwise deterministic system' (Davis et al. 1966, p. 351). In more sophisticated later work that tests both political and environmental determinants of expenditure, they conclude 'the disturbances to the normal situation were the result of exceptional, probably non-recurring events' (Davis et al. 1974, p. 438). Moreover, even when there is punctuated equilibrium there are long periods when a more incremental pattern prevails (Howlett and Migone 2011). The difference to incrementalism is that the punctuated equilibrium model relates stability to negative feedback processes, whereby decisions are protected from change by the monopolistic power of institutional actors and key interest groups in a given policy sector. Change is associated with positive feedback that results from new definitions of issues and the intrusion of new actors into formerly closed decision-making arenas. As existing institutional arrangements break down, the issue receives more attention. One implication is that long periods of stability in decision-making can contribute to the intensity of policy change. Institutional and cognitive frictions can inhibit the expansion of the policy agenda (Baumgartner et al. 2009a; Jones and Baumgartner 2005a, 2005b). When the pressure for change exceeds a certain threshold, it exhibits disproportionate changes manifested by positive feedback and the transfer or cascades of agendas moving across jurisdictions and different arenas for decision-making. When agenda change occurs, there can be large shifts in the attention of policy-makers to particular issues. The punctuated equilibrium model has been tested with aggregate data on budgets (e.g. Breunig 2006; Breunig and Koski 2006, 2012; Jensen 2009; John and Margetts 2003; Jones *et al*. 1997, 1998; Mortensen 2005; Robinson *et al*. 2007; True *et al*. 1999), and on data from a wider range of institutional venues (Alexandrova *et al*. 2012; Baumgartner 2006; Jones *et al*. 2003; Jones and Baumgartner 2005a, 2005b; Walgrave and Nuytemans 2009) as well as qualitative and mixed method studies (Busenberg 2004; Baumgartner and Jones 1993, 2009; Pralle 2003; Repetto 2006; Resodihardjo 2009; Walgrave and Varone 2008).

Applied to public policy, the approach is not without its critics. Prindle (2006, 2012) argues that Baumgartner and Jones's approach elides the causal processes behind punctuations. Researchers are not able to attribute causal processes in quite the same way as the biological theory on which it is based even though, as we shall discuss below, the statistical work it inspires moves in that direction. Prindle (2006, p. 11) complains that Baumgartner's and Jones's 'formulation has no grounding in operational definitions of stasis and sudden change and is therefore a metaphor rather than a causal theory', that is, Baumgartner and Jones describe the changes but do not explain them. Cashore and Howlett (2007) argue that there is a more complex set of processes to observe, some of which point to the radical change indicated by Jones and Baumgartner, but which require close empirical examination.

Focused adaptation

This book aims to develop a heuristic for examining the evolution of policy attention that builds on the foregoing approaches. There may be a series of changes happening across the policy agenda that may, respectively, have characteristics of incrementalism or issue attention or policy punctuations. Of interest is whether such changes are sustained in time, reflecting a change in the underlying structure of the mechanism that generates policy priorities. Our approach has the following criteria.

1. A re-election-seeking government controls a mechanism that generates substantive attention to public policy topics in spite of significant pressure on the policy agenda from the media and public opinion.
2. A landscape, or population, of policy problems exists and that voters are concerned that government allocates attention to those policy problems, though not all problems impact all voters.
3. Government searches this problem landscape to learn its characteristics. This search includes assessing information about mass and elite views of the relative importance of particular problems.

4. Armed with that information, government adjusts its policy-making attention mechanism to reflect what it has learned to pursue its electoral goals.

This search and adjustment process, captured by these four elements, continues iteratively, filling the policy agenda with topics over time.

There are three characteristics of policy-making systems that affect the search process. First, institutions such as political parties create pre-commitments to particular policies that can inhibit adaptation. Second, the length of electoral cycles means that certain policy attention choices are bound to be made in greater haste—and on the basis of less information—than others. Third, the pattern of the policy problem landscape can play a role. If it is very coarse, namely, involving clusters of very different problems, the government can get stuck on some problems and miss others, including key emergent problems that can cause shifts or later searches. If the landscape is very fine-grained, the government can adapt more easily as it is not as difficult to identify and understand the importance of the various problems the country faces.

When government's adaptation process is poor because the characteristics just discussed are too important, the policy agenda resembles the expectation of the punctuated equilibrium model. By contrast, good adaptation resembles tactical statecraft, using information gleaned in search in the service of responsible government that shifts with the needs and wants of the public, not in big lurches. We call our heuristic focused adaptation. This occurs when policy-makers, in response to exogenous conditions and to information acquired by searching the policy landscape, use their discretion to alter the agenda. In essence, it is a theory of decision-making that captures how focusing events compel policy-makers to rationalise the landscape of policy problems. This can happen in different ways, but is detectable by looking for structural breaks in the time series of attention to the issues on the policy agenda. That is, a shift in the average value of attention to a policy domain defines a new epoch in it, raising or lowering its priority. In Chapter 6, we present a method to capture structural breaks that allows us to identify these epochs.

Focused adaptation stands in contrast to incremental patterns that do not lead to large changes in policy, or seasonal oscillations or transient punctuations where attention returns back to its overall mean level. Members of the policy elites, who are at the centre of the mechanism of agenda formation, have the discretion to create lasting changes in policy attention. These actors update their information as the policy environment changes, but as the information flow changes and new signals arise they may be forced to adapt to external events and adjust their conclusions about what those events mean. Much of the time it may involve small adjustments that continue the regime from before, such as slowly rising expenditure, for example; but from time to time it may force decision-makers to review their options and set off on a new course of action that defines a new era for the policy agenda. This might not necessarily take the form of a massive shift or leap in attention. The ship of state may maintain its course, with government making adjustments for tides and storms, but heads in the same direction until a discretionary change of course occurs which alters the underlying structure of attention, steering the vessel in a different direction.

Focused adaptation has some similarities with the punctuated equilibrium model in its attention to—but not its theory of—periods of stability and change. Indeed, if one examines the origins of the studies of punctuated equilibrium in the work of Padgett, the adaptive model of decision-making is quite similar. This is also shown in the work of Carpenter (1996, p. 286) who posits a data-generating process behind decision-making whereby policy-makers update their prior choices in light of new information. As policy-makers update their decisions, they give less weight to information the longer it is in the past: 'They slowly adjust their behavior in response to new signals, tempering their reaction in light of signals yet to come... a variable moving average of past [changes] in order to interpret the current one, in order to set it into context' (p. 287). Our model assumes that decision-makers operate within an updating adaptive world, but where the force of new information can cause them to change course at a particular decision-point. This returns to classic themes in decision-making as articulated in the work of Herbert Simon (1955) and others.

In our claims regarding governments' searches of the policy landscape, we are sympathetic to the work of Kollman et al. (1992, 1998) on adaptive political parties, which models parties' searches of the electoral landscape with the use of artificial intelligence routines. Kollman et al. (1998) offer different strategies for learning, such as random search, hill climbing (where the party uses a search close to the original platform) and a genetic algorithm that mimics evolutionary adaptation. The decision-maker uses information to gradually move toward an optimal policy position; but this is not certain, as there are local equilibria in which she or he may become stuck and that are not the best option overall. The process of adaptation is not perfect, but the decision-maker usually moves to a better position on the basis of it.

This relates to our claim that governments search for policy problems, adapting their strategies to yield the most electoral benefit. It does not predict that small steps do not lead to significant policy change. In some cases the adaptation can be quite quick—as in a sudden move from a local equilibrium—which captures the focusing idea in which we are interested. Under the guise of focused adaptation, an understanding of epochs in British politics must capture changes in the mechanism by which government allocates its attention to substantive topics.

Each model of the policy agenda provides a lens through which to examine the policy process, and we will return to them during this book. There is of course, the issue of how to confirm or reject them from the data we have—or from other data. In Chapter 3 we discuss how we might do this, using a variety of statistics and forms of observation. There are a number of difficulties in adjudicating when a process has the characteristics of the model, as each is concerned with the pattern of change and stability, and in distinguishing focused attention from the others. In Chapter 6, we elaborate a statistical method that is able to capture such shifts. Before we do that, we need to set out the institutional context within which policy prioritisation takes place. This comprises the rules, practices and cultures that operate in a jurisdiction like a nation state, which guide decision-makers in what is possible and set limits and opportunities for them when seeking to change the agenda. Moreover, in seeking to understand how such institutions and practices work and intersect with decision-making, we can start to find out how focused adaptation can be enhanced by the way in which institutions operate, which is particularly apposite in the UK with its unique constitution.

Policy-making in British politics

Policy prioritisation and adaptation take place in a context, where the formal means of making decisions—political institutions—structure the content and sequence of policy-making. Moreover, there are informal rules of the game that are important in shaping behaviour, which are sustained through shared norms and values. Both formal and informal rules are tied together by constitutional arrangements and understandings, particular laws and constitutional conventions (Marshall 1984), which reflect beliefs about how the political system should work. The rules of the game and the constitution are themselves underpinned by a deep-rooted political culture that creates expectations of what can be done in politics. All these features of political systems vary across nations, creating some unique aspects to decision-making and affecting the content of the policy agenda.

Institutions sustain the generic features of policy-making, which have to do with providing for a regular supply of policy options, creating the means for selecting and authorising those options, and turning those options into implemented and enforced policies (Smith 1976). This is a representation of the stages model of the policy process (see DeLeon 1999; John 2012; Lasswell 1956), but which here describes the formal authorisation and implementation of policy rather than being an indicator of the direction of causation down the decision-making chain. At the same time, political institutions may affect the processing and aggregating of information, and the type of decisions that are made, especially if they give autonomy to certain decision-makers or spread decision-makers across many veto players. In this way, the prevalence of models of decision-making—as set out above—may be affected by institutional design, so that some political systems experience punctuations, while others have more gradually changing patterns.

In this book we look at the political system in Britain, which has both unique and generic features. Its particular form of decision-making, what is known as the Westminster system or model, has been of great interest to political scientists and other scholars, particularly during the twentieth century (Beer 1965; Bevir 2008; Bevir and Rhodes 2003; Dunleavy 2006; Heclo and Wildavsky 1974; Lijphart 1999; McLean 2010; Neustadt 1969; Saalfeld 2003; Wilson 1994), and has often been used for comparison with nations with different political institutions.

Britain's distinctive political system came about from its origins and development. Over many centuries, Parliament gradually asserted its power, and then over time the democratic mandate, bolstered by successive extensions of the franchise, became vested in the first chamber of the legislature, the House of Commons. Parliament holds legal sovereignty, so if one or more political parties elected under a first-past-the-post electoral system get a majority of seats in the House of Commons (and can get measures through the House of Lords—the assent of the sovereign to legislation has not been in doubt since the early twentieth century), then they have access to a nearly unlimited legal power to do things (bar observing common law principles in the implementation of statutes, such as reasonableness and natural justice). Partly due to convention and partly due to the lack of a codified constitution, the other branches of the state do not play a significant role in decision-making. Since the early twentieth century, the Crown has not involved itself in politics; the bureaucracy has been the servant of the government; the courts have not (at first) sought to be policy activists; and there are no constitutional checks from lower levels of decentralised government. The system does require centralised and disciplined political parties—one or more of which form the government—to control the business of Parliament (Cox 1987; King 1976; Norton 2005, 2011), but these have been in operation for much of the twentieth century. This means that Britain became the classic example of party government (Rose 1974).

The party with the majority not only dominates the business of lawmaking, it has access to the resources and powers of the state. The strong state that emerged since the sixteenth century remains in place in the authority and powers of the ministers of the Crown. In particular, the Prime Minister has powers of appointment and dismissal of ministers. Thus power is effectively delegated from Parliament to the leading ministers of the party in government, who make decisions in the Cabinet. By virtue of the party control of Parliament and a centralised state, policy-making in Britain is concentrated in an executive led by the Prime Minister.

Some observers claim that British government was always more differentiated and pluralist than this stylised account acknowledges (see Rhodes 1988, 1997). There are complex policy communities that dominate decision-making way beyond the control of the Prime Minister and Cabinet (Richards and Smith 2002). The gaze of the executive rarely extends to policy implementation, to the delivery level where the key decisions are made, as it is focused on day-to-day crises. Some writers developed the concept of a core executive to describe the complexity of the central state and the factions within it (Burch and Holliday 1996; Dunleavy and Rhodes 1990; Smith 1999). Even though the key decision-makers who operate the system believe in the Westminster model, many academics writing on British politics believe reality belies these beliefs (see the summary in Judge 2005, pp. 24–26).

There are some stronger criticisms. McLean (2010) powerfully argues that the British constitution was never founded on parliamentary sovereignty; and that there are veto players in the second chamber of the legislature in the form of the House of Lords, which was able to delay legislation for two years and hence, was able to derail the business of a government halfway through its term in office. Membership of the EU and then accession into law of the European Convention on Human Rights (ECHR) in 1998 finally undermined the legal power of Parliament and exposed the fiction of the Diceyan tradition of parliamentary sovereignty under the rule of law.

The most common attack on the operation of the Westminster model is the claim that it has changed out of recognition from a variety of parallel trends that complement each other: membership of the EU and the associated Europeanisation of British political institutions and policies limit freedom of manoeuvre; the exigencies of the global economy and competition have promoted delegation to structures of governance (Cerny and Evans 2004); the devolution of power to entrenched legislative institutions constrains policy-making in Whitehall (Hazell 2010); a significant delegation of power to semi-independent agencies and institutions alters political-decision-making (Bertelli 2008; Flinders 2008, 2009); a more powerful judiciary can strike down government policies (Ewing 2009); and a more assertive and influential second chamber can modify decisions coming from the House of Commons (Russell 2010). Britain now seems to have a separation of powers, quasi-federalism, a codified constitution, a multiparty system and regular coalition government (Dunleavy 2006). Moreover, the glue that held the system together—party unity—has eroded in recent years with a greater number of backbench rebellions. The government can be less confident of getting its measures through Parliament (Cowley 2002). Others argue that members of the governing elite have less commitment to and understanding of the constitution so the system of government does not operate as effectively as before (Johnson 1975; King 2007). Even the business of law-making has become less assured and competent, so bills increasingly have to be amended because of poor drafting (Foster 2005).

But in spite of these changes it is important not to underestimate the power of the existing institutional system to shape relationships partly from entrenched beliefs about them and the deep roots of the institutions themselves, which is Judge's (2005) argument. Britain remains—in spite of many arguments to the contrary—a parliamentary state (Judge 1993). The Westminster system has adapted to the changes keeping the logic and rationale of the old system, as has happened with the response to the EU, for example (Featherstone 2009). Moreover, a few key actors in government still determine the direction of policy. In fact, the experience of Britain in coalition government since 2010 shows the resilience of the system that can adapt its structures to a coalition: policy promises are put into a coalition agreement and few central actors—the Prime Minister and deputy Prime Minister—determine the course of policy. There will always be complexity in any political system but what matters is whether the constitutional rules and traditions vest key powers with some actors who can drive policy through if they want to. In Britain, those key features of the system remain in place, such as the power of the Prime Minister to hire and fire ministers, which is used extensively (Berlinski *et al.* 2009), and the way in which key policies need Cabinet authorisation to get through. Moreover, for most of the period between 1945 and the late 2000s, many of the traditional features did apply to British government and politics (the period from the 1940s to end of the 1960s is not discussed in McLean's book). So Britain still retains a single chain of command, where there is a clear delegation of power from the electorate to Parliament, and to the Prime Minister and Cabinet, even if some aspects of this system of government have weakened in recent years (Saalfeld 2003).

Policy selection in the British system of government

Once we look at the selection of key policies then the key aspects of British politics and its institutions come to light. Once appointed into office, the Prime Minister and members of the Cabinet need to have a programme of government, part of which they have promised in the party's manifesto. This meets the first criterion of focused adaptation as it is the mechanism for generating substantive policy attention controlled by a re-election-minded government. The implementation of a programme of policies is integral to being in government. The Prime Minister and Cabinet also face a number of problems and issues that may already be in the system when they take office, such as existing proposals from government departments, hangovers of legislation and half-implemented policies from the previous government. There will be issues raised by experts and official reports, pressures to act from debates in the media, and the demands and requirements from international organisations. Interest groups too will have their concerns, as do party workers and members of Parliament. These policy proposals fall into a set of categories such as health or education—the building blocks of the policy agenda and represented as such by the names of government departments and interest groups that occupy the policy subsystems.

All of these policy proposals—far more than could ever be implemented—aim to provide solutions to a range of public problems. This long list is what we call the policy landscape. This second criterion of focused adaptation is very familiar to students of public policy, especially as they figure strongly in the prominent work of Kingdon (1995) cited at the start of this chapter. Often, the policy landscape contains requests for new laws or increases in the level of public expenditures in a policy domain. There is then a selection issue: how to select policies to fit the existing timetable of the legislature and the amount of budget that is reasonably available. This is where the institutions come to help those in charge to select the right number of policies at particular points in time which fall into main functional categories of economy, health and so on. These institutions vest power in a limited number of actors defined by their institutional office who we call the core decision-makers (which in Britain vary according to the venue of decision-making but always include the Prime Minister). The clearest venue for the search for policy problems, the third criterion in focused adaptation, is the procedure to determine the list of laws that will be introduced into Parliament; the other venue is the means to decide how much public expenditure will be allocated to each kind of public problem. The government has other more diffuse venues for decision-making, such as the decision to provide information or to alter the organisation of the bureaucracy (see John 2011), but laws and budgets are crucial as they are the key tools of government (Hood 1983; Hood and Margetts 2007). So it is no surprise that only a small number of people are allowed to make the final decisions about their allocation.

In the British system there are many channels that influence the selection of policies, the final criterion in focused adaptation, and a complex internal machinery of departments and agencies, but most departments need authorisation of these policies and often need a new law to be passed. For that they need to make a proposal to the centre of government, which controls which laws can be submitted to Parliament. This occurs in the Cabinet Office, a government department that works to support the Cabinet. One part of the Cabinet Office, the Economic and Domestic Affairs Secretariat (Legislation), receives proposals for bills and is tasked with finding the time in the legislative programme of government. This is not a technical process, but is fundamentally political and involves the balancing of multiple demands for new policies with the need to implement the government's promised programme. The government and its advisers need to react to the demands of the day in the form of public opinion, what is in the press and what is worrying their party supporters, which is a balancing act that results in the policy agenda the government wishes to follow. The Business and Legislation Committee, a Cabinet Committee chaired by the leader of the House of Commons, selects the legislation going forward in consultation with the Prime Minister, who may attend.

Most political systems have a formal statement of the executive's programme for the year ahead (Breeman *et al.* 2009; Cohen 1995; Hobolt and Klemmensen 2005, 2008; Mortensen *et al.* 2011). In part this is driven by the timetable of the legislature, which has sessions and years with clear beginnings and ends, which give a natural sense of the business that is to come. It is also attractive to a government because it wants to signal its agenda and make a credible commitment to policies, setting out a policy programme that it can follow. In turn, the public can judge if the government is adhering to its agenda. It also gives government the ability to offer a narrative of events to be picked up in the media; and it encourages Parliament to pass the laws and the bureaucracy and other agencies to implement them.

In Britain, the tradition that the monarch gives a speech to open Parliament, the Speech from the Throne, more commonly known as the King's or Queen's Speech, is a major political event that serves to open each session of Parliament, and usually happens each year (Herman 1974; Jennings et al. 2011a; Namenwirth and Weber 1987).[2] It is an established means for setting the agenda of British government. In this, the government unveils its legislative programme in the form of a long list of proposals read out by the sovereign; but the speech also contains a substantial non-legislative element where the government conveys its approach, and identifies key problems facing Britain and the world. It sets out the policy agenda of government and is reported on, and commented about, extensively in the national media. The government also issues briefing notes that tie each line of the speech to the detail of policy and to the responsibilities of government departments.

In spite of the pomp and ceremony, the construction of the speech follows a policy selection model whereby the key decision-makers select the proposals that go forward and leave aside the ones they do not want. This is because the speech has to be—within small margins—a set length, which is dictated by the expectations of the Palace and the logistics of the occasion, and there is only so much time in the parliamentary year that follows. Although the departments of state lobby for their legislative proposals to be included, there is not enough space for them all and it is the Prime Minister and members of the Cabinet who select which ones go forward. The speech is prepared by the Cabinet Office on behalf of the Business and Legislation Committee, but the Prime Minister determines the themes and content of the speech, especially closer to the event, when the drafting of the text takes place. The Prime Minister (and since 2010 the Deputy Prime Minister) agree the final wording of the speech, which is then usually approved, without any major changes, by a meeting of the full Cabinet.[3] The speech then drives the agenda of Parliament and is reviewed at the end of the session for any bills that do not go through as listed in the Prorogation speech.

The central message of this narrative is that only a few people—the leading politicians or more often just the Prime Minister—can shape the content of the speech in spite of all the effort that is taken by government departments to secure a place in the speech and the consultation in the Cabinet and across Whitehall about its content. The Prime Minister and a few other leading politicians make decisions about which topics on the policy agenda to focus on, which they can do right up to the last moment when the speech has to be written on vellum about a week before the opening of Parliament.[4] In this they are not just driven by pressure from external events, but can adapt to them, taking political decisions about how to adjust the policy agenda in light of those events. This is something that all political systems vest their leaders with discretion to do, but in Britain that discretion—the monopoly of decision—is closely guarded by the Prime Minister and protected by the Cabinet Office.

The political direction of the policy agenda characterises the general selection and timing of legislation through the House of Commons and Lords. This is partly because it is structured by the Speech from the Throne, but the Cabinet's Business and Legislation Committee considers all proposals for bills and decides them in accordance with the government's overall strategy and in response to political considerations as well as the arguments put by the sponsoring departments. Even though the civil service influences the legislative proposals of government (Page 2003), the core political decision-makers select the final list of bills. This centralised control of the agenda applies to budgets as well, which are prepared by the Treasury, but are subject to political authorisation and pass through Parliament without amendment (see Chapter 9 for a discussion of budgeting). In the key venues of decision-making discussed in this book—speeches, laws and budgets—politicians at the centre of government have the discretion to shape the policy agenda and to adapt to events in a focused way. That is not to say other decisions are not relevant, such as over delegated legislation, circulars and regulations, but these three key venues are particularly important. Government is highly attached to them and gives them a high degree of emphasis. This is why we pay so much attention to them in representing the policy agenda of British politics.

Conclusion

This chapter has introduced the concept of the policy agenda, and has explained how public policy scholars have used it to understand government decision-making. As a result of three decades of the study of policy-making and agenda setting, there is now a body of work that examines the way political systems prioritise topics in public policy, and seeks to explain why attention changes over time. Three different frameworks have been widely used to understand stability and change in the policy agenda: incrementalism, the issue attention cycle and punctuated equilibrium. We propose a fourth, called focused adaptation, which draws on the insights of these approaches but is based on understanding the changes that may lead to structural breaks in the policy agenda.

While focused adaptation is a general claim about policy-making systems, we also argue that the structure and operation of political institutions shape how it works in practice. For this reason, we have introduced the core features of the country under scrutiny in this book, that of Britain. Like every country, political institutions create rules and conventions that determine how policies are selected for inclusion on the policy agenda, which reproduce the general features of the policy process, that of policy formulation, selection and implementation. But there are very special features of British politics remaining today that ensure that only a few politicians, operating within a number of institutional constraints, have power to determine the content of the policy agenda. We contend that these persistent institutional rules and practices have structured the content of the policy agenda, even though the policy challenges political leaders faced have changed dramatically in our period of study.

To explore the historical context, next in Chapter 2 we review approaches to studying politics and policy in Britain. We ask, what are the implications of this institutional structure for the policy agenda, and which of the four models of policy agendas fits best (though focused adaptation is our favoured candidate)? In Chapter 3 we provide detailed information about our data sources and policy content coding system, guide readers to our project website (see www.policyagendas.org.uk) and offer helpful information about how to access and use the data. Chapters 4–6—the analytic heart of the book—explore the content of the Speech from the Throne and Acts of Parliament using different methods. Chapter 4 describes the data for each domain, whether it is defence, education, health and so on, and examines fluctuations in attention. Chapter 5 provides an assessment of the punctuated equilibrium model in post-war British politics. In Chapter 6, we employ a Bayesian change point model to uncover structural shifts in issue attention, which is our main test of focused adaptation. In Chapters 7 and 8, we examine the non-governmental policy agenda as represented, respectively, in public opinion and the media. The penultimate chapter of the book discusses the implementation of policies down the line, in budgets. Here we graphically represent trends across all the series, which allows us to make an assessment about the nature of the different policy agendas, and serves as a bridge to Chapter 10 where we synthesise our argument and make some general conclusions about policy agendas in British politics.

2
Policy-Making and British Politics

Does British politics demonstrate a stable pattern of issue processing, rather like the incremental model, or is it characterised by something more like the rare but substantial fits and starts of punctuated equilibrium? Do its institutions promote stability or change—or both? Surprisingly, there is no clear answer to these questions from studies of British politics. No single dominant narrative about the operation of British political institutions prevails; and several have emerged depending on the particular literature and approach to study. One of the key junctures is between scholars who suggest that British politics reflects a strong pattern of continuity and inertia and those who emphasise the frequency of large changes and recurrent reversals in public policy. We set out the main lines of this debate in the section below, but they are preludes to our claim that data on the policy agenda of British government provide potential answers to these questions. In subsequent chapters we offer empirical evidence about whether governments did indeed maintain similar sets of policy topics over time, or whether they tended to change course and used the discretion of office to make large changes to public priorities.

Stability and change in British politics and policy

A common assumption is that policy-making in Britain is largely stable and follows particular large contours because of its unique features. This is a recurring theme of some analyses of political systems, which tend to operate according to long-lasting institutions and associated cultures. The historical institutionalist approach to public policy, which became influential in the 1990s, embodies competing claims that institutions act as coordination mechanisms that preserve equilibria (e.g. North

1990) or depend on temporal mechanisms that keep them stable (e.g. Pierson 2004), though of course it is possible to use an institutionalist approach to examine policy change (see Streeck and Thelen 2005).

There are several reasons that scholars identify for the dampening effect of political institutions on the policy process in Britain. One is rooted in the fact that British political institutions are typically characterised as being stable, having evolved from medieval times in a pattern of gradual adaptation as we reviewed in Chapter 1. There have been no large breaks in recent British political history, like a revolution, or regime change, or invasion by foreign forces on the core territory of the UK, as is more characteristic of continental European countries. The nation only gradually democratised its institutions (Birch 1964), while vesting a considerable amount of power with the executive. This meant that the habit of slow change and of adapting to an established way of doing business became entrenched in Britain, which affected both how the members of established institutions, such as civil servants, saw themselves, but also how new participants, such as interest groups, behaved. This is not to say there were not violent episodes in British political history, such as the demand for voting rights. For example, in the period before the Great Reform Act of 1832, the Prime Minister, the Duke of Wellington, and his followers fiercely responded to political violence of the time and refused at first to accept an extension of the franchise (Brock 1973). But many members of the governing elite had a more pragmatic reflex. They preferred to adapt to change rather than resist it at all costs, as was shown by the passing of the reform act itself. The conservative nature of British politics ensures continual re-invention of institutions and policies while the basic framework and distribution of power remains in place. The Conservative Party has been master of these exercises in pragmatism, but the other political parties do it very well too if less overtly.

The Westminster system incentivises a high degree of continuity in the policies it produces—in spite of regular turnover in partisan control of government. The institutional framework provides for a constant processing of issues raised by constituents, but allows the machinery of the state to present policies for authorisation. A long line of scholars have argued that the rules and conventions of the British political system condition the behaviour of the parties who occupy office by ensuring they are prepared for government and present themselves to the electorate as an incoming team with the competence to govern (McKenzie 1955). This socialisation means that opposition parties do not seek to challenge the system or to embark on radical new policies.

This has been particularly marked with the Labour Party, which started as an extra-parliamentary movement, but evolved into a party of government seeking a majority in the House of Commons, where its leaders present themselves to the public as capable of being members of the next government. According to this line of thought, powerful constitutional conventions constrain the behaviour of elected politicians by promoting accountability through their responsibility to Parliament and the smooth running of Cabinet government (Marshall 1984). All this should constrain policy-making and make for a stable management of issues, whereby each department of state gradually develops policies to present to ministers, which can then get included in the Speech from the Throne.

The conservatism hypothesis

Counterbalancing the alternation of political parties in government are powerful organs of the state that also help to stabilise policy-making, such as the civil service, whose members do not usually change with the government in power. Civil servants channel policy problems to government and brief ministers accordingly. If institutional parameters are subject to little change, we may reasonably expect considerable stability in decision-making, sustaining an underlying conservative trajectory of public policy. This conservatism hypothesis has been the cause of complaint by radicals such as Tony Benn. Drawing on his experience as a minister, Benn believed that systemic solidity prevented ministers from bringing about change because civil servants would always promote policies that kept the existing set of priorities in place (Benn 1980), although his bigger rivals were often his Cabinet colleagues, such as Prime Minister Harold Wilson.

Beyond the formal structure of government lie the routines and interests that affect each sector of activity, the topics of the policy agenda. The decision-making world divides these into domains of activity, such as health, education and welfare, although there are elements of crossover and some linkage among the sectors. Within each sector of activity, there are demands to attend to its particular problems, whether it is poor health, the need for better education or the demand for more spending on welfare. Interests are determined by the problems themselves, their priority by the public and the media, and the opinions of experts; but they are also articulated by public officials and private interests that specialise in providing solutions to these problems and who advocate more attentiveness to them. Policy advocates may work in representative associations within the service-providing bureaucracies or even within government itself. For example, farmers' representative organisations, the food industry, the specialists and experts who work for universities, the civil servants who work for government and the MPs who specialise in farming interests benefit from increased public attention to food production problems. Within political parties, some members have interests in one particular policy area rather than another, and this may be expressed in selection for ministerial posts and shadow ministerial roles in opposition. The legislature itself is specialised through its committee system, which is divided into distinct policy areas for the purposes of scrutiny and investigation. Specialisation according to domain is found throughout the policy process and influences the agenda.

At the subsystem level, such as a domain like housing or education, rather than finding a general sense of left-right, scholars have referred to the different and contrasting political relationships in these areas and to the way in which much business is often done behind the scenes, away from public scrutiny. In fact, one of the most influential accounts of policy-making in Britain came from this kind of analysis. Richardson and Jordan in *Governing Under Pressure* (1979) presented case studies of the power of interest groups in the political system that supported this point of view. They argued that policy-makers always strive for consensus, no matter how controversial an issue. Even if consensus is disputed, the basic aim of policy-makers is to return to the stable processing of political issues.

The conservatism hypothesis complements Heclo and Wildavsky (1974), who described the club-like and village aspects to policy-making centred on the Treasury, an account that re-appeared in Thain and Wright's (1995) study of public finances. Rose and Davies (1994) presented considerable evidence that policy programmes of British government tend to stay in place over time and that budgets change only incrementally. Rose's (1980) earlier work went somewhat farther, declaring that parties 'do not make a difference'. One of the main sources for a change in issue emphasis in government, that political parties enter power with their own preferences, has therefore not been thought to be as influential in the British political system which encouraged more responsible government rather than responsive government (Birch 1964). The stable routines of government augur against large lurches in policy. The elite adhered to constitutional conventions of ministerial responsibility that made for restrained decision-making, and upheld the right of Members of Parliament to scrutinise the executive (ministerial responsibility) or encouraged minsters to adhere to a line that had been argued and agreed to in Cabinet (collective responsibility). More generally, in the tradition laid out by Dicey (1917), the potential harshness of the doctrine of parliamentary sovereignty is softened by adherence to the rule of law, such as respecting the rights of those involved in decision-making (natural justice) or acting with good information and evidence (reasonableness). Such rights, for some, were embedded right through the operation and decision-making in the legal system (Allan 1994) so feed back into political decision-making. These institutions act as a commitment so that citizens, pressure groups and elites know the rules of the game and respond relatively predictably. In this view, institutions drive the incremental pattern of government decision-making.

Linked to the institutional argument is a view about the stable orientation of Britain's political elites. Its political classes were able to adapt to a changing world from running an empire in the early part of the century, to responding to the working-class vote, to fighting world wars, to creation of the welfare state, to dealing with the economic crises of the 1960s and 1970s and to the new politics of growth in the 1990s. Rather than resisting change at all costs, British elites tended to respond to new problems and to incorporate them. Even large changes in British politics, such as the election of a Labour government in 1945, reflect a longer-term adaption. Many British historians argue that the developments in the 1930s and the policies and politics of wartime led to the Labour programme (Addison 1982; Pugh 2002), and that political consensus emerged as the Conservative Party also came to accept many of Labour's key platforms and reforms. The Tory programme maintained a compromise between views of the different wings (Middlemas 1979, p. 420; Seldon 1981). The post-war climate had induced Conservatives to attend to issues of housing, social policy and economic growth regardless of their convictions about the role of the state. While Labour and the Conservatives hardly agreed on all policy matters (see Glennerster 2000; Jones 1996), there was a fair degree of consensus on the content of the policy agenda that there should be housing policies beyond reconstruction of post-war damage to homes, and so on. This political agreement also reflected, as Addison (1982) argues, a Whitehall consensus on the role of the state in economic management and the provision of welfare. It was sometimes known as Butskellism, a hybrid name containing the names of the Conservative and Labour chancellors of the exchequer, Rab Butler and Hugh Gaitskell, who were supposed to follow very similar policies in spite of being from different political parties. More generally, it was seen to apply to the acceptance of the institutions of the welfare state by the Conservative Party and the realisation by the Labour Party of the benefits of the mixed economy and a balance between public and private ownership. This had been thought to have been established in wartime (Addison 1982; Marwick 1968) and had been fostered by moderate politicians, such as Bevin (Bullock 1967), and even Churchill when in government again in the 1950s (Seldon 1981).

The question to ask of course is whether this classic picture captured in the foregoing discussion ever really existed in British politics apart from what is described in textbooks, and whether there was more division and policy change in the system right through the twentieth century (see Jones and Kandiah 1996). Some writers question the extent of consensus (Pimlott et al. 1989). Studies of policy-making by Kelly (2002) and Glennerster (2000) suggest much more partisan conflict than the consensus would indicate. Political parties reverse each other's policies when entering office, such as nationalising and de-nationalising steel; economic policy experienced many twists and turns not entirely consistent with a stable consensus (Rollings 1996). Yet many scholars continue to believe this kind of temporal classification proves useful (Harrison 1999; Seldon 1994) and it still appears in histories of twentieth-century politics (e.g. Kavanagh 1989; Middlemas 1979). Even though political parties threw mud at each other, there was much agreement among bureaucrats and among other elites about what type of policies that should be produced, for example Keynesian economic management and social policies (Hennessy 2007). In the 1950s, the policy topics of the welfare state—for example, health, education and housing—became regular features of government programmes. For example, in the 1950s and 1960s governments were under pressure to announce new housing construction programmes (Dunleavy 1981). These new issues emerged partly through the party system that tended to respond to new issues whereby political parties tended to converge on many policy issues and themselves were subject to pressure to attend to items on each policy topic in their election manifesto.

During the latter part of the twentieth century, Britain had to respond to a gradual change in its circumstances, such as the demand for independence of the colonies and migration of new populations to its shores. Management of the dissolution of the former, in the end, required some effort, and it would not be expected that these issues would fall off the agenda in the short term (Darwin 1987, 1988; Owen 1996). Governments of the left and right had to respond in the same way. Many histories of British politics present an account of accommodation with the forces of change. In particular they stress the constraints placed on the social-democratic party, the Labour Party, which tended to assume the code of the government elite and responsibly steer the economy, while at the same time introducing reforms and a gradual extension of the provisions of the welfare state (Miliband 1991). Middlemas's (1979) history also presents a picture of accommodation to a corporatist consensus, whereby labour unions bought into a governing code and economic and industrial policy predominated. However, such writers do identify alterations to the course of British politics. Even Middlemas argues that the consensus had started to break down in the mid-1960s.

The relative power hypothesis

Some accounts of agenda setting claim that structural factors systematically cause certain policies, and not others, to be on the agenda (Bachrach and Baratz 1962; Crenson 1971; Gaventa 1980; Lukes 1974; Schattschneider 1960). The distribution of power in society and in the economy is reflected in the policy outputs of government, a view held in neo-pluralist accounts of the distribution of power in market societies (Lindblom 1977). The relative power hypothesis expects issues of poverty and the powerless to give way to the interests of the economy. This literature expects a hierarchy of issues that follow from the interests of the most powerful, so that economic performance and foreign affairs always take precedence. Bulpitt's (1983), in his account of the politics of the central government and its elites, discusses the way in which powerful national elites were concerned with managing a central support system of a successful economy and foreign policy. When following such concerns, the Westminster elite gave itself autonomy to follow national policy by delegating more routine policy matters to subnational elites, and so governed without challenge. The relative power hypothesis expects poverty, social policy and territorial issues to be much lower down the policy agenda and rarely to take precedence. The same old problems dominate policy-makers and institutional routines, and standard debates in the media reinforce this inherent conservative bias for a small number of problematic topics to remain on the policy agenda.

The economic emphasis hypothesis

Preoccupation with the economy is a critical claim in many histories of British politics in the twentieth century. The economic emphasis hypothesis expects a high level of attention to economic matters. Most states see it as their role to provide conditions for economic development—even in a minimalist way—through managing monetary policy and international trade. A central role government plays is in the management of monetary policy, although this can be delegated to an independent central bank, the Bank of England, as the UK government did in 1997. The post-war period was fraught as elites were concerned about the relative decline of the British economy's productivity and competitiveness, which had started to preoccupy policy-makers since the 1960s (Moran 2003). Many commentators expressed this sentiment: for example, Bacon and Eltis in *Britain's Economic Problem: Too Few Producers* (1976) contend that the UK had lost is productive base and was relegated to an inferior economic status. Such a concern continues to this day, such as in the 2010 coalition government's desire to rebalance the economy toward the private sector.

Attention to the economic agenda is only one part of this problem as elites reformed policy areas like education and institutions such as the civil service in an attempt to modernise the country and to make it more globally competitive. In the 1960s policy-makers believed the nation was experiencing an economic crisis in light of a relative decline in economic performance, and they sought to respond to it (Clarke 2004, p. 3), often through institutional reforms designed to make central and local government more efficient and professional. Some historians claim this owes to the influence of a belief or discourse about economic performance rather than an objective analysis (see Tomlinson 2009). A perception of poor economic performance and stagnation drove the reform policies of Conservative governments elected in 1979.

Trade unions were believed to be one of the causes of the perceived crisis, a belief that increasing trade union militancy contributed to worsening economic conditions and ultimately led government to introduce reforms to the law on trade unions. For example, the government appointed a royal commission to examine industrial relations in 1965: the Donovan Commission. The Labour government attempted to reform industrial relations in 1969, followed by the proposed reforms to economic planning and industrial policy of the Conservative government of Edward Heath from 1970–1974 (Moran 1977, 2009). For Britain, the 1970s was a period of sustained political crisis. Deterioration of industrial relations and widespread strikes, continuing economic problems, such as rising unemployment and inflation, and the cost of living interacted with ideological conflict between political parties (Whitehead 1985). Both the Conservative (1970–1974) and Labour (1974–1979) governments of the era were preoccupied with economic problems and attempts to solve them. At the same time, certain elements of the early post-war politics—attempts to build a structured relationship with business in tripartite arrangements and interest in social policies and progressive reforms—continued to the end of the decade in spite of the economic crisis (see Holmes 1985). Many of these problems, such as over economic fundamentals and industrial disputes, which dominated the 1970s continued into the 1980s. And some might argue they were still present in the 1990s.

The foreign affairs emphasis hypothesis

Narratives of twentieth-century history widely describe policy-makers who had to deal with a diminished foreign policy role, with the decline of empire and with the loss of Britain's role as a military and world power. It is hard to underestimate the sense of anxiety felt in the 1960s and 1970s, associated as it was with the decline of the influence of Britain in the world, the relinquishing of its empire (especially after the humiliation of the Suez crisis) and a sense of being out of date with trends toward modernisation—a word that continually appears in the language of new governments. Partly from international commitments and also because of a wish to retain global influence, foreign affairs remains a core part of the policy agenda like the economy. The foreign affairs emphasis hypothesis expects that this domain receives much attention from the elite as it gets dragged into successive crises and adventures. In this sense, there is a similarity between Eden in Suez, Thatcher in the Falklands and Blair in Iraq.

Structural hypotheses

The 1960s was also a period of change to British social structure and attitudes (Fielding 2003), which altered the climate of policy-making encouraging the government to introduce new legal rights and to propose to open up key institutions in Britain, such as the civil service. In this way, we expect the policy agenda to adapt to this new structure; and commentators believe the modernising Labour government of 1964–1970 did just that, even if not as much as advocates for change would have wished (Dorey 2006; Fielding 2003). At the same time it still attended to more traditional social policies in housing and welfare, while at the same time adding new areas such as urban policy (Thane 2000, p. 108), which targeted a package of policies to urban areas to assist in mitigating deprivation. Therefore, even the processes making for strong changes in British politics did not lead to such radical shifts in policy as might be expected as these new policies needed to be accommodated to existing interests entrenched within political parties.

Another consideration is whether the stability in the post-1945 period was short-lived, as Britain had a multi-party system before 1939 and this had begun to reappear in the early 1960s with the revival of the Liberal Party and the Scottish Nationalist Party, the growth of a more assertive interest group politics and the increasing fragmentation of decision-making. As Chapter 1 discussed, since the 1960s there has been a greater number of access points for other actors and veto players, from the European Economic Community (EEC) beginning in 1973 to the devolution of power to Scotland, Wales and Northern Ireland. If there ever was a consensus within the governing elite about how policy should be made, learnt in the cosy world of 'club government', it had lost this sense of the governing code upon which stability rested. Taking its place is another form of government where personnel change very quickly, and where policy is created on the hoof, subject to influence to new public management ideas and the input of consultants. This decline in club government was originally noted by David Marquand in a number of publications in the 1980s (1981, 1988); then Michael Moran (2001a, 2001b, 2003) further developed the idea linking it with the loss of institutional knowledge and the growth of new forms of managerialism. In the view of Moran, this approach has itself been a source of fiascos in public policy-making, in particular a failure to regulate effectively. So even if institutional change has an element of truth, it lasted for a very a short period of time, what the French call *Les Trente Glorieuses*. This was a temporary period of decision-making, occurring between more ideological periods of conflict. British politics returned to its norm of instability and conflict after the early 1960s.

However, if the period of greater pluralism has arrived in British politics, it is not possible just to predict instability if some of the established contours have broken down. If there is more multi-partisanship or greater access points from new devolved institutions, this may limit, as Hazell (2010) argues, the policy options of the centre. It may create gridlock because the centre is not able to force through a policy. If Rhodes (1988) and others are right, that the UK has always had a complex implementation system, then it was always hard to implement policy, with gridlock not far beneath the surface. In that sense the move to institutional change should slow down policy-making and make it more stable.

The punctuation hypothesis

An alternative line of work suggests a punctuation hypothesis, which expects that the British policy agenda has always been subject to discontinuity and change, bursts of activism, which contrasts with the picture of stability presented in the conservativism hypothesis. As with the conservativism hypothesis there are different proposed mechanisms for the effect, not all of which are complementary. One uses the constitutional argument presented above, but comes to the opposite conclusion. Because the executive of the day can monopolise the law-making process if it commands a majority of votes in the House of Commons, and has the patience to get things through the House of Lords, it can act at will in enacting policy change. This institutional feature introduces the possibility of radical change because the party with a majority of seats in the House of Commons can force laws through the legislature that are opposed by other parties.

While this point is made by Tsebelis (1995, 2002) in examining the relationship between the number of veto players and policy stability, several generations of writers in British politics have accepted the idea, fearing what they call elective dictatorship (Hogg 1976). The control of Parliament by either of the two main centralised political parties for most of the period since 1945 meant that governments had almost complete control over the content of legislation and policy implementation (cf. Cox 1987; Norton 2005, 2011; Rose 1974). In this milieu, parties can ensure that their policy priorities are taken into effect, without directly accounting for the preferences of the opposition, or that of political actors in separated institutions. Of course, if the governing party does not want to change policy, then such a system of decision-making can hold up change and lock-in monopolies of decision-making, a strength of the system as seen by the older generation of scholars discussed above. That is, it could restrain change, but not smoothly. It does mean that if the governing party wants to introduce a series of measures in a policy area, say as the result of an ideological programme, then no other party or branch of government can stop it provided the party of government has a secure majority in the House of Commons.

Analyses of party government in Britain share the spirit of this literature. A line of work in British politics claims that the party-in-government has a powerful incentive to introduce an ideological programme during its first four or five years in office. It will seek to reverse the programme of the previous government. The electoral system provides this incentive for even a party elected with a minority of vote to govern in this fashion, without consulting other groups and establishing cross-party consensus. Such was Finer's (1975) critique of adversarial politics, made in the 1970s. This informed a recommendation for electoral reform, which would inject more pluralism into the operation of Britain's political institutions. The implication of this suggested reform is that politics would operate much more according to consensus. These ideas appear in comparative approaches to the study of politics and policy, such as Lijphart's, *Democracies* (1999), which admired the 'gentler, kinder' politics of more inclusive political systems, and criticised the opposite in more majoritarian systems.

Thus, dates when parties enter office do matter, and it is possible to identify important party-based forms of government, such as the election of Labour in 1964. A more right-wing Conservative government elected in 1979, under the leadership of Margaret Thatcher, introduced a series of reforms to labour markets and privatised various state-owned companies and public utilities. During the 1980s certain aspects of public policy were subjected to reforms, either through privatisation, or through introducing private-orientated principles into the management of public services. Many scholars see 1979 as a key turning point in British politics, a moment when the policy agenda shifted irreversibly because of the change in party in government with the new party headed by a strong leader. Some studies regard the post-1979 period as a dramatic shift in policy-making (e.g. Gamble 1988) while others, which support the point of view of the previous section, see a more incremental and pragmatic character to policies of the time.[1] In the former view, students of public opinion identify the late 1970s as the post-war high point of conservative attitudes among the electorate, with reduced support for collectivist policies making the public more ready to embrace the policies of the Conservative government (Bartle *et al.* 2010, p. 270; Crewe *et al.* 1977). In political terms, the industrial conflict of 1978 and early 1979, the 'Winter of Discontent', marked a key moment when Keynesian policies, corporatism and the consensus of the provision by the welfare state had been questioned (Hay 2010). Governments in the 1980s prioritised economic reform along with a new focus on social problems like crime and policies to support the family, which some term authoritarian populism (Hall 1980). In the latter view, Thatcher's leadership was more pragmatic and incremental as the government set about a gradual process of reform and realignment (Bulpitt 1985; Kerr 2001; Marsh 1995). This debate continues and it is hoped that the analysis of data in this book can shed some light as to whether 1979 really marks a key change point in British politics in terms of the policy agenda.

The election of Labour in 1997 may also have marked a turning point in policy. A reinvented Labour Party was determined to reject older ideological forms of policy and to govern middle England under the leadership of Tony Blair, who argued for a focus on education in the iconic speech that introduced this book. Decline in attention to foreign policy after the end of the Cold War, the improvement of economic conditions and rising house prices (the 'long boom') meant that economic problems did not dominate the agenda. The shift was from a concern about fundamentals to worrying about Britain sharing in worldwide economic growth. The 1990s saw an easing of pressure on the policy agenda that made the trade-off possible. The Labour government paid considerable attention to health and education, increasing public spending in these areas (for review of the policy contexts see Driver and Martell 2006; Hay 1999; Toynbee and Walker 2010, and for the electoral context, Heath et al. 2001). Its programme for government, while seeking to be a competent manager of the economy, promoted considerable investment in public services and their delivery, and attempted to address social and economic inequality and discrimination.

Labour displayed a modernising spirit, rather like its 1960s predecessors, in reforming political institutions, giving independence to the Bank of England, incorporating the European Convention on Human Rights (ECHR) into law, introducing devolved government in Scotland, Wales and Northern Ireland, providing an elected government for London, (a few) mayors for local government and reform of the House of Lords, which were not traditional socialist policies but more liberal in inspiration. From the beginning of the twenty-first century, Tony Blair became bogged down in foreign policy, and stymied on the domestic front by a long-running political conflict with the chancellor of the exchequer (see Rawnsley 2000, 2010). Under the leadership of Gordon Brown from 2007 to 2010, shocks to capital markets at the beginning of the global financial crisis returned economic problems to the top of the government's agenda. Labour's initial response was as Keynesian as anything in the *après-guerre*, meant to stimulate the economy through a variety of spending programmes. But the 1980s had made budget consciousness an essential part of economic policies in Britain, the US, Germany and many other nations. Labour was planning to scale back public spending in social policy domains even as the 2010 election approached. However, in spite of the Labour government responding to external concerns and seeking to adapt to change, Blair and Brown were closely allied in seeking to follow a political agenda that was unique to them and different from the Conservative governments from 1979 to 1997.

At its most extreme, the punctuation hypothesis is undergirded by the claim that the British political system stumbles from one controversy to the next. Britain is claimed to be prone to policy disasters (Dunleavy 1995), which owe much to the power of the central executive and the role of ministers, driven by the electoral incentives discussed above, who wish to bring about radical change. Another example comes from budgeting, where the conventional view of Rose and Davies (1994), who find relatively stable budget series with few programmes that were cancelled, was challenged by John and Margetts (2003) who produce evidence that budgeting in the post-war period supports the punctuation hypothesis. British politics offers many examples of large policy changes, which often have turned into disasters. An example that is regularly cited is the experiment of British government with local government finance, which resulted from an increase in attention to rising local taxes and the central government's obsession with local government spending. This led to the introduction of a controversial per capita local tax, the poll tax, an explosion of protest and the policy's eventual withdrawal in 1991 (Butler et al. 1994). All political systems are subject to disjunctures in the political agenda, but we expect Britain to exhibit these large shifts all the more because of the characteristics of its institutions and political culture.

Ironically, the logic supporting the punctuation hypothesis in the British context is at odds with the argument of Baumgartner and Jones (1993). They argue that the presence of veto players should increase the tendency for policy departures or large punctuations because pressures for change must overcome institutional friction before change is possible. We investigate whether Britain is subject to policy disruptions later in this book, but one line of argument suggests that Britain has more veto players than one might think, as argued by McLean (2010). In that sense, there may be more institutional stickiness in British politics, reinforced by strong constitutional conventions and the power of the civil service. Either way, the literature is inconclusive on the question of whether the presence of veto players increases or decreases the tendency of the British political system to display stability.

Models of British politics and the policy agenda

So how do theories of agenda control map on to these accounts of British politics? It is useful to summarise the different claims being made in the literature. Table 2.1 puts all the claims into two lists: one suggesting stability and the other suggesting change. In Table 2.2, we can observe how the same claims can be arranged by their predictions regarding the policy agenda, mapped as to whether the institutional

Table 2.1 Summary of accounts of British policy-making

Stability
1. Conservatism hypotheses—political institutions slow down change
2. Relative power—stable relationship between interest groups limit the space for new agenda items, and unorganised, poorer interests lose out to organised, wealthy ones
3. Dominance of economic interests—the high level of resources and threat of sanction of private capital
4. Search for a stable international support system—prioritisation of international affairs
5. Monopolistic stability—programmes kept in place until change in government
6. Non-monopolistic stability—loss of power leads to gridlock

Instability
7. Institutional loss of norms—change in institutions have induced stability
8. Monopolistic instability—government has freedom to stumble from error to error and is not punished
9. Non-monopolistic instability—where many actors create policy changes

Table 2.2 Instability and stability of attention and institutions—accounts of British politics

		Attention Stable	Attention Unstable
Institutions	Stable	1. Conservatism hypothesis 2. Relative power 3. Economic dominance 4. International support 5. Monopolistic stability	8. Monopolistic instability
	Unstable	9. Non-monopolistic instability	7. Institutional loss of norms

arrangement is stable or not. It can be seen that the bulk of claims about British politics expect that stable institutions produce stable policies, but use different causal mechanisms to arrive at the same relationship, such as issue processing through interest groups or the effect of constitutional arrangements or monopolistic power. This classification exercise demonstrates that some of these claims are observationally equivalent. The monopolistic account of decision-making suggests that agenda-controlling governments keep their priorities in place to get re-elected

Table 2.3 Instability and stability of attention and institutions—possible expectations of models of decision-making

		Attention	
		Stable	Unstable
Institutions	Stable	Incrementalism Punctuated equilibrium	Issue attention cycle Punctuated equilibrium Focused adaptation
	Unstable		Focused adaptation

next time, maintaining manifesto commitments, thus promoting stability. More commonly, the monopolistic approach is used to describe instability while occupying a stable set of institutions. But institutions change too, producing instability in one account and not in the other.

It is also possible to map the four agenda setting approaches into the same quadrants to see how they are suited to these environments—see Table 2.3. Incrementalism occupies the stability–stability quadrant, but so does punctuated equilibrium as it seeks to explain stability. Quite a few approaches can account for instability—such as the issue attention cycle, punctuated equilibrium and our focused adaptation account. The theories are less well adapted to understanding institutional change, but here focused adaptation suggests that policy-makers might seek to operate in contrasting environments.

The focused adaptation hypothesis

Some of these representations of policy-making in Britain are rather extreme. The account of monopolistic party government as almost out of control (Finer 1975) is something of a stereotype. The British political system is complex despite its unitary tag, and contains many actors exercising influence, if in an elite-dominated set of institutions. In practice the Prime Minister and Cabinet have significant resources, but they need to operate in a complex system. Neither is the account of complexity or pluralism a sensible position, nor the loss of governing norms. A more balanced approach is to consider the factors that lead to both continuity and change in the agenda, which is partly accounted for in the punctuated equilibrium model.

As discussed in Chapter 1, it is possible to argue that the policy agenda may be characterised by periods of stability, but with bursts of change as new issues enter onto the agenda. The reason for this is the factors mentioned above that tend to lock in change for long periods of time because the agenda is set and political interests seek to prevent change. But the fundamentals of political attention may shift, and when they do, the result may be rapid and mark a break point from one period to another. It is not so difficult to see the sources of the lack of change in British politics owing to the pressures for incoming governments to process issues from powerful bureaucracies, the logic of international commitment and the perpetual crisis of the economy. Added to that, policy may be seen to shift dramatically because of the rise of new issues on the agenda, the priorities of new governments and new crises that need to be solved. Moreover, such attention to both change and stability is still consistent with a moderate degree of institutional change as decision-makers can adapt to a new environment. As they occupy the same institutions they can act to protect their power. The attraction of data such as ours is that we can observe and analyse these discontinuities and periods through systematic mapping of the policy agenda.

Building on our previous work (John 2006a; John and Bevan 2012; John and Jennings 2010; John and Margetts 2003), we depict Britain as an adaptive political system. In seeking to develop a form of statecraft, Britain's political elites sought to be pragmatic in the face of changes (Bulpitt 1983, 1986). Rather than resist change, such as challenges to the hegemony of empire, they sought to accommodate change to maintain their autonomy and power, developing the art of statecraft to do so. In this way, the focused adaptation hypothesis expects that that governments experiment with policies, following on successes and avoiding failures. In part, this mechanism is conservative, as we noted above with the primacy of the economy and foreign policy, but it is also adaptive, and is a form of managing change. In short, we claim that the best way to describe British politics is consistent with the account of focused adaptation we present in Chapter 1. We do not expect continual small changes as predicted by incrementalism, because the central state is capable of imposing change when it wants to do so. We also do not anticipate the dominance of policy monopolies and stasis implied by the traditional models of British politics (and elements of the punctuated equilibrium model) because of the power of the centre to break down established centres of power when it wants to (Marsh and Rhodes 1992a). Neither do we expect many large leaps in attention.

Returning to the election of the Conservative government led by Margaret Thatcher, it is possible to see it as an important, but gradual step, toward larger policy changes, whereby her leadership was characterised by compromise as much as by large ideological initiatives (Marsh 1995), at least at first. Kerr (2002) describes the gradual evolution of these policy changes during the post-war period, within which the Thatcher reforms are but part of the story. Hay's (2007) account of Thatcherism also emphasises the gradualism of the changes. Rather than create a free-market state in 1979, the government gradually moved to reform institutions such as trades unions, and was willing to try new ideas, such as privatisation, and build on any successes that occurred. In this way, the government committed to change, but change governed by an adaptive mechanism. New Labour, elected in 1997, behaved similarly; it did not seek to overturn all aspects of the status quo, but to find a strategy that would work and would deliver successive election victories. Pragmatism, then, is central to British policy-making, which means we expect the shape of the policy agenda to be neither rigid in its stability, nor to show overreaction to each new challenge or set of party preferences.

Conclusion

This chapter has explored contrasting accounts of how public policy is made in Britain. It discusses conflicting themes in the literature: one that stresses policy stability and constant information processing through pressure of interest groups and institutional routines; and the other approach that emphasises instability. The argument in this chapter casts doubts on both these perspectives. It suggests that adaptive politicians govern Britain. As a result the policy agenda exhibits tendencies for both stability and change.

It is hard, nonetheless, to predict how recent changes in British politics feed into changes in public policy, whether the veto players from Europe, the courts and the devolved territories will slow down decision-making or whether they will—as Baumgartner and Jones suggest—increase the likelihood of policy punctuations. Our data offer a record of the how the British state responded to the key problems of the second half of the twentieth century and are explored in subsequent chapters of the book. We use them to explore the claims that were described in this chapter.

3
Measuring the Policy Agenda: Policy, Public and Media in Britain

To begin to assess our claims about focused adaptation in British politics against competing claims discussed in the preceding chapters, we construct a dataset that captures the substantive content reflected in different venues of agenda setting and policy-making (i.e. policy domains or sectors). To do this, we have adapted the coding scheme of Jones and Baumgartner (2005a, pp. 291–292) for the case of Britain as summarised in Table 3.1.[1] Within the period of policy-making since the Second World War, 1945–2008, the venues we explore are the annual programme of the executive presented in the Speech from the Throne, Acts of the UK Parliament, functional budgetary expenditure, public opinion and the print media. In this chapter we provide more detail about these data and their coding, taking each series in turn. To start, we set out the background to the Policy Agendas Project and to the coding system it created.

The Policy Agendas Project

In recent years, the efforts and projects of Frank Baumgartner and Bryan Jones have developed an approach to measuring and understanding policy agendas, with the explicit aim of testing the punctuated equilibrium model. Their studies of the US (e.g. Baumgartner and Jones 2002; Jones and Baumgartner 2004; Jones et al. 2003), which culminated in the book, *The Politics of Attention* (Jones and Baumgartner 2005a), were followed by studies of the policy agenda across nations (for reviews see Baumgartner et al. 2006, 2011; John 2006b).

In *Agendas and Instability in US Politics* (1993, 2009), Baumgartner and Jones examined policy-making in selected policy sectors in the US, such as nuclear power and urban policy, which they compared in order to

42 Policy Agendas in British Politics

Table 3.1 UK policy agendas major topic codes and abbreviations

Topic	Abbreviation	Name
1	Economy	Macroeconomics
2	Civil	Civil rights, minority issues, immigration and civil liberties
3	Health	Health
4	Agriculture	Agriculture
5	Labour	Labour and employment
6	Education	Education
7	Environment	Environment
8	Energy	Energy
10	Transport	Transportation
12	Law	Law, crime and family issues
13	Social	Social welfare
14	Housing	Community development, planning and housing issues
15	Commerce	Banking, finance and domestic commerce
16	Defence	Defence
17	Science	Space, science, technology and communications
18	Trade	Foreign trade
19	Foreign	International affairs and foreign aid
20	Gov't	Government operations
21	Lands	Public lands, water management, colonial and territorial issues

examine changes in the policy agenda. To this end, Baumgartner and Jones collected longitudinal data according to policy topic, such as the number of regulations, the frequency and tone of congressional hearings, articles in the print media and opinion polls. They mapped out the agenda and set out the key relationships. These procedures were the first steps in a systematic data-collection exercise. Even though each topic made different demands on the data (Baumgartner and Jones 1993, p. 254), there were similar coding procedures for other policy areas—including pesticides, smoking and tobacco, alcohol, drugs, urban affairs, nuclear power, automobile transportation policy and child abuse.

After *Agendas and Instability in American Politics,* and related papers (e.g. Jones and Baumgartner 1991), the authors 'thought the ideas that we initially developed there could be expanded into a more robust understanding of decision-making' (Baumgartner and Jones 2002, p. vii). With a National Science Foundation grant supplemented by local sources of funding—helped by a large number of coders, PhD students and academic collaborators—they began the project of coding the agenda of the US government according to topic, covering congressional budgets, congressional hearings, *Congressional Quarterly* (CQ), almanac stories, presidential executive orders, media coverage in the *New York Times*, public opinion and public laws. The researchers developed a codebook,[2] which enabled them to allocate the content of documents into 19 categories on major aspects of public policy from the economy to education and beyond, as well as sub-codes within these categories, which now total 225. What allowed the research to proceed was the flexibility in the way that codes could be added and modified (see Baumgartner *et al.* 1998 for a full account of the methodological issues), creating a massive dataset including 88,000 Congressional hearings, 19,883 public laws, 4,092 executive orders and 8,920 Supreme Court cases coded according to policy content. This links to work on Congressional bills, which uses the same coding system (Adler and Wilkerson 2013).

The Policy Agendas Project has generated general information, tests about the workings of US politics, and studies of how agendas are shaped and linked to punctuations, such as the Baumgartner *et al.* (2000) work on the evolution of congressional jurisdictions. The chapters in Baumgartner and Jones' (2002) edited volume showcase the project, with essays on telecommunications (MacLeod 2002), immigration (Hunt 2002), health care (Hardin 2002), science and technology (Feeley 2002), national security (True 2002), general surveys of the policy agenda (Talbert and Potoski 2002), the use of omnibus legislation (Krutz 2002), detailed studies of Congressional committees (Adler 2002), policy windows in health care policy (Wilkerson *et al.* 2002) and the agendas of Congress and the Supreme Court (Baumgartner and Gold 2002). The publications using the dataset continue to grow in number, such as Sulkin's (2005) analysis of issue uptake in Congress, looking at the link between the content of Congressional campaigns and the policy agenda; Jones and Baumgartner's (2004) study of representation, the link between public opinion and the content of policies; and Sheingate's (2006) study of biology technology policy, Baumgartner's (2006) account of environmental policy and analysis for the Congressional bills project (Adler and Wilkerson 2013). There is a lot that can be learned from the coding of policy documents about policy-making in the US, and the natural extension of this is to extend the policy content coding system to other countries, such as Britain, as this book does. What the coding system does is reliably measure the policy agenda, albeit to a predetermined coding frame, enabling the observation of polices on the basis of such measures and analysing how they change over time to make an assessment about the key changes in a political system, such as British politics. It is of course not the final word on how policies can be coded and others favour a more flexible approach that is determined by linguistic recognition of the policy topics and the use of software (Quinn et al. 2010). However, it is generally true that most countries' political systems make the distinctions between the basic policy areas that are similar to those of the policy agendas framework.

The coding system measures the attention of government, the media and the public to certain topics of public policy rather than ascertains their left-right position in relation to those issues. We are, therefore, not tracing whether the policy agenda moved to the left or the right under a particular government or whether the tone of media coverage was positive or negative. We are interested in cataloguing the subjects expressed through these venues during our period, whether they concern health, education, the economy and so on. This coding system ensures consistency over time and permits reliable comparisons to be made between each of these agendas, both qualitatively and quantitatively. For example, attention of the public, the media, the executive and the legislature to macroeconomic issues are all coded in the same way allowing the issue to be observed from one decision-making venue to another.

The comparative agendas projects

Even though this coding system originated in the US, most of the major and minor topics translate very well to other national contexts and require little adaption. Using major topics and sub-topics of public policy in the US coding system as a general guide, national codebooks have been developed with additional instructions and examples to aid coders.[3] Such was our practice for Britain.[4] This is because certain aspects of the US institutional system have no direct parallel in other countries, and comparative applications need to be sensitive to this. Other political systems do not tend to have such a powerful and differentiated legislature as the US, so certain procedures defined as legislative in the US are classed as executive policy-making elsewhere. There are also sets of institutional functions, which exist only in countries outside the US. Another major difference for policy is the range of state activities between the US federal government and the national governments of Western Europe, reflecting a less well-developed welfare state and the strength of US federalism. This means that some topics have a rather different emphasis or interpretation for a non-US audience. For example, countries that have universal welfare systems tend to use the sub-topic on comprehensive health reform to refer to reforms to health systems already in existence, though in practice a careful use of the US coding framework can incorporate most topics. National customs and institutional frameworks can also influence which major topic a particular sub-topic is included under: for example, immigration is bundled with labour and employment issues in the US, but tends to come under the major topic of citizenship rights and minority issues in most European countries, which reflects how the topic is dealt with in public debate and the kinds of institutions involved. Outside the US, terrorism is often not international in origin, and tends to fall under the categories of law and crime or defence. In the few instances where there is a gap in the coding system, research teams in the comparative project have created new categories for their own system, such as for fisheries in many European countries, including Britain. Another issue is that the topics have been developed and specialised because of the amount of attention they receive from policy-makers in the US, which leads to more detail in some areas of policy than others. In practice, due to the generalisable nature of the coding system, it is usually possible to allocate a topic code that relates to the functional equivalent for policies and institutions, which reflects the universal nature of many policy problems in Western societies.

The topic codebook for the UK Policy Agendas Project—colour coded for additions and modifications to the coding system developed in the US—is available on our website (www.policyagendas.org.uk). In this book, we analyse policy at the major topic level to explore general patterns of attention to the issues listed in Table 3.1.

While our datasets reflecting the policy, media and public venues share the coding scheme described above, their content and the process by which they were collected vary considerably. Each dataset is discussed here in turn, detailing the key differences, such as source and unit of analysis. Particular detail is provided for the media and public opinion datasets, not because they are of greater importance than policy agendas in other institutional venues, but because their gathering was particularly complex. The datasets are summarised in Table 3.2.[5]

The Speech from the Throne

As Chapter 1 discussed, the Speech from the Throne is a major venue for agenda setting and each speech can be assessed for policy topic content according to the policy agendas code scheme. It is divided into executive and legislative parts. The first consists of a series of statements about

46 Policy Agendas in British Politics

Table 3.2 Summary of UK Policy Agendas Project datasets

Dataset	Years	Unit of analysis	Source	Coded
Speech from the Throne	1945–2008	Mentions	Hansard/Hansard Prototype	Double-blind
Acts of Parliament	1945–2008	Acts	legislation.gov.uk	Double-blind
Budgetary expenditure	1951–2007	Yearly spending	UK *Blue Book*	Recoded categories
Public opinion	1960–2008	Per cent responses	Gallup (1960–2000); Ipsos-MORI (1980–2008)	Recoded categories
Media	1960–2008	Headlines	*Times* Digital Archive (1960–1985); Microfiche (1986–1991); Lexis-Nexis (1992–2008)	Double-blind

matters of executive interest or concern. This portion of the speech tends to be quite general in tone and contains few direct promises of legislative action.

The second part of the speech communicates specific details of the programme of the bills that the government intends to enact during the forthcoming session of Parliament. For instance, in the Queen's Speech of 1974 it was stated: 'Measures will be placed before you to amend the Trade Union and Labour Relations Act 1974; and to establish the Conciliation and Arbitration Service on a statutory basis and to protect and improve working conditions generally.' This language of measures, bills and other terms related to policy production are contained throughout the legislative section of the speech, indicating a clear purpose and specific legislative action. Furthermore, the transition between the two sections of the speech is marked by formal and standardised language. For example, between 1945 and 1997 this language was as follows:

> Members of the House of Commons,
> Estimates for the public services will be laid before you.
> My Lords and Members of the House of Commons,...

In 1998, the Labour government changed the order of the items of the speech putting the legislative promises first after a general policy statement. Now the state visits and other general statements appear at the end.

The Speech from the Throne data has been coded according to quasi-sentences (or policy mentions). A quasi-sentence constitutes an expression of a single policy idea or issue while not necessarily a complete sentence (Volkens 2002). Generally, this unit of analysis is identifiable from the punctuation marks and from conjunctions. The transcripts of the Speech from the Throne were blind-coded by two researchers, first to ascertain whether each quasi-sentence contained any policy content and then to assign a major topic code to the quasi-sentence. This procedure led to 90 per cent inter-coder agreement for most years.[6] The remaining differences were resolved by the project leaders, which led to a consistent and valid dataset of the policy agenda of the executive. For this book we use data for each parliamentary session for the period from 1945 to 2008.[7] Figure 3.1 shows the total length of the speech since 1945 in sentences.

Acts of Parliament

Acts of UK Parliament represent the final passage of bills originally proposed in the Speech from the Throne. While not all proposed or government bills become law and many bills are not mentioned in the

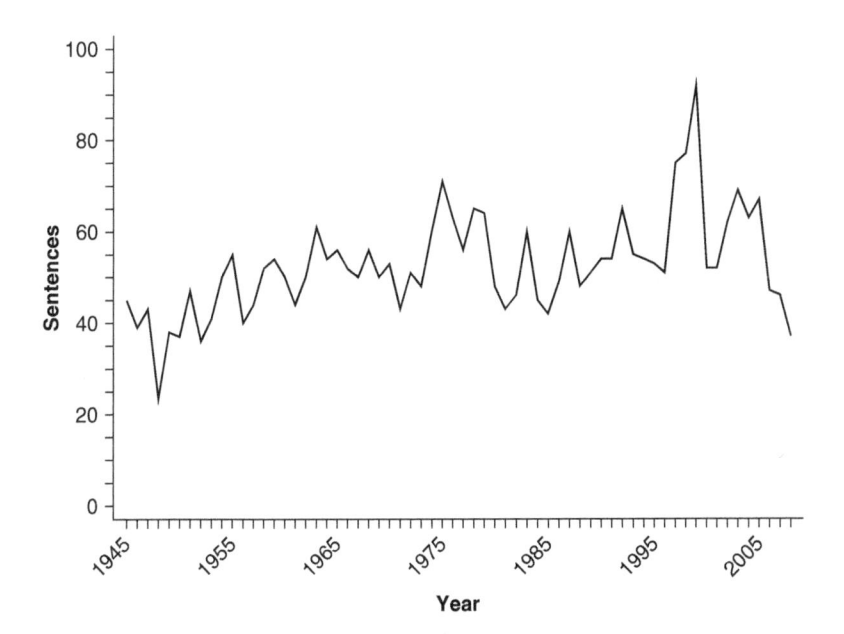

Figure 3.1 Number of sentences in the Speech from the Throne

speech, the vast majority of these bills do result in an Act of Parliament (House of Commons Library 2009, pp. 7–8). Even the few that do not are usually carried and passed in the following session. This high passage rate is in part due to single-party government of Britain in our period of 1945–2008 (the Lib-Lab pact of 1977–1978 excepted). Even the recent coalition government gets much of its programme through, though it suffers from some rebellions (Cowley and Stuart 2012), suggesting that it may be the Westminster system and not single-party rule that leads to such a high passage rate. Compared with most other nations, however, the amount of primary legislation passed in Britain is quite low with an average of just 58.8 acts passed a year between 1945 and 2008.[8]

We hasten to note that acts do not fully capture all legislative output of the British government, as many decisions can be implemented by delegated legislation (statutory instruments, rules or orders) that do not require line-by-line approval by Parliament. However, acts are the primary instrument of public policy, and it would be unlikely that a government would introduce major changes to policy without announcing it in Parliament and ensuring debate on its measures. Policy changes enacted through delegated legislation are also constrained by the terms of the original act (Page 2001).[9]

Acts of Parliament were blind-coded by two researchers according to the long and short title of each act. The short title is the formal name of the act, while the long title is either a brief or several sentence summary of the purpose of the legislation. A comparison of the content of acts and their long titles proved that the short and long title were more than sufficient to assign an appropriate major topic code to each act. Researchers assigned a single major topic code to each act leading to an 85 per cent inter-coder agreement with the remaining cases resolved by the project leaders. For each act the date of royal assent is the observed time point, in other words when an act has officially become law. Since all acts in a parliamentary year receive royal assent prior to the beginning of the next parliamentary session, each act can be associated with the Speech from the Throne in which it may have first been mentioned (Figure 3.2).

Budgetary expenditure

While government spending is one of the more easily understandable aspects of public policy, budgeting can be a complex process of trade-offs among different programmes. What is more, functional spending estimates in Britain tend to suffer from poor data quality owing to

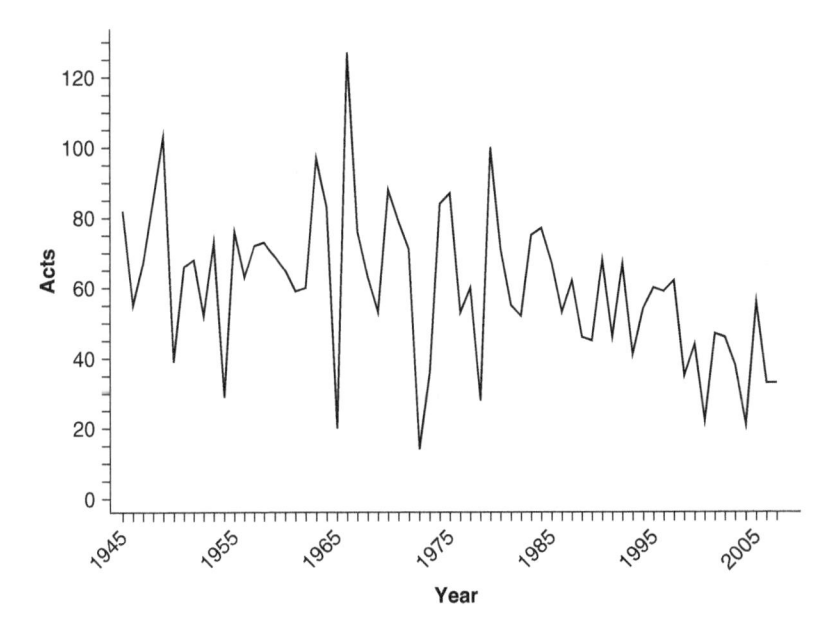

Figure 3.2 Number of Acts of the UK Parliament

changes in functional definitions and repeated re-calculations of spending figures (see Soroka *et al.* 2006). While the minutiae of the British government's spending on particular sub-functions are potentially interesting, for the purposes of this analysis the total amount of government spending is aggregated to the major topic level. Each UK *Blue Book* on government expenditure—our data sources for the budget series—contains several years of data updated to account for inaccuracies and additional expenditures not initially included upon first publication. To obtain a time series of the annual expenditure of British government from 1951 to 2007, we used data originating from the *Blue Book* for 1962, 1971, 1980, 1989, 1997, 2002 and 2008. The *Blue Book* for 1962 was the first comprehensive list of financial statistics published by the national government through the Central Statistical Office that was established to create better accounting procedures for the national government following the Second World War. We then coded these data according to the scheme in Table 3.1.

In 1996, the Office of National Statistics was formed out of a merger of the Central Statistical Office and the Office of Population Censuses and Surveys. This led to a format change in how expenditure was reported after the 1997 *Blue Book* with the addition of a category for recreation and an unclassified category for expenditure over several years. Despite the change of format, spending data across a number of important policy domains was reported consistently during the 1951–2007 period. *Blue Book* data for the period 1945–1950 are not reliable.

The major topics of government expenditure examined in this book are: macroeconomic issues, health, education, law, order and family issues, social welfare, housing and defence. Unfortunately, public expenditure on other issues, such as agriculture and transport, was neither reported nor is sufficiently disaggregated to be usable for the whole period, so can only be used for a shorter period than the others. However, those issues for which functional expenditure data is available are of sufficient importance that it enables a meaningful and wide-ranging investigation of the policy agenda in the budgetary agenda of British government.

Public opinion

Our measure of the public agenda is comprised of a combination of survey data on issues that are of importance to the public from the opinion pollsters Gallup and Ipsos-MORI (previously MORI) fielded between 1960 and 2008. In Britain, the longest-standing measure of the public agenda are aggregate-level survey responses to the open-ended 'most important problem' (MIP) question that Gallup asked according to variants of the wording, 'Which would you say is the most urgent problem facing the country at the present time?' between 1960 and 2001. (Its historical counterpart in the US asks about the 'most important problem', hence the label MIP has taken hold.) Between December 1959 and December 1964, Gallup asked a prompted version of the question, 'Which of these is the most important problem facing the country today?' The Gallup data used in this book compiles data from surveys reported in *British Political Opinion, 1937–2000* (King and Whybow 2001) and the original monthly *Gallup Political and Economic Index* (Gallup 2001). Since 1977, Ipsos-MORI has asked a similar open-ended question, 'What would you say is the most important issue facing Britain today?' The 'most important issues' (MII) data was obtained from Ipsos-MORI's monthly *Political Monitor* from 1998 to 2008, with the data for the period between 1977 and 1998 collected with the kind assistance of Professor Roger Mortimore of Ipsos-MORI. The problem/issue categories used by each survey organisation (e.g. unemployment, national health service) were re-coded to correspond to major topic codes with additional codes for 'don't know' and 'other' response categories.[10] Both the

MIP and MII measures were aggregated according to calendar year and parliamentary session as the time interval, to ensure that the time intervals correspond to those for the relevant policy or media agenda series. The MIP and MII data are described in full in Jennings and Wlezien (2011). Limited by the lack of a single continuous measure of the public agenda between 1960 and 2008, we employed a combination of MIP and MII responses to capture the issues of concern to the British public at a given moment in time.[11] While there are clear similarities between these measures, they are not, as Jennings and Wlezien (2011, p. 554) note, 'perfect substitutes' and one 'cannot simply splice the two series together to construct a continuous measure'.[12] It is crucial, then, to take great care in constructing our measure of the public agenda. Among the options for combining the MIP and MII data to mitigate the slight difference in the measures that we considered, two emerged as reasonable. The first option is a simple break point in the series when it moves from using MIP data to MII data. For this method, any transition year from 1980 to 2001 would be possible.[13] The second method estimates the average of MIP and MII responses for the overlapping time period (from 1980 to 2000). The latter has the advantage both of dampening the effect of the transition between MIP and MII (in 1980), although it adds two transition points instead of one, and of incorporating all available information concerning the public agenda during that period. While there is potential for variation in the measures due to 'house effects' (i.e. survey methodologies), sampling error, and the coding of MII or MIP responses by fieldwork agents, the measures provide a comparable indication of the underlying issues that are on people's minds (Jennings and Wlezien 2011, p. 555). This generates a continuous source for the public agenda from 1960 to 2008, aggregated at the major topic level, for both calendar years and the parliamentary sessions.

The media

In Britain, two national newspapers have historically gained a reputation as being 'newspapers of record', delivering high standards of journalism and providing authoritative content: *The Times of London* and *The Daily Telegraph*. While both match our general criteria, the availability of a longer historical record for *The Times* made it a more reasonable choice for measuring the media agenda over time, and it has been used in other studies of media attention (e.g. Soroka 2006). Furthermore, its appeal to readers with a wider cross-section of political views than the usually Conservative Party-supporting *Daily Telegraph* (see Ipsos-MORI 2005) is another important reason for use of this single source of media content. Further, our data on the media agenda of *The Times* focuses on the content of front-page news. The front page not only provides a measure of the content of the media agenda and events, but also indicates the prioritisation of issues by the media. Because of this, the prioritisation that is inherent to a front-page agenda better captures the attention of the media to issues (Boydstun n.d., pp. 30–32).

In addition to the use of front-page news content, a sampling strategy was used to make the coding of such a large number of news stories over an extended time period possible. Since our measures in this book are aggregated to the annual level (or according to the parliamentary session), the main requirement was that the sampling of the media agenda captured the overall content throughout the year. Front-page news stories from Wednesday each week were collected for the period 1960–2008.[14] The headlines[15] of these stories were then blind-coded by two researchers according to the major topic codes,[16] with comparisons finding 80 per cent inter-coder reliability and with disagreements resolved by the project leaders. This created a database of 21,854 front-page headlines from every Wednesday edition of *The Times of London* from 1960 to 2008.[17]

Between 1960 and 2008, two key changes in the format of *The Times* occurred. The first was the move to a standard broadsheet format on 3 May 1966, the second was the change to a smaller tabloid format in November 2003. Sampling the front-page agenda during the broadsheet era was straightforward, with the front page defined as all headlines printed on the first page of the newspaper ranging from 8 to 11 headlines a day on average. Prior to this change, *The Times* took its role as a paper of record rather literally, presenting information on births, deaths, marriages, sport results, play and concert reviews, and even television schedules on the first several pages of the newspaper. As a result, the section titled 'News' started anywhere between 5 and 17 pages into the paper. An extensive review of stories that headed the 'News' section demonstrates that these matched what would typically be thought of as front-page news, with the biggest and most important news headlines of the day listed at the start of the section. In the pre-broadsheet era, the front page of *The Times* is defined as all 'News' stories on the first full page of the 'News' section in the newspaper each day.[18]

The tabloid format presents a further set of challenges as no clear delineation between front-page news and the remainder of news existed, as had been the case during the broadsheet or pre-broadsheet eras.

Often, the front page of the tabloid format of the newspaper consisted of a single headline, and in general no more than three headlines on any particular day. A brief 'Inside' overview also printed on the front page summarises stories throughout the paper and not just front-page news as normally understood. The second page of the paper contains two or more editorial pieces covering general concerns of the day, human interest stories and other matters, and cannot be equated with front-page news. The third and fourth pages of the tabloid format contain many additional 'News' headlines and, as such, can be considered an extension of the front page. To measure the media agenda of the 'front page' during this period, all stories were gathered from the first, third and fourth pages from November 2003 to December 2008, leading to a noticeable over-sample (i.e. an excessive number of front-page stories than observed in earlier years). However, the exclusion of news stories from the fourth page led to a systematic under-sample, which would represent a more significant methodological problem, and in light of this we opted to use stories from the first, third and fourth pages of the tabloid format of *The Times*.

The Times does not provide a continuous measure of the media agenda between 1960 and 2008. Like a number of newspapers at the time, *The Times* experienced a dispute between management and unions, leading its owners to shut down the paper from 1 December 1978 to 12 November 1979.[19] For nearly one year, no editions of the newspaper were published and this gap is reflected in the dataset. This prevents analysis of the media agenda at the weekly, monthly or quarterly level when including this period. An aggregation of the media data to an average for the calendar year only masks this issue because the inclusion of a sample of just six front pages in 1979 leads to dramatically lower absolute levels of media attention and variance than in complete years. The use of percentages of attention instead of frequencies addresses this issue in part, but 1979 remains an analytic concern. Unlike many data issues in the social sciences, these observations are not missing and represent true zeros for the number of front-page stories in *The Times* over this period, adding an additional complication to analysis.

With that said, techniques for dealing with missing data for the strike period can be appropriate depending on how the data is conceptualised. For example, if the media agenda is conceptualised as a measure of salience or events it can be treated as missing and imputed, but if it is conceptualised strictly as a measure of the content of media during this period it should be treated as zeros, as no media attention from *The Times* actually existed. However, imputation of missing observations systematically under-count the amount of attention to labour issues and to the media during this time period as both the number of strikes and the concern over disruption to the national media cannot be measured. An imputed series can therefore be used for quantitative or qualitative analysis, but the downward bias in attention to these issues must be kept in mind.

Conclusion

This chapter has detailed how a common policy content coding system—the policy agendas coding system developed by Baumgartner and Jones—has been applied across a wide range of institutional venues. The sorts of data gathered and coded for each venue can be quite different (e.g. speeches, titles of legislation, budget categories, opinion polls, newspaper front pages). The main characteristics of each of these datasets are summarised in Table 3.2, which can be used to serve as a reference guide for the reader. This reports the name of the dataset, the time period it covers, the source of the data, how it was coded and the unit of analysis. Throughout the analyses presented in this book, we explain how these data series are constructed and matched. Any changes to these formats are noted in each relevant chapter.

4
Change and Stability in Executive and Legislative Agendas

In this chapter—and in the two that follow—we statistically uncover major and minor epochs in the post-war British policy agenda. Our focus is items in the Speech from the Throne and the topics of Acts of Parliament, which as we have discussed above, provide an important portrait of the executive agenda. Attention to laws and to speeches correlates highly for many, but not all, policy topics. So, with the data described in the preceding chapter, we are able to appraise the different accounts of agenda setting, namely, incrementalism, the issue attention cycle, punctuated equilibrium and focused adaptation. Much of the chapter reports on the trends, changes and cycles in major policy topics during the post-war years. Our inspection reveals periods of large changes in the content of the agenda, which reflect the emergence of new policy problems and the setting of new priorities by political parties after winning elections. In fact, what is so interesting about these data we present—for topics like agriculture, civil rights, health, education and crime—is how much they change in importance across the decades since 1945.

To assist the task of interpretation and explanation, we relate the patterns in the data to accounts of the period written by historians, public policy scholars, political scientists and other informed observers. Our data reflect important periods of British political history about which much has been written. By representing the data over time, this chapter (and chapters 5, 6 and 9) create a policy history of British politics. Rather than tracing British political history through a sequence of events, crises, personalities, wars and institutions, we explore how decision-makers in government coped with the large number of subjects and problems facing them, choosing to commit more of their attention to a given issue relative to the others. In particular, we aim to find out how and why government policy priorities changed over time as a means of assessing the competing expectations set out in the preceding chapters. It is likely the changes we observe will correspond to what historians consider to be well-known events in British politics, such as in 1979, when Margaret Thatcher took office, or in 1997, when Tony Blair led New Labour into power. These dates are assumed to be important because new leaders entered office with an intention to establish a particular approach to policy-making, but there may be other factors shaping the policy agenda at other times. We expect the findings to differ from the standard histories for the functional topics that do not so often make it into the history books. Our analysis can find out what changes beyond the narrative of grand events, in what citizens consume from government in the form of public policies focused on building roads, expenditure on missiles or doing something about the environment. In this sense, we can add to the historical record by reporting and discussing changes in the policy agenda, which may occur at different periods, to classic accounts of crises or partisan shifts in British politics. In this way, our analysis presents important new information about the impact of the retreat from empire, the building of the welfare state, the economic crisis from the 1960s to the 1990s and the re-discovery of social policy since the 1990s — the overall contours of the policy agenda. The examination of the historical record may then be used to interrogate the four models of agenda setting.

In the following sections, we first examine the patterns of policy-making attention according to the 19 main topics. These figures are reported as percentages in the text, but Tables 4.1 and 4.2 show the raw figures for all the topics. Once we have given a brief picture of the change we engage in a more detailed examination.

Core activities of government

Our analysis commences with policy domains that consist of the key services that every state is under pressure to provide for its citizens. These core topics, the economy, international affairs, defence, government operations and law and crime, are usually prominent on the policy agenda (Jennings et al. 2011b).

Macroeconomics

Figure 4.1 plots the attention of British government to macroeconomic issues from 1945 to 2008. This includes the percentage of the Speech from the Throne assigned to this topic, which includes mention or

Table 4.1 Summary statistics of speech policy topic attention by year, 1945–2008

Topic	Abbreviation	Mean	Minimum	Maximum	SD
1	Economy	7.02	0	17	3.48
2	Civil	1.83	0	12	2.29
3	Health	1.66	0	6	1.55
4	Agriculture	2.08	0	7	1.68
5	Labour	2.55	0	7	1.78
6	Education	3.06	0	11	2.35
7	Environment	1.09	0	5	1.17
8	Energy	1.14	0	7	1.43
10	Transport	2.22	0	7	1.75
12	Law	4.69	0	17	3.60
13	Social	2.14	0	7	1.98
14	Housing	2.48	0	11	2.05
15	Commerce	2.03	0	9	1.86
16	Defence	5.85	0	26	3.76
17	Science	0.46	0	3	0.81
18	Trade	2.54	0	9	2.09
19	Foreign	15.85	0	31	5.97
20	Gov't	5.49	0	18	3.49
21	Lands	7.55	0	17	3.17

Table 4.2 Summary statistics of acts policy topic attention by year, 1945–2008

Topic	Abbreviation	Mean	Minimum	Maximum	SD
1	Economy	7.17	0	19	3.19
2	Civil	1.14	0	4	1.03
3	Health	2.48	0	6	1.44
4	Agriculture	3.05	0	9	2.32
5	Labour	1.85	0	5	1.57
6	Education	1.71	0	5	1.43
7	Environment	1.60	0	10	1.62
8	Energy	1.69	0	4	1.18
10	Transport	4.22	0	17	2.95
12	Law	8.40	0	21	4.31
13	Social	1.68	0	7	1.46
14	Housing	3.26	0	10	2.41
15	Commerce	4.54	0	15	2.89
16	Defence	2.03	0	12	2.39
17	Science	1.14	0	4	1.12
18	Trade	0.71	0	4	1.01
19	Foreign	1.98	0	5	1.47
20	Gov't	6.68	0	20	4.22
21	Lands	3.54	0	15	3.28

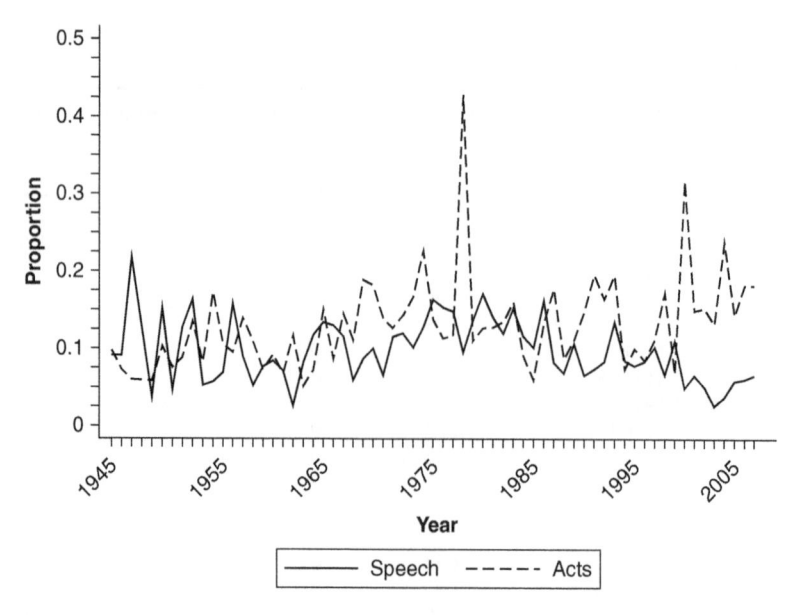

Figure 4.1 Incrementalism in macroeconomy in speeches and laws, 1945–2008
Note: Pearson correlation coefficient between speech and laws series is −0.14 ($p = 0.26$).

policy proposals on inflation, the economy, money supply, the national budget and debt, taxation, price control and industrial policy. Against this is plotted the percentage of Acts of UK Parliament on the same topic. It is to be expected that there is a correlation between the speeches and laws because the Speech from the Throne often signals pieces of legislation in advance or contains promises that legislation is to be expected. When considered over time and across all topics, this relationship is strong (Bevan *et al.* 2011). However, this speech–laws link is not observed for the economy since 1945. It may be the case the speech indicates more general attention of British government to macroeconomic issues that need action whereas legislation is not the main vehicle through which fiscal and monetary policy is set (that is the Chancellor's budget speech), but tends more to be about industrial policy.

Overall, the economy is an important area of attention taking up 9.7 per cent of the Speech from the Throne in the post-war period, and 13.1 per cent of Acts of UK Parliament. Figure 4.1 suggests little difference between the two in terms of the level of attention but the laws receive statistically more than speeches ($t = 3.6$). There is not that much variation in the series either, with the standard deviation being

4 per cent for speeches and 6 per cent for laws, although the former has a high point of 42 per cent in 1978, well above the average. With the exception of some years when there are large leaps in attention in laws such as in 1978, attention is quite smooth over the decades. This depicts a pattern of decision-making that resembles incrementalism, or attention change through small steps.

The patterns depicted are consistent with the expected attention to this core policy issue in the post-war years, with a higher level of attention in the early 1950s, which then declines in the period when Britain's post-war economic problems receded. From the early to mid-1960s the level of attention to macroeconomic issues started to increase, with increasing pressure on the level of the currency. Using simple inferential statistics it is possible to assess whether these years marked a shift in attention to a state in which the economy increasingly dominated British politics. We see no such evidence. In part, this could be because in the mid-1990s, the economy moved off the agenda again, partly because economic conditions started to improve with rising employment and better growth through the 1990s and 2000s. This was the period when Labour Chancellor Gordon Brown famously declared that a Labour government would not see a return to the era of boom and bust,[1] although the years of economic crisis had already started to recede during John Major's premiership following Britain's exit from the Exchange Rate Mechanism (ERM). However, attention is higher after 1991 than before: 12.1 versus 15.7 per cent (t = 2.1). So while attention to economic issues in the speech is falling, its presence in acts is higher than before. In 1997, New Labour's attention to acts is higher than the preceding period (t = 2.3).

From their low correlations for macroeconomic issues, it appears that Acts of Parliament and the Speech from the Throne series are measuring different things. In 1966, for example, there were a large number of institutional changes that appeared under the major topic for macroeconomic issues, such as laws on the national debt—changes to the consolidated fund—and changes in taxation. The Prices and Incomes Act instituted control of prices and incomes, and the Industrial Development Act set up arrangement for the giving of grants to industry. In a similar vein, the Industrial Re-organisation Corporation Act 1966 established a public corporation to promote development of an industry. In other words, the economic policy of the then Labour government was targeted at a number of rule changes and was connected to industrial policy. In 1967, it was much the same, with the Iron and Steel Act 1967 that established the National Steel Corporation. In 1993, we find the government making promises in the speech about promoting budgetary discipline in the EEC, then statements on macroeconomic policy. A high point of attention to the economy occurred in the Queen's Speech of 1986, when the level of attention to macroeconomic issues reached 16 per cent with attention to EEC economic matters, monetary and fiscal policy, and specific policy initiatives such as privatisation and employment. In other words, the Speech from the Throne is a means to convey general attention to macroeconomic policies that do not necessarily require legislation. The budget speech can be used to announce policies, such as new programmes and spending which also do not require legislation, and which has been used as a measure of economic policy-making (Hakhverdian 2010).

The peaks and troughs of the legislative agenda tend to relate to special policies, which were very much in evidence in the post-1965 period as successive governments embarked on a series of structural reforms of the British economy, which included industrial policy but then successive privatisations in the 1980s and 1990s. If attention to the macroeconomy diminished from 1993 on, attention of British government to structural reforms did not. Consistent with expectations set out earlier, the party in office does not affect the level of attention ($t = 1.6$). All governments attend to this issue, given its fundamental importance to the state and to parties seeking re-election. However, there are differences for New Labour right at the end of the period: it talked less about the economy than its predecessors at an average level of attention of 6.3 per cent compared with 10.4 per cent ($t = 3.3$), but passed more acts on the topic at 16.8 per cent of the total, a substantial number compared with the rest of the series at 12.3 ($t = 2.3$). This lack of attention in the speech perhaps reflected the economic growth of most of the period, in particular between 1997 and 2007.

International affairs

In the Bulpitt (1983) scheme of state priorities, foreign affairs takes a central place because of the need for the state to create an external support system so it can maintain its autonomy. In the case of Britain, external factors are prominent because of the legacy of overseas commitments from empire, its role as a global power with a military capability and its representation in the governance of international institutions (Sanders 1990). Given these roles, any large crisis of international affairs is bound, at least in part, to become the concern of government. Even decolonisation leads to a large amount of activity of the state in order to get measures through Parliament. Likewise, changes to international

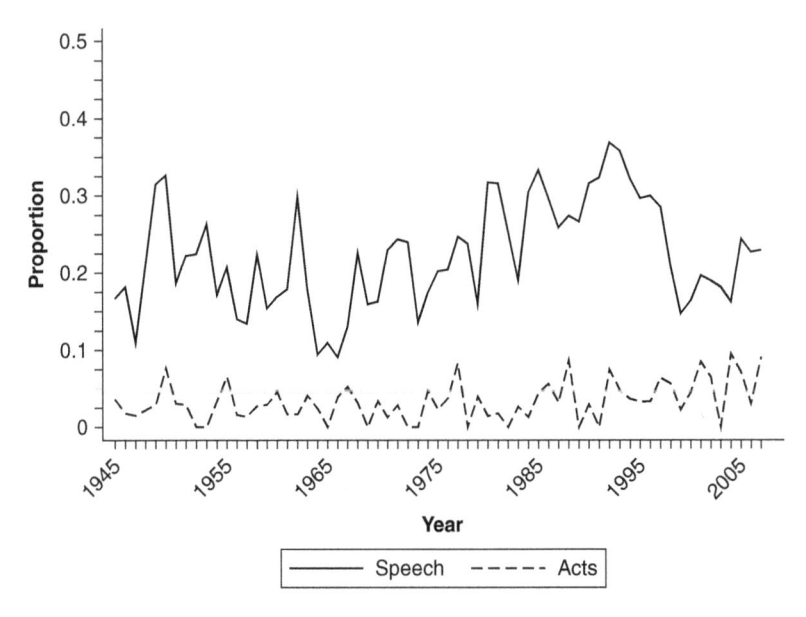

Figure 4.2 Focused adaptation in international affairs and foreign aid in speeches and laws, 1945–2008
Note: Average attention in speeches is 22.3 per cent, but only 3.4 per cent in Acts of Parliament. The series are uncorrelated ($p = 0.6$).

treaties may require a lot of government activity, such as entry into the EEC (Figure 4.2). However, it is important not to exaggerate the extent to which the share of foreign policy differs from other comparable states, as Britain has similar external preoccupations as other large European countries (Smith and Smith 1988).

As with the economy, the British government does not primarily use legislation to respond to and act in international affairs, the average share of the agenda for the Speech from the Throne and Acts of Parliament is very different, with very few acts being included in this category. The speech conveys substantial information about government policy in general, foreign policy concerns including overseas aid, the exploitation of international natural resources, policies toward developing countries, international finance and polices in relation to different parts of the world, such as Africa, China, Western Europe and North America, with some other issues such as matters about Britain's embassies and diplomatic service.

The attention to international affairs in the speech is subject to some variation with a standard deviation of 7 per cent, but this is less of a proportion of the average than for macroeconomic issues, which suggests there are elements to the Speech from the Throne that are stable over time, such as giving notice of visits by the head of state to foreign countries. Patterns in the Speech from the Throne are consistent with focused adaptation as they show several changes in attention levels and no long periods of stability. The trend in attention over the period resembles that for the economy, with a high level of policy-making attention in the early period that declines, but where there is a growth of attention to the issue in the 1960s that continues until the 1980s. This early drop in attention can be linked to the settling down of international affairs in the period following the Second World War. There are a few jumps of attention, such as after the Suez crisis of 1956. Then there is the gradual rise in the pre-occupation of British government to international affairs from the mid-1960s up to the late 1980s. Then foreign policy starts to diminish steadily during the 1990s. Seeking to explain this trend one can first observe the need to attend to matters pertaining to the European Community as this became more important when the Wilson government sought to prepare Britain for entry. For example, the Queen's Speech of 1967 contained the declaration, 'My Government look forward to the early opening of negotiations to provide for Britain's entry into the European Communities.' There were successive international conflicts and crises, such as the war in Vietnam, even though Britain was not militarily involved. International security and disarmament appear on the agenda during this period too, which explains the later decline. In particular, possible conflict between the superpowers was a major cause of concern for British government from the 1950s up until the fall of the Berlin Wall in 1990. These data show changing focus on international affairs as issues rise and fall in importance rather than a decline. The changes tend to be more dramatic than for the economy, which may reflect the nature of international affairs, and the extent to which it is possible to have distinct eras when policy attention changes, rather like a structural shift.

Defence

Defence refers to provision of collective security through the application of resources and employment of personnel and technology that can threaten and carry out acts of force on other states, either in defence or in attack. Figure 4.3 shows the trends in the Speech from the Throne and Acts of Parliament for this topic. The policy activities relating to defence include military budgets, the intelligence services, the army, navy and air-force personnel, military aid, weapon sales, provision for veterans,

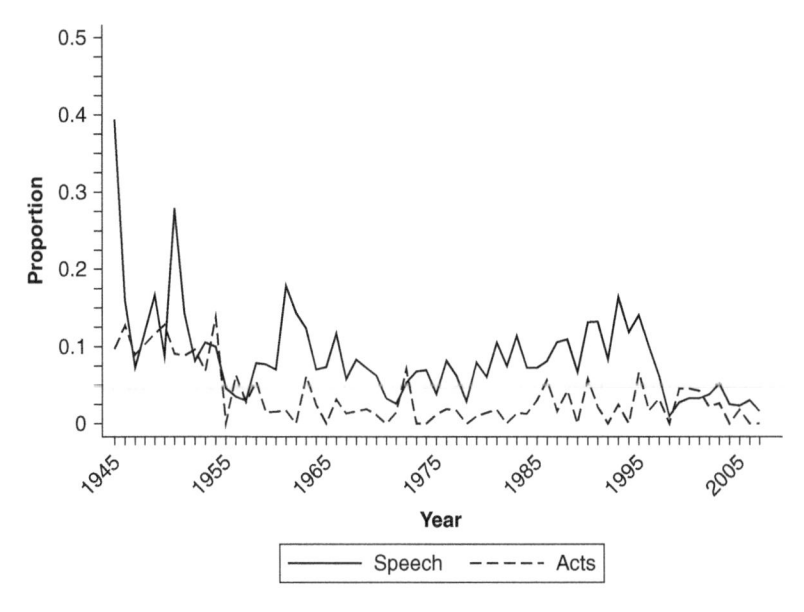

Figure 4.3 Punctuations and focused adaptation in attention to defence in speeches and laws, 1945–2008

Note: The speech and laws series have a Pearson correlation of 0.46 ($p < 0.01$). Laws on average take up 3.5 per cent of the total legislative agenda but 8.7 per cent of the speech. Standard deviations for speeches (3.7 per cent) and laws (6.2 per cent) are relatively large.

procurement, installations, reserves, nuclear weapons, civil defence, the conduct of war and international terrorism and its control. These factors, of course, remain relevant to government in the absence of military conflict, but they are expected to rise sharply when conflict becomes more pronounced and countries consider that they need to be prepared for war as well as wage it. Here defence is core to the state and its survival so it is no surprise that governments wish to prioritise this topic, though not all conflicts threaten territorial integrity. In terms of our measures of the policy agenda—speeches and laws—defence is expected to be a normal but usually quite minor part of the Speech from the Throne, but to receive more attention from government during wartime as it makes statements about the defence of the nation and Britain's military action overseas. With legislation there may be changes to the regulation of the armed forces, but these too tend to receive more attention during periods of conflict.

Speech and Act series for defence, plotted in Figure 4.3, display a lower correlation than in the case of international affairs, suggesting that government uses the speech to signal the introduction of legislation about the armed forces rather than to offer general policy statements. Greater dispersion in the series is predictable because governments are under pressure to attend to this area at certain times, such as the outbreak of conflict or when pressured to conduct reviews of defence capabilities and regulations. What is striking from this is the large amount of attention dedicated to defence in the early post-war period, which captures the early years after the Second World War, the need to wind down wartime regulations and manage continuing international matters associated with the war. The King's Speech of 1945 included references to the end of the war, such as the surrender of Japan and the demobilisation of the armed forces. By 1946 there was discussion of the organisation of central government on defence and by 1947 the organisation of civil defence. From that point, attention of government to defence dropped dramatically as the Atlee government focused on other issues. It rose again with the onset of the Korean War in 1950, then declined in prominence during the 1950s. Acts of Parliament exhibit a similar pattern of decline after 1945, following a number of pieces of legislation dealing with the aftermath of war, such as War Damage (Valuation Appeals) Act 1945 and the National Service (Release of Conscientious Objectors) Act 1946.

The other large jump in the attention of British government to defence in the speech is observed in the late 1950s, which reflects Britain's involvement in international treaties at the time, which were not addressed in legislation. Examples were references to the North Atlantic Treaty Organization (NATO), which had been established in 1949, occurring in the speeches of 1953, 1954 and 1959. The Geneva Conference in 1959 was mentioned in the speech of the same year alongside other international negotiations.

What is striking in that immediate post-war period is how the attention of policy-makers to defence dropped off suddenly both for speeches and laws, even though there have been numerous military conflicts across the world in the period since. The attention of both speeches and laws to the issue of defence continued to decline until the mid-1970s, increasing gradually until the late 1980s before dropping away again. Similar to the early 1960s, the decline in attention to defence in the mid-1990s is steep. Clearly this represents an important change in the agenda, and reflects the decline—if temporary—in international tensions after the end of the Cold War.

Partisan effects on the policy agenda might be expected for this topic as the Conservatives are expected to be more concerned with defence matters, putting 'guns before butter' (Soroka and Wlezien 2005, p. 676), though of course military conflicts can occur under any government. It is possible that right parties prefer defence for historical reasons and consider international affairs to be more important as it is about the nation, which is core to the identity of the party and reflects its history of support for empire. There is no statistically significant difference for laws, but Conservatives attend to defence more in speeches with its share of the agenda averaging 24 per cent of the speech compared with 19 per cent for Labour (t = 3.5). However, this difference could just be due to chance in that conflicts happened during the 1950s and 1980s when the Conservatives were in power. On the other hand, in spite of its military interventions in Kosovo, Afghanistan and Iraq, New Labour emphasised defence much less in its policy agenda than its predecessors: with 3.1 per cent of speeches relating to defence compared with 9.8 before 1997 (t = 3.5), although the 2.1 per cent of laws on defence under New Labour compared with 3.7 per cent (t = 1.4). Overall, trends suggest support for the claims of punctuated equilibrium in 1945 and 1998, and focused adaptation during the period 1955–1998.

Government operations

The third of the five core activities of government is government operations. This relates to public policies about the structure and management of government, including such things as budgeting systems, intergovernmental relations (including local government), government efficiency and the civil service, the powers of the House of Lords and other legislative procedural matters, the regulation of political parties, and the monarchy as well as other sub-topics, such as political scandals (Figure 4.4).

The low correlation between these series suggests how the British government can announce major changes to the running of government not attached to legislation. Moreover, a good proportion of the legislative agenda is focused on the machinery of government, or at least these issues take up the legislative timetable. Indeed, it is possible to argue that some reorganisations and reforms of British government take place neither through the Speech from the Throne nor Acts of Parliament given the royal prerogative of ministers so this is only part of the total activity.

At the start of the post-war period there were a large number of acts relating to government operations, including a series of small reforms, such as of local government, of ministerial salaries, of Northern Ireland and of the post office, the need for reorganisation after war and secondary and indirect effects of the programme of nationalisation. A spike

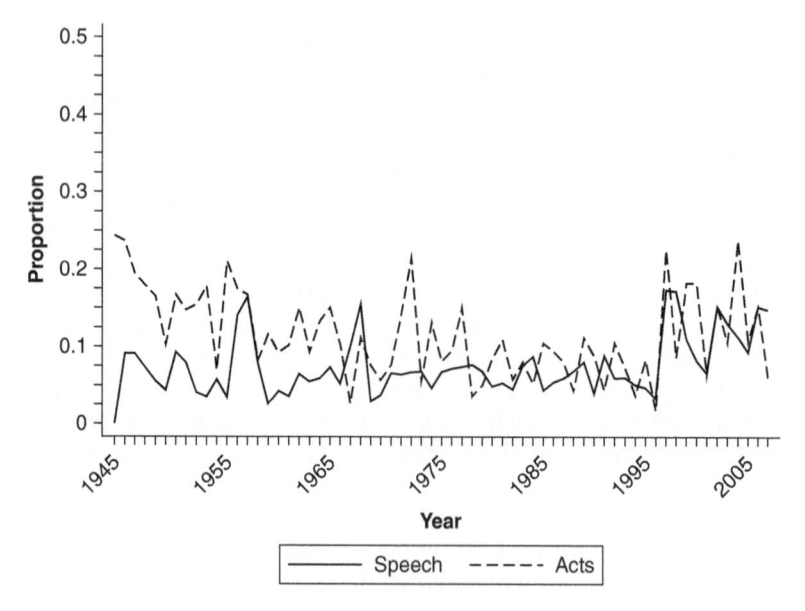

Figure 4.4 Punctuation, focused adaptation and issue attention cycle in government operations in speeches and laws, 1945–2008

Note: Pearson correlation between the series is 0.16 ($p = 0.12$). The speech series has a mean of 7.5 and standard deviation of 5.6 per cent compared with 11.4 and 3.8 per cent for laws.

in the early 1970s is due to a combination of factors, such as changes to the administration of Northern Ireland in response to the troubles there, which led to a number of reforms to government institutions, such as the Northern Ireland Assembly Act 1973. This was the power-sharing agreement that established a decision-making assembly, which Protestants eventually scuppered through the Ulster Workers Council Strike of 1974. Local government reforms also occurred during this period, so the upsurge in attention may be thought of as the legacy of the reforming Labour government 1964–1970, which sought to modernise British politics, and the acceptance of this programme by the Conservative government 1970–1974.

A punctuation is evident in both the speeches and laws associated with the reforms of the late 1990s when Labour entered office with pledges to modernise and reform Britain's institutions, which included local government and devolution, the reform of political parties, provisions for referendums and further changes to the governance of Northern Ireland.

Law and crime

The final pillar of core state activities—the goods that matter to the lives of all citizens—is protection against crime and the provision of law and order. Without authoritative instruments of the state to punish and deter illegal and anti-social behaviour, society and the economy could not function. The policy agendas topic of law, crime and family issues, is one of the categories that have caused some debate among scholars because of the conjunction of family policy with criminal justice issues. It covers the Home Office, the judiciary and the agencies charged with targeting crime, white-collar crime, crimes relating to illegal drugs, the courts, prisons, juvenile crime, child abuse, police and fire, the criminal code and public order issues. Family issues include the battery of women and child custody, which veers toward social policy issues or could be categorised as a gender issue. Here it might be advisable to analyse such issues separately as feminist scholars have done (Annesley et al. 2012), but they do not greatly affect the trends explored here in the aggregate.

Figure 4.5 maps out the policy agenda for law, crime and family issues in the same fashion as the other topics. Here it is possible to observe how the agenda of the speech and of the acts track together, which is expected because the natural outcome of the attention of government to law and crime is a legal change, often achieved through primary legislation.

Before discussing Figure 4.5 it is useful to speculate on the extent to which policy changes might be expected on crime and related issues. It is a subject that may attract government attention from time to time because the legal system needs regular reform, such as to adapt to new forms of crime or to respond to changes in the role of the courts. However, it is not quite the same kind of topic as the other four sets of core government activity as attention can be very low. On the other hand, it is a topic that can appear frequently in the media (see later discussion) and is of public concern, and is an example of where the agenda can shift linked to popular and media perceptions. In addition, it is possible to have shocks from crime because of citizen lawlessness, such as the urban riots which occurred in England in 1980, 1981 and 1985, which can impact on the public agenda and on policy (see John 2006a).

The policy agenda on crime and law follows a relatively stable trend at a low level of attention for most of the post-war period up until the mid-1990s, with a few dips when there was not much concern in government to the issue. The rise in the attention of policy-makers to crime occurred during the late 1990s and 2000s, increasing sharply for the

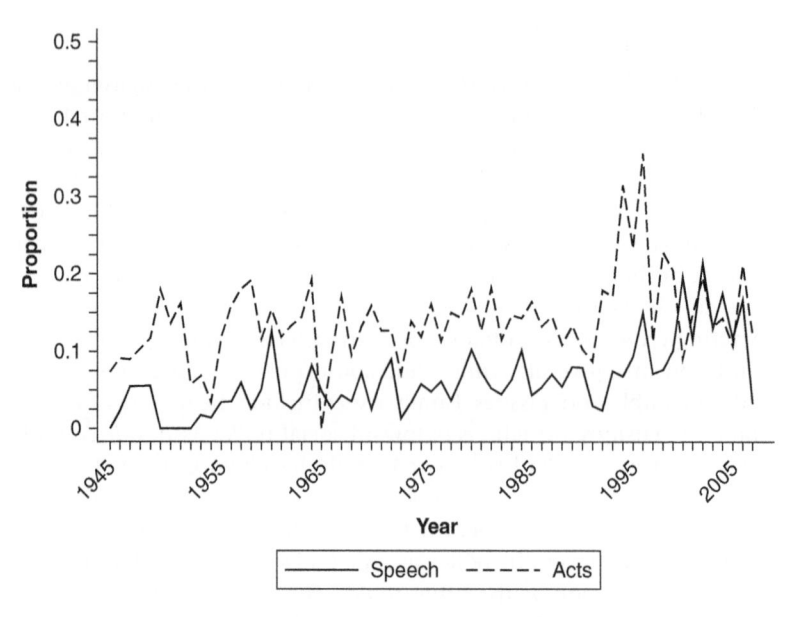

Figure 4.5 Focused adaptation and issue attention cycles in attention to law, crime and the family in speeches and laws, 1945–2008

Note: The Pearson correlation between the series is 0.36 ($p = 0.004$). The speech series mean is 6.5 and the acts mean is 14.1 per cent. The standard deviation for speeches is 4.7 compared with 5.6 per cent for acts.

speeches and more gradually for laws, stabilising after 2004. In fact, the leap during the Major government looks from first inspection rather like an issue attention cycle, when Michael Howard was home secretary, at a time when there was much legislation on criminal justice going through Parliament. This period included altering penalties on crime, such as the Offensive Weapons Act 1996 and the Sexual Offences (Conspiracy and Incitement) Act 1996. There are no differences for acts by party in office.

Social policy activities

In the next sections we move to the goods that provide social benefits, often associated with the welfare state, although, of course, they were provided to citizens long before then. The wartime coalition and the Labour government of 1945–1951 extended social benefits and consolidated the collective provision of them. Most British governments since 1945 have been heavily committed to these policies and they figure prominently in party manifestos at election time. Governments may like to be seen to be doing something on areas that the public care about, such as health and education. As with other policy sectors these issues also are subject to change or reform from time to time, such as to improve efficiency, to raise standards or to ensure that structures and processes are consistent with other administrative structures or international rules. It also may be the case that these issues have grown in importance because government wants to deliver benefits to the population to win elections, or there may be pressures to spend more because of technological change (see Chapter 9). If other items on the policy agenda decrease in importance, such as the economy, defence and international affairs, will governments be tempted to push other items onto the agenda, such as crime, social welfare or health? The argument is that such a movement did occur in the policy agenda in the 1990s, which the Conservative Party initiated under the leadership of John Major, but the largest beneficiary was New Labour elected in 1997, which sought to shape the policy agenda of British government in many ways to distinguish it from its predecessors and respond to the changing political environment.

Health

Both speeches and laws experience years when health attracts attention from policy-makers and years when it does not, as indicated in Figure 4.6. In spite of the large amount of public spending devoted to it (see Chapter 9), health receives less attention from British government than crime. It is also surprising that the speech and law attention series are uncorrelated, given that health reforms tend to require legislation.

Up to the 1970s, the data do not show a distinct pattern of attention, which suggests that focus of the government on health was spasmodic, and the policy field attracted the attention of policy-makers when it needed reforms or when particular problems came along. Once dealt with, the policy area returned to a normal pattern of low attention. In fact, in the years between 1945 and 1975 there was no space given to health in the Speech from the Throne for some 12 of the 30 years, whereas this was the case for just 5 years for acts. In the 33 years since that time, only five speeches assigned no attention to health. The eye can discern the growing preoccupation of government to health in both laws and acts over this period. From the mid-1970s they rise hand in hand, peaking in the late 1990s. This is the period of health reforms in which successive governments sought to reform the National Health Service, with market- or target-based reforms (see Bevan and Hood 2006, Greener 2008). This builds on the period since the 1970s when

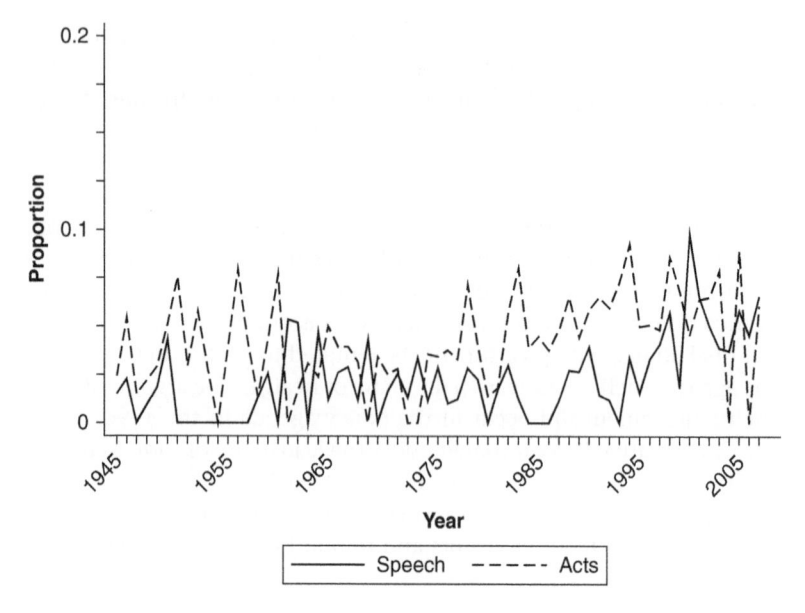

Figure 4.6 Focused adaptation in attention to health in speeches and laws, 1945–2008

Note: Average values are 2.3 per cent of the speech and 4.3 per cent of acts with standard deviations equal to 2.1 per cent and 2.5 per cent for speeches and acts respectively. The two series have Pearson correlation at only 0.08 ($p = 0.51$).

successive governments had reorganised the health service to try to get more rationalisation and modern management techniques (Hann 2007; Klein 2010). The figure suggests a pattern consistent with focused adaptation, where the government responds to increasing problems in the health arena with a possible structural shift in attention beginning in the Major government.

There is a difference according to the party in government, with Labour tending to emphasise health more in its policy agenda at 3.4 per cent of the speech compared with the Conservatives at 1.4 per cent ($t = 4.2$), although there is no difference for laws. The statistical significance of this break point falters if we remove the New Labour years after 1997, although it remains if we accept a 90 per cent confidence level ($t = 1.9$). Labour governments offer policies on health even if there is no difference in the amount of legislation that each party produces when in government. For laws, the peak is in the late 1980s and early 1990s and the difference becomes non-significant after 1994. The legislative action was in an earlier period, compared to the more general policy activism of New Labour after 1997. The resulting picture for health is less clear than for crime. There is this same rise in attention to the topic, with a leap in the last part of the series, but it is less like a punctuation from a previous equilibrium. Instead, the series are moving in different ways.

Education

Education is another important social policy topic in the post-war era that is predominantly within the ambit of the state.[2] This major topic includes all levels of education: higher, elementary (primary) and secondary education, specialist forms of education (e.g. vocational, for minorities, for children with special needs). It also includes attention to research and development (which overlaps with science policy to some extent). Education is typically considered an important issue by government, but it is not usually considered to be as important as the economy and other policy areas, which is perhaps why Tony Blair felt the need to emphasise it as a priority. Education often requires legislative action for policy change as it is governed by a statutory framework. It has been subject of reform, such as in the 1960s to end selection for secondary schools (see Saran 1973), but this did not require legislation at first as it was implemented by Circular 10/65 in 1965. Since the 1970s, in particular since Prime Minister James Callaghan's speech at Ruskin College, Oxford on 8 October 1976, governments have argued that education needs reforming to make it more responsive to the economy, to take into account advances in teaching methods and to increase performance and results (see Ball 1990; Cole and John 2001; Ranson 1989). Conservative governments in the 1980s sought to reform education to improve standards, introduce competition and reform the curriculum—which was part of a critique of state provision and suspicion of professional control of public services. Then under New Labour there was growing attention of government to early education and childcare, which in the past had tended to be left to private providers, while the focus on standards and performance continued (Chapman 2009).

Figure 4.7 is consistent with a low level of government attention on the topic of education as well the expectation that drawing attention to education in the Speech from the Throne is associated with subsequent legislative action. It is possible to observe that the fluctuations in attention to education over time in Figure 4.7 are consistent with issue attention cycles, that is, bursts of attention that reduce to near the original levels. There was a rise in interest of British government in the issue in the 1950s with reforms to the system of technical

72 *Policy Agendas in British Politics*

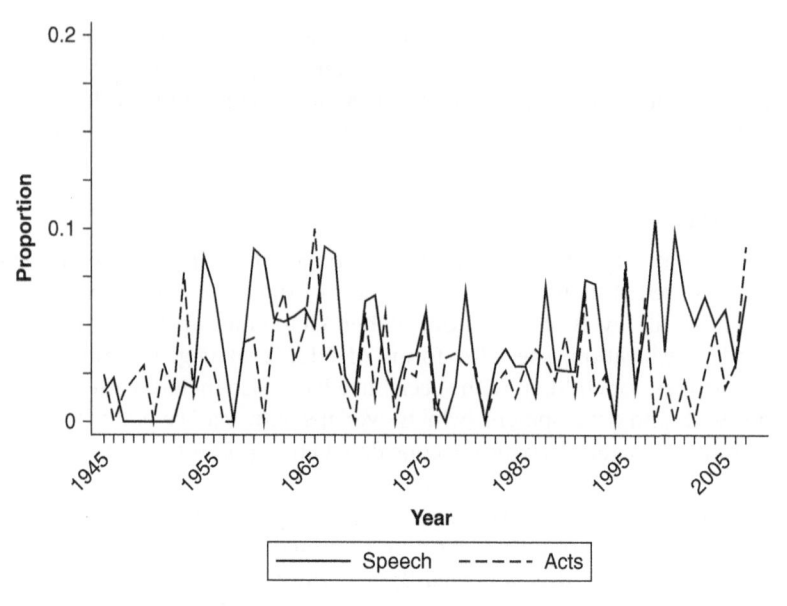

Figure 4.7 Issue attention cycles in attention to education in speeches and laws, 1945–2008
Note: Means values are 4.1 per cent of the speech and 2.9 per cent of the acts with standard deviations of 2.9 and 2.4 percentage points respectively. The series correlate at 0.27 ($p = 0.03$).

education and new school buildings announced in the Queen's Speech of 1955. One notable trend is an increase in education policies during the 1960s. Governments had become convinced that education needed reforming. The Wilson administration of 1964–1970 promised action to promote comprehensive education (in the speeches of 1965 and 1966), as well as introducing initiatives in higher education. Such policy concerns reflected the meritocratic and modernising impetus of the early period of office of the Wilson government (Dorey 2006). The next rise of policy-making attention to education (from a low base) occurred under the Conservative leadership in the 1980s. Several education acts were passed, most notably the 1988 Education Reform Act, which introduced the national curriculum and gave autonomy to school heads and governing bodies. There were successive acts on teachers' pay and student grants. After a lull in the policy agenda during the early 1990s, there was growing attention of government to the issue of education even before Labour came to office under Tony Blair, with a further series of education acts. This interest in education was sustained into the 2000s.

Overall the evidence shows some growth in attention to education on the policy agenda over the post-war period as the British government identified it as a policy problem, linked to modernisation of the economy and to achievement of wider social objectives, such as increasing mobility. However, overall these movements are relatively small, and confined to the speech rather than the laws. There are phases of interest, such as in the 1970s, which fall off; then the recent rise places it back to where it was as a policy topic in the 1960s. It is possibly one of those issues that cycle rather than go through large changes in attention.

The pattern shows that governments promised education policies, but did not necessarily do the same in terms of percentage of legislative attention. This applies to the reforming New Labour government with an average of 6.1 per cent for speeches compared with 3.7 per cent before 1997 (t = 2.7), whereas it legislated on education just the same as previous governments (both at 2.9 per cent, t = 0.01). There is no difference in the policy agenda overall according to the party in power, both for acts (t = 0.07) and for speeches (t = 0.1).

Social welfare

A related topic in social policy is social welfare, which includes programmes on social assistance to deprived and disadvantaged groups, anti-poverty measures, programmes for the elderly, social services and support for charitable work. As with the other social policy areas, it does not receive a high level of attention from British government, but is a persistent subject of both the Speech from the Throne and Acts of Parliament, as Figure 4.8 shows.

Social welfare is one of the big spending items of government (see Chapter 9), and the primary way in which the state ameliorates the conditions of disadvantaged people (see Baldock *et al.* 2007). This major topic includes the budgets of the social security ministries, food aid, anti-poverty programmes, means-tested benefits, such as tax credits, support for the elderly, help for the disabled, social services and voluntary support. But attention to both speeches and laws is far lower than the amount of government activity involved. Nor is there a great deal of difference in the mean level of attention to social welfare in speeches and laws. This pattern is consistent with sudden bursts of attention that are not sustained over time—issue attention cycles—but also shows a possible structural shift in the mid-1970s that is suggestive of focused adaptation. In the latter case, the policy landscape appears to include social welfare problems on a continuing basis with government attention adapting as a consequence.

74 Policy Agendas in British Politics

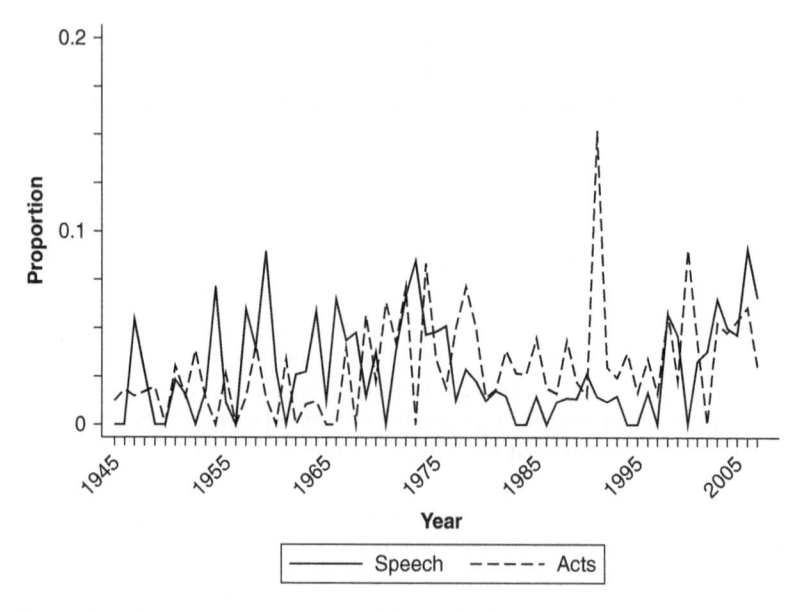

Figure 4.8 Issue attention cycles and focused adaptation in attention to social welfare in speeches and laws, 1945–2008
Note: Mean values for speeches and laws are 2.8 and 3.0 per cent with standard deviations equal to 2.5 and 2.6 per cent respectively. The series have a Pearson correlation −0.04 ($p = 0.76$).

It may be the case that the speech and laws are not related in the sense that the speech may be drawing attention to general matters relating to social welfare while laws are dealing with specific and technical changes. For example, the Speech from the Throne tends to include general statements about the provision of welfare, such as in the 1962 speech: 'My Government will promote further improvements in the social conditions and in the housing, health and welfare of My People', as well as specific promises. Acts of Parliament relating to social welfare tend to be specific provisions, such as the Family Income Supplements Act 1970, which created a new benefit for families with low incomes, exempted them from health service charges and allowed their children to claim free school meals.

Overall, the level of attention to the topic of social welfare tends to remain at a low level for most of period with a large peak in 1992, but this was caused by a number of Acts of Parliament on social security in Northern Ireland rather than a national initiative. The main change is at the end of the period, with a rise of attention from 1995 onwards.

This is largely due to New Labour's particular emphasis on social policy and anti-poverty policies. The pre-1997 legislation on social welfare tended to be about combatting fraud whereas the post-1997 acts were about provision of social security, such as the Child Support, Pensions and Social Security Act 2000. The Labour government increased support for the poor and many (but not all) measures reflect this. For example, in the Queen's Speech of 1998, the government emphasised its wish to have 'made clear their determination to modernise the welfare state upon clear principles of work, security, fairness and value for money'. In fact, in this period the speech contains a large number of legislative promises about social welfare, such as in 1999: 'To build on my Government's modernisation of the welfare system, a Bill will be introduced to reform child support so that money gets to children more speedily and effectively.'

Over the whole time period, Labour governments average 3.7 per cent for speeches compared with Conservative governments at 2.1 per cent (t = 2.6). If the post-1997 period is excluded, the difference drops to less than 1 per cent and is not statistically significant. As with other policy issues discussed so far, it is the New Labour period that stands out as marking an important shift in the policy agenda.

Community development, planning and housing

The next social policy topic considered here relates to housing, but in the policy content coding system it is a hybrid category that encompasses infrastructure and investment policies, as well as support for housing. This topic includes government funding and provision of social housing for the less well-off, such as for the elderly and the poor, but also includes urban economic development, the planning system, house building, rental controls, rural economic development and regulation of the mortgage market.

Figure 4.9 reveals housing and planning to be an important issue, receiving as much attention from government in both the speeches and laws compared to what might be thought to be the major issues of health and education. Low levels of attention might reflect the detailed statutory provisions that are needed in the planning field. There is slightly less variation in the policy agenda in the Speech from the Throne compared with the other topics discussed so far, which suggests there is some connection between the emphasis on the issue of housing in the Speech from the Throne and subsequent legislative action in Parliament.

76 Policy Agendas in British Politics

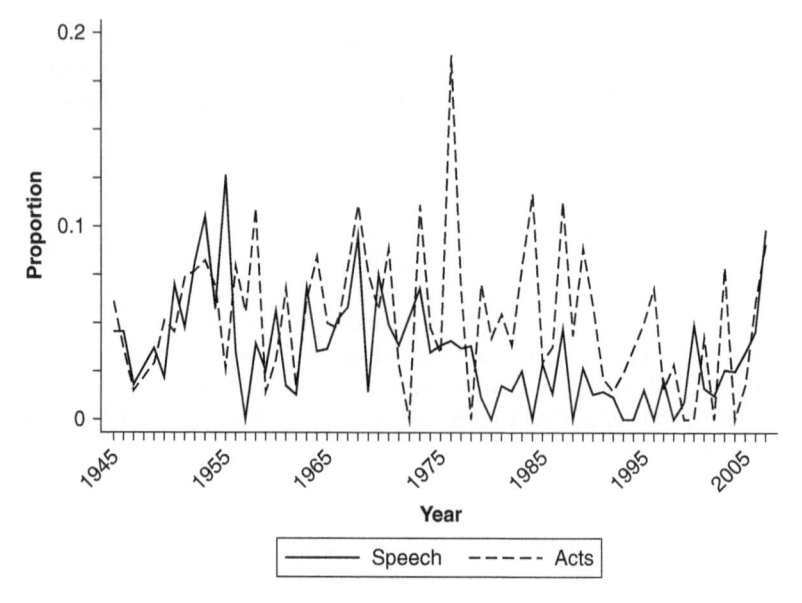

Figure 4.9 Incrementalism in attention to housing and community development in speeches and laws, 1945–2008

Note: Mean levels are 3.5 per cent for speeches and 5.3 per cent for acts with standard deviations of 2.8 and 5.3 percentage points respectively. The series have a Pearson correlation equal to 0.25 ($p = 0.04$).

Over the whole period, the attention of government to housing in speeches and laws does not exhibit an overall trend, but suggests a pattern of incrementalism distinct from the bursts and retractions in the issue attention cycles we have seen in the last series. During the early post-war years, there was a steady growth in the proportion of speeches and laws dedicated to this topic, which relate to housing provision and some changes to private ownership. The speeches contained general promises to build houses, even the first Speech from the Throne of the Churchill government in 1951, which demonstrates that the parties were competing on this issue. There were some important landmark pieces of legislation, such as the New Towns Act 1946 and the Town and Country Planning Act 1947. The latter piece of legislation defined the local planning system for many decades to come. After a dip in attention of government to housing in the 1950s there was a general rise in interest from the 1960s. There were quite a few changes to the planning system during that period, further reforms to New Towns, and changes to private renting and leasing associated with reforms introduced by the second 1966–1970 Wilson administration. For the remainder of the period, the issue remained at quite a low level on the policy agenda except for a spike in the legislative agenda in 1977 when a whole series of rent and housing laws were passed in the same parliamentary session, which again reflected Labour's interest in the issue. However, over the whole time period there is no statistical difference in the level of attention that Labour and Conservative governments assign to the issue. Further, New Labour is no different from previous governments with respect to the Speech from the Throne, and there was a lower proportion of acts passed on housing since 1997 (3.0 per cent) than before (5.8, t = 2.4). Overall, it is hard to interpret the trends with a general model of agenda setting, but it is possible to see gradual changes in response to shifts in policy responsibilities.

Transport

A topic that is related to planning is transport, which includes public transport, the building and maintenance of roads, railways, policy on airports and ports, and traffic safety. As with housing and planning, what is surprising is the amount of attention that transport receives from government in speeches and laws. It is an issue that governments often emphasise as part of their policy agenda due to its strategic importance, but which tends to require a higher volume of legislation because of the detailed regulation of transport. Further, there is no correlation between the series, indicating that attention to transport in the speech is not closely tied to subsequent legislation. There is a fair amount of variation in the series. The policy agenda for both speeches and laws, shown in Figure 4.10, falls to zero in some years and rises to around 15 per cent in a few peak years for laws. This pattern is indicative of bursts of legislation on transport matters, such as in 2001, which was one of the peak years of New Labour activism on new policy topics. There are a series of peaks not unlike the issue attention cycle.

The policy agenda on the issue of transport appears consistent with issue attention cycles from the immediate post-war period through the late 1980s and then incrementalism afterward. For example, in 1954 and 1955, the Conservative government announced policies on roads as part of the Speech from the Throne. However, the legislation passed in each year related to a series of specialist measures, such as Public Service Vehicles (Travel Concessions) Act 1955. In the early 1980s there was another burst of attention to transport in the Queen's Speech combined with legislative action. The Thatcher government passed a key piece of legislation, the Transport Act of 1980, which privatised municipal transport,

78 Policy Agendas in British Politics

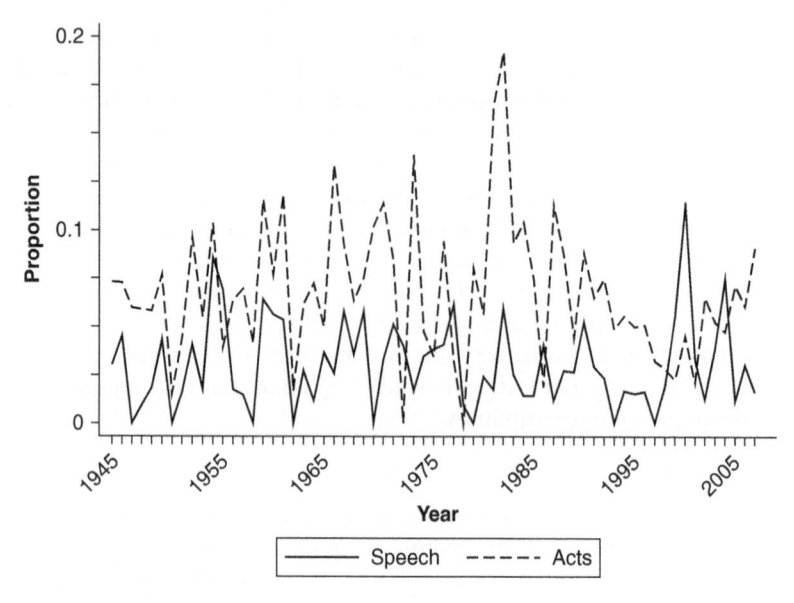

Figure 4.10 Issue attention cycles and incrementalism in attention to transport in speeches and laws, 1945–2008
Note: Mean values are 3.1 per cent for speeches and 6.9 per cent for laws with standard deviations of 3.1 and 6.9 for speeches and laws respectively. The Pearson correlation between the series is 0.12 ($p = 0.34$).

along with introducing reforms to civil aviation and the privatisation of British Aerospace. Transport was a focus for the reforming and ideological agenda of Conservative governments in the 1980s. The attention of government to transport issues lessened during the 1990s and only revived slightly toward the end of the period. There are no break points in the speech series, indicating a lack of change, but acts are different. Although there is no difference for the early part of the series, the topic emerges in 1985 with an average of 7.6, which falls to 5.7 afterwards (t = 2.0), then continues to 1998 when the difference becomes non-significant again (t = 1.7). There is also no difference in the level of attention according to party, which is not altogether surprising since transport is an issue that does not tend to be owned by a particular party.

Environment

Often linked with transport and planning is the environment as a form of regulation of infrastructure, which includes policies relating to water, waste disposal, air pollution, climate change, recycling, forest protection, land and coastal protection. Once again, this is not a core issue for government, but has a number of specialised sub-fields that require regulation or reform as circumstances change (and can also be part of other policy fields, such as agriculture and transport). It has risen up the agenda in recent years because of climate change, public concern and international and transnational coordination, such as from the EU and international treaties (Jordan et al. 2003).

Governments do not tend to emphasise the environment in their annual programme, but are more likely to introduce specific legislation to address the issue, which may be due to the regulatory nature of the problem or the transposition of policies decided at the EU or international level. There is a reasonable amount of variation in speeches and laws because attention to the environment falls to zero in many years. This is consistent with successive bursts of policy activity in response to regulatory demands and external pressures with a return to near initial levels.

The policy agenda of government on the environment, plotted in Figure 4.11, exhibits stability at the start of the post-war period, with the issue receiving little or no attention from policy-makers. There is a spike in attention in 1970 and 1971 when Parliament passed a large amount of anti-pollution legislation, which followed the earlier emergence of the environment as a political issue in the 1960s. A number of policy measures coincided—rather like Downs' (1972) issue attention cycle. This is not a major policy shift, however, especially when compared to the massive surge in government attention to the environment in both speeches and laws in 1990 and 1991. Legislation on the environment reached 15 per cent of the total legislative programme of government in 1991. The EU has been increasingly active in this area, especially after the Single European Act 1986. When the EU passes directives, such as on the environment, national parliaments such as Britain's must turn these into law (also known as 'transposition'), some of which appear in the measure of the legislative agenda. For example, the Environmental Protection Act 1990 was mainly about the implementation of EU directives. This was also a period when the public had become more interested in the environment, with the Green Party winning a record 15 per cent of the vote in the 1989 elections to the European Parliament. But did the environment then return to its previous level of salience on the policy agenda (recall that Downs says the level of attention does not go back to the level before the cycle)? For speeches, the answer is no, as the average following this peak after 1993 is significantly higher than

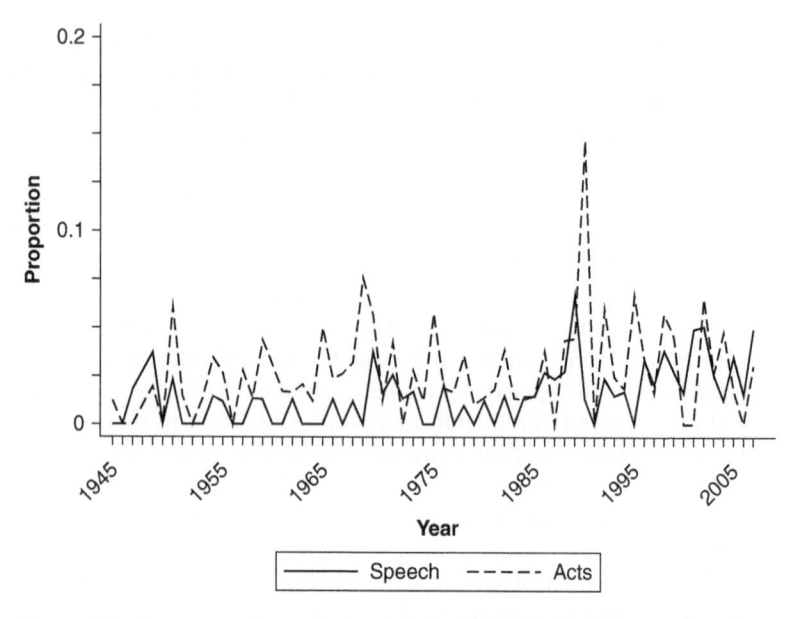

Figure 4.11 Issue attention cycles in attention to the environment in speeches and laws, 1945–2008

Note: Average levels of attention for speeches are 1.5 and for acts 2.8 per cent with standard deviations of 1.5 and 2.5 per cent respectively. The Pearson correlation between the series is 0.20 ($p = 0.11$).

the period before: receiving an average level of attention of 1.1 per cent before 1993 and 2.7 per cent afterwards (t = 3.8).

The conclusion is that, while there has not been a significant shift in the amount of primary legislation passed in relation to the environment, the issue has received growing levels of attention in the government's agenda communicated in the Speech from the Throne. This might be to do with reliance on delegated legislation and regulation in this particular domain. Further, there do not appear to be party differences in emphasis on the environment when in government, which is suggestive of the problem-oriented nature of environmental policy.

Public lands and water management (territorial issues)

The category of public lands, water management and territorial issues is a hybrid that relates to how the state manages and governs its lands and territories, and links to the infrastructure class of topics we have been discussing above. These include the management of national parks and historic sites, water resources and matters concerning the administration of government of the member nations of the UK, Scotland, Wales and Northern Ireland as well as administration of Britain's territories and dependencies which survived the end of empire, as well as Commonwealth affairs. The Speech from the Throne tends to capture such concerns as the government will highlight international matters such as the Commonwealth, which rise and fall on the policy agenda over time, and provide details of planned state visits to other countries.[3] Plotted in Figure 4.12, this topic is subject to bursts of attention from government combined with a long-term downward trend. The early post-war period was preoccupied with the dismantling of the British Empire and development of the Commonwealth. For example, the Speech from the Throne of 1947 announced the introduction of measures 'to enable the future governance of Burma to be in accordance with the free decision of the elected representatives of its people', while the speech in 1953 noted: 'My Government attach the utmost importance to continued consultation with their partners in the Commonwealth and will

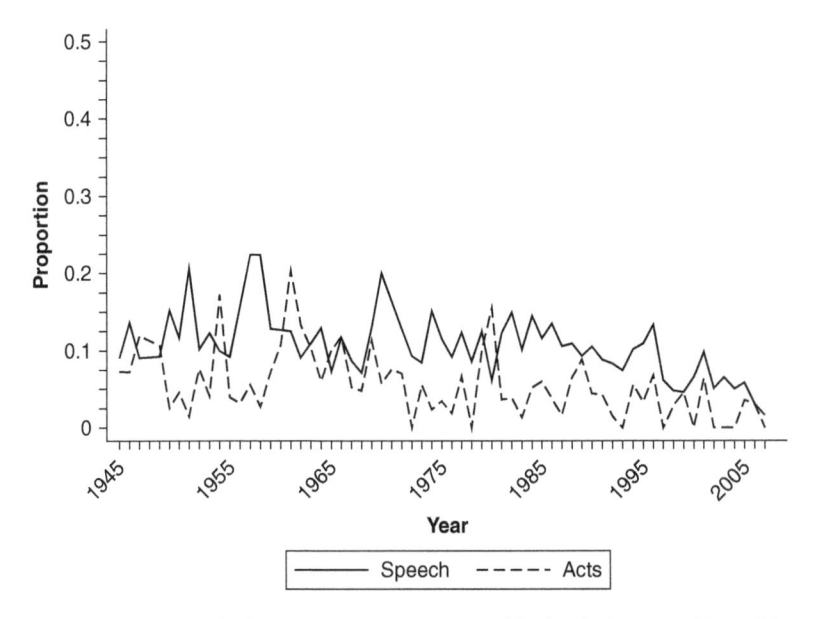

Figure 4.12 Focused adaptation in attention to public lands (territorial issues) in speeches and laws, 1945–2008

Note: Mean values are 10 per cent of attention in the speech and 5.5 per cent of legislation and standard deviations of 4.2 and 4.4 per cent respectively. The Pearson correlation between the series is 0.15 ($p = 0.25$).

take part in the Conference of Commonwealth Finance Ministers which will be held in Australia in January.' Throughout the period, Acts of Parliament were also passed that adapted legislation for Scotland and Wales, such as the Forestry (Sale of Land) (Scotland) Act 1963.[4] There is a burst of legislation on territorial issues in the early 1960s linked to the wave of decolonisation that occurred during that period (in particular with reference to the granting of independence to a number of countries in Africa and the West Indies). However, legislation relating to decolonisation was passed on quite a regular basis continuing into the 1970s as smaller territories gained independence, for example, the Malta Republic Act 1975.

Overall, as shown in Figure 4.12, attention to this issue trends downwards toward a new epoch of low salience beginning in the Thatcher years, when there was more attention in the speech than in legislative outputs. The shift reflects a pattern of focused adaptation to the contours of the policy landscape. Territorial issues (and public lands and water management, which tend to be less important sub-components of this topic in Britain compared with the US) are an important focus for the Speech from the Throne, although it should be noted that this in part consists of the official announcement of state visits to Commonwealth countries. However, this topic includes more of the legislative agenda than some of the main topics of social policy. While much of the legislation is procedural, it still takes up parliamentary time that could have been spent on other topics. Speeches and laws do not correlate, so appear to relate to different sorts of policy-making attention and activities, with legislation tending to be passed in waves. Toward the end of the period, this topic had become less prominent on the political agenda, despite the devolution of powers to Scotland, Wales and Northern Ireland (although it is possible that part of the decline of this issue on the agenda is due to there no longer being a need to pass duplicate legislation for Scotland and Wales on top of the original act). Attention falls to zero in some years during this period. This secular change suggests structural change in the agenda, marking what appears to be a real break in the institutional equilibrium, and may create opportunities for other issues to take its place. The next domain discussed is another that has suffered a secular decline due to structural factors.

Agriculture

In recent times, agriculture has not tended to be such a prominent issue on the policy agenda due to the relatively low level of employment in the sector. Much agricultural policy is now delegated to the

EU. This was not always the case, though, especially in the period soon after 1945 when British government was concerned about food security and had direct control over agricultural policy. This topic includes matters relating to agricultural trade, subsidies, food inspection and food safety, animal welfare and fishing. There has been a shift in emphasis on agriculture as from the 1990s there was a greater focus on the environment and a greater emphasis on food quality/safety. More recently food security has re-emerged because of rising and more volatile prices, and long-term shifts in supply and demand. All these changes get recorded with the major topic unless primarily in another topic like the environment.

Attention to agriculture in speeches and laws is shown in Figure 4.13. This is higher than might be expected, especially for legislation. However, it could be due to the prominence of agriculture in the earlier period after the Second World War rather than an indication of the long-term salience of the issue. Further to this, there is not a high level of variation in the policy agenda. There is a strong connection between the

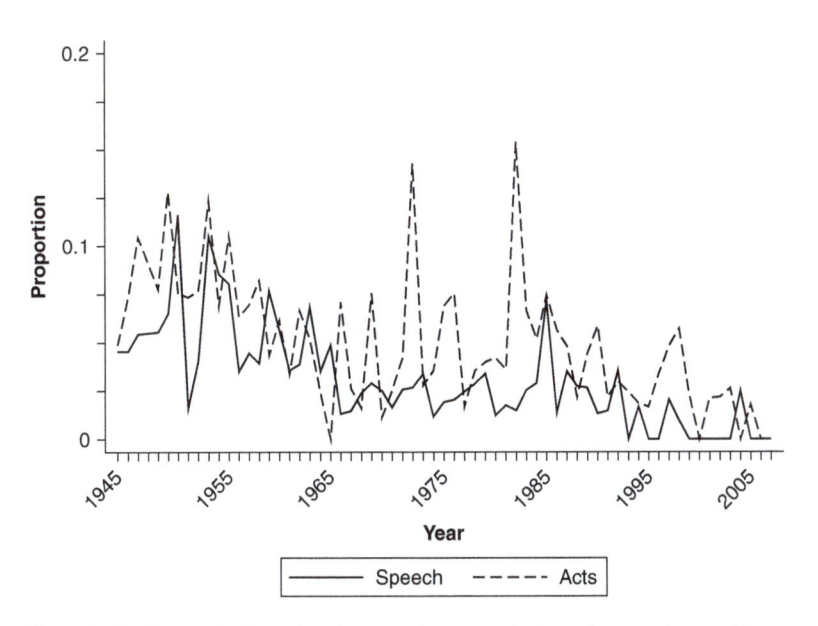

Figure 4.13 Focused adaptation in attention to agriculture in speeches and laws, 1945–2008

Note: Average values are 3.0 per cent for speeches and 4.9 per cent for laws with standard deviations of 2.6 and 3.5 per cent respectively. The series have a Pearson correlation of 0.46 ($p < 0.01$).

emphasis on agriculture in the Speech from the Throne and subsequent Acts of Parliament.

The most significant change in Figure 4.13 is the steady decline in importance of agriculture over time, which captures an apparent structural change consistent with focused adaptation. In the late 1940s and early 1950s, attention to agriculture in the Speech from the Throne exceeded 10 per cent of the agenda and received even a larger proportion of Acts of Parliament. This early period was a time of reform and the creation of a subsidy regime. Through the speeches, government promoted self-sufficiency and achieving decreases in volumes of imported food. For example, the 1949 King's Speech stated the aim of the policies: 'The economic difficulties of this country have emphasised the need for renewed effort to expand the production of food from our own soil', and: 'My Government will continue to take all practical steps to encourage our agricultural population to increase output by every efficient means and to make better use of marginal land.' Acts of Parliament set up systems for regulating agriculture, such as the Cotton (Centralised Buying) Act 1947.

The decline in attention to agriculture was steady from the early 1950s to the 1970s. There were spikes of legislation with very specific aims, such as series of acts designed to regulate fishing in 1972 and 1973, then a large fall despite a series of agricultural and food crises during the Major and Blair years (most notably the BSE (Bovine spongiform encephalopathy) crisis under the Major government and the foot and mouth outbreak under the Blair government). An interesting question that remains is whether the decline in influence of the agriculture industry as an organised interest and its relocation to the EU level created a gap for other issues to fill, although there is no sign in this series that 1973 or adjacent years marked a break point, or where the rate of decline accelerated. Nor is there any evidence of a return to importance with new issues hitting agriculture, such as the environment and food security. There is no evidence of party differences in attention to agriculture in either speeches or laws.

Energy

Energy has often been a peripheral topic for policy-makers, especially when compared with the larger core policy topics, such as social policies and even infrastructure. This topic includes nuclear power, the generation and supply of electricity, gas and oil, coal and alternative forms of energy production. It is a constant because energy is always needed, but it remains possible this is an area that will grow in importance over time due to structural changes in the wider geo-political environment. Energy has become a pressing concern for governments in recent times due to fears over the supply of oil and the depletion of other natural forms of energy resources, as well as concerns with climate change and the need to reduce of harmful emissions. Demand for energy is interlinked with economic growth and adoption of new forms of technology, while there is growing awareness of the interdependence of energy demand with other countries and the possibility of interruption of supply. As energy becomes scarcer, then potentially dangerous forms such as nuclear power come under consideration even though there is demand to develop alternative sources.

The attention of government to the issue of energy is plotted in Figure 4.14 and shows what appears to be trendless variation. The average for speeches is low. There is substantial variation in the series as is evident from the figure. There is no correlation between speeches and laws. There are a few spikes in attention to energy during the early 1970s because of the oil price crisis, but these are not as large as might be

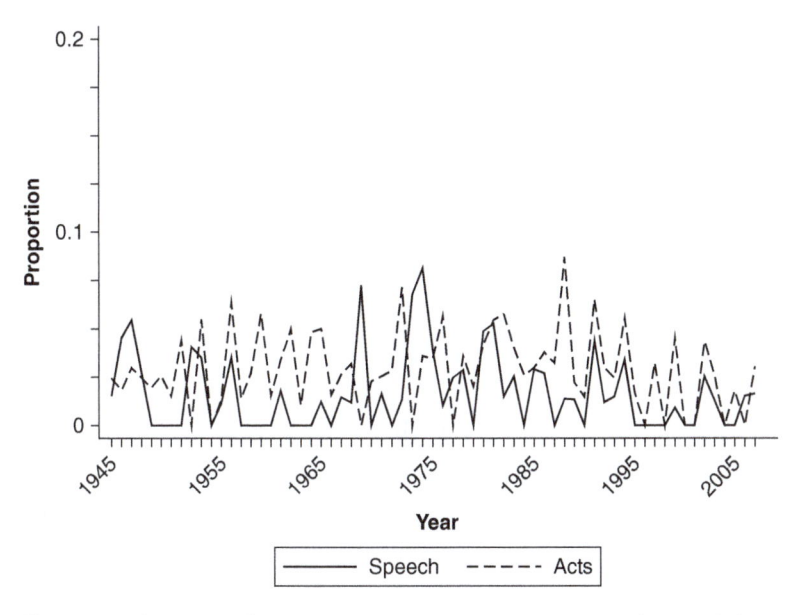

Figure 4.14 Incrementalism in attention to energy in speeches and laws, 1945–2008
Note: Mean values are 1.5 for speeches and 2.0 per cent for laws with standard deviations of 1.9 and 2.0 per cent respectively. The Pearson correlation between the series is 0.14 ($p=0.27$).

expected. There does appear to be a slight decline in attention toward the end of the period in the mid- to late 1990s.

Civil rights, minority issues, immigration and civil liberties

Another set of issues concern rights, which is an ongoing area of concern in liberal democracies. The struggle for the right to vote and to assemble has a long history in British politics although, arguably, its salience has increased as groups increasingly use the language of rights. In our coding system, however, we place immigration in this topic, which might in some views be seen to be a curtailment of rights. However, they form the same topic of legal rights and obligations for groups of citizens. While liberal reformists tend to focus on only some of the sub-topics, right-wing groups usually support immigration control. Labour has been interested in both sets of agendas at the same time, strengthening rights at the same time as changing the law on immigration, which is what occurred during the 1960s and 2000s.

The level of attention to civil rights, minority issues, immigration and civil liberties is plotted in Figure 4.15. This topic is another set of policies that does not attract very much attention and is statistically the same in

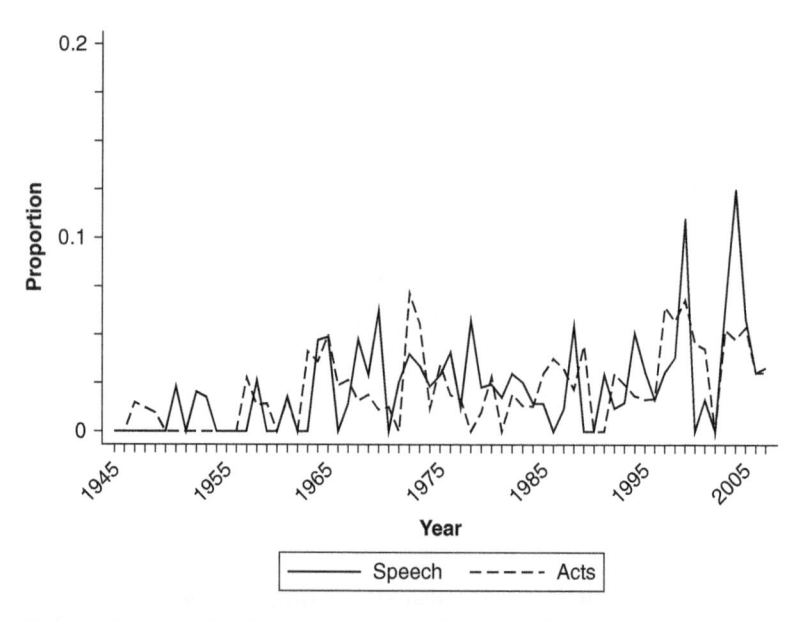

Figure 4.15 Issue attention cycles in attention to civil rights, minority issues, immigration and civil liberties in speeches and laws, 1945–2008

Note: Averages are 2.3 per cent for speeches and 2.1 per cent for the laws with, respectively, 2.6 and 2.2 percentage point standard deviations. The series correlate at 0.48 ($p < 0.01$).

speeches and laws (t = 0.4). This is not a major policy item for British governments in spite of recent changes in attention. But there is some variability to the topics, about the same as the mean level of attention. The series are correlated, which is not surprising given that the legal nature of the topic suggests that the policy content of the Speech from the Throne would tend to indicate the same topic as legislation passed in the same parliamentary year.

Figure 4.15 does show a pattern of a rise in the prominence of these issues on the agenda toward the end of the period, but is suggestive overall of issue attention cycles that culminate with the domain being removed from the agenda. From the figure it is possible to observe a rise in attention to the issue during the reforming Labour government of 1964–1970. Then there is another steep increase at the end of the period under New Labour, which is also due to the attention of that government to immigration policy (Jennings 2009). There is a party difference in emphasis on the issue in the Speech from the Throne with Labour governments averaging 3.2 per cent over the entire period compared with the Conservatives at 1.7 (t = 2.4), which is perhaps not surprising given that Labour tends to represent less advantaged parts of society but accounts less for the higher level of interest in immigration (although the each government was highly active in policy on asylum and immigration throughout the 1990s and 2000s, see Jennings 2010). There is a similar relationship for acts (2.9 per cent for Labour compared with 1.6 per cent for the Conservatives, t = 2.7). However, if one removes the observations under the Labour government elected in 1997 there is no difference statistically whatsoever for acts or laws. The strongest pattern in the series is the rapid rise in attention under New Labour.

Labour and employment

A more traditional area of social policy is the topic of labour and employment, which includes a series of regulations about worker safety, training, employee benefits, trade unions and parental leave. There is no difference in attention levels between speeches and laws statistically speaking (t = 0.61). This is evident in Figure 4.16. The speech is either promising laws or reflecting the same concerns.

The pattern over time suggests trendless variation rather than periods of rising or falling attention, consistent with an incrementalist account of policy-making in this domain. A significant decrease emerges in 1979 where the average was 4.0 per cent of attention in the period before and reduces to 2.8 per cent afterwards (t = 2.1), which continues for subsequent years until 1996 (t = 1.6). This spans nearly all the years

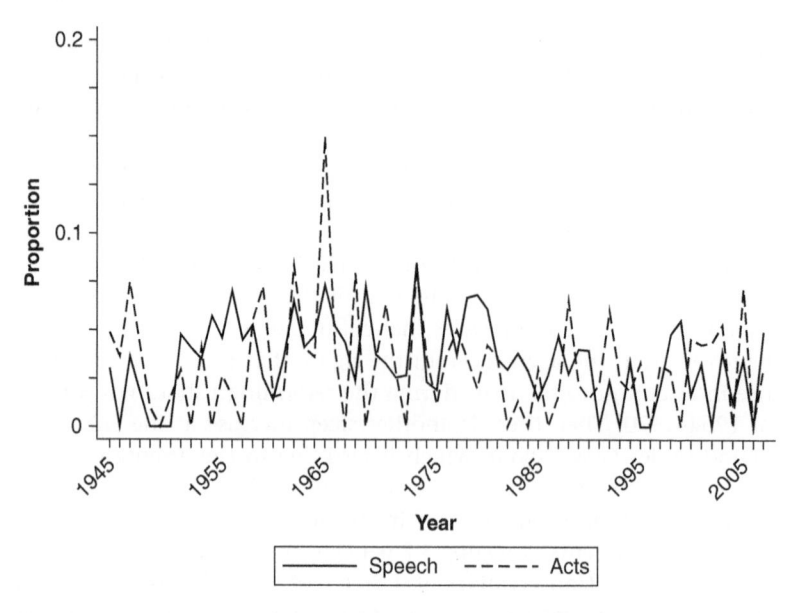

Figure 4.16 Incrementalism in labour and employment in speeches and laws, 1945–2008

Note: The average for speeches is equal to 3.4 and for laws 3.2 per cent with standard deviations of 3.4 and 3.2 per cent respectively. The series display a correlation of 0.27 ($p=0.03$).

of Conservative rule and may reflect the lack of interest from a right party to labour issues, which is in spite of the reforming efforts of Prime Minister Thatcher to reduce the power of the trades unions. There is no reversal of this pattern under the Labour government elected in 1997. Despite labour and employment being an issue that Labour would traditionally be expected to 'own' (Budge and Fairlie 1983; Petrocik 1996), there are no party differences in the speeches and laws.

Other topics

The final section briefly reviews some less prominent topics to complete the picture of the shape of the policy agenda of British politics over the post-war period. The first topic is banking and domestic commerce, which includes banking, securities regulation, consumer finance, mortgages, insurance, debt and bankruptcy. Since the financial crisis of 2008, this topic has shifted up the agenda, which is an interesting phenomenon in itself, but falls outside our period of analysis. The topic

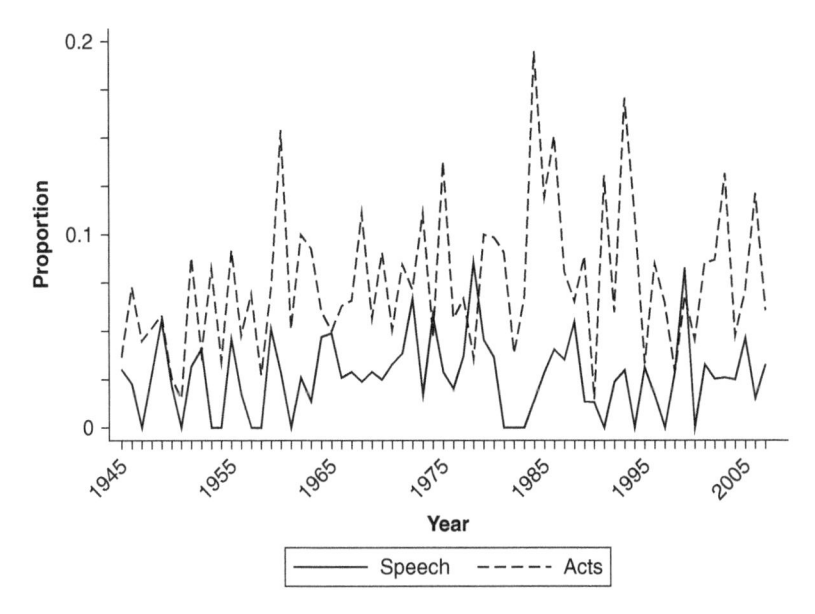

Figure 4.17 Issue attention cycles in attention to banking in speeches and laws, 1945–2008

Note: The topic receives 2.6 per cent of attention in the speeches and accounts for 7.7 per cent of laws with standard deviations of equal to 2.0 and 3.8 per cent respectively. The series have a Pearson correlation of −0.01 ($p = 0.93$).

still receives a fair amount of attention from government, as shown in Figure 4.17.

Business and commerce is an area that is fast changing and requires regulation in a statutory framework: hence there is greater attention to the issue in acts rather than speeches. There is no correlation between speeches and acts either in the same year or with a lag of acts in the year following the speech. Nor is there a statistically significant difference between the parties in attention to this topic. There is growth, however, in the number of related acts during the period, with the issue receiving an average of 6.2 per cent of the agenda before 1966 and 8.4 per cent afterwards (t = 2.2). Perhaps the most distinctive feature of Figure 4.17 is a peak in 1985 when there were a series of market reforms, such as the Company Securities (Insider Dealing) Act 1985, and the privatisation of the Trustee Savings Bank. Overall, the episodic changes seem to indicate that banking reforms issue attention cycles.

Science—space, science, technology and communications—is a distinct policy area, which covers policy and regulation for space agencies,

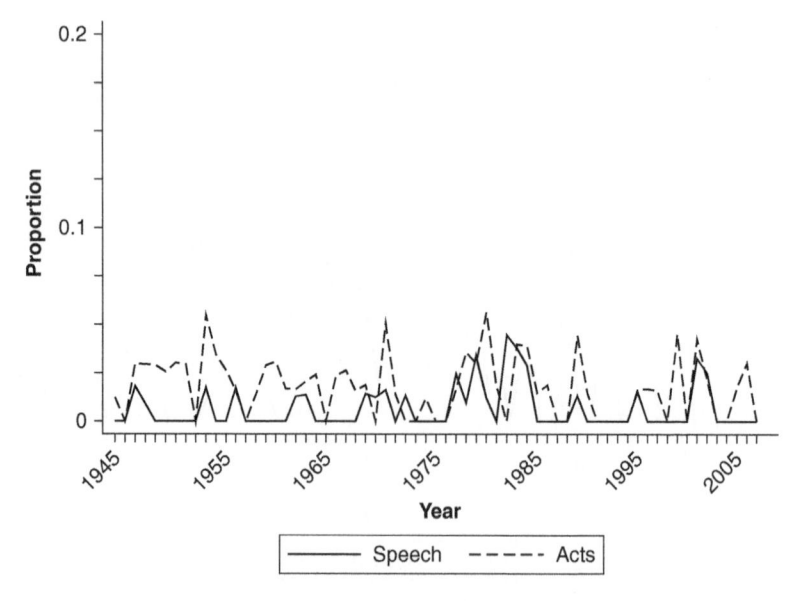

Figure 4.18 Incrementalism in attention to science in speeches and laws, 1945–2008

Note: The mean for speeches is 1 and for laws 1.8 per cent with standard deviations of equal to 1.1 and 1.5 per cent respectively. The series have a Pearson correlation of 0.35 ($p = 0.01$).

satellites, technology, telephones, broadcasting, weather, computers and research and development. The prioritisation of this issue is plotted in Figure 4.18. It shows that the level of attention in speeches and laws is rather spasmodic, which is to be expected given that this is a low salience and technical/specialised set of subjects.

The average level of attention is very low. Consistent with the episodic nature of the policy area, there are no differences across the series for break points or according to party. This is essentially trendless or a series of issue attention cycles.

Another specialised area of public policy is foreign trade, which includes trade negotiations, export promotions, productivity and exchange rates. Figure 4.19 shows the pattern of attention to foreign trade over time. In this case, averages do not convey the full picture as the topic was much more important in the 1950s. There is a good deal of variation in the series and they do correlate quite highly. The pattern appears consistent with focused adaptation with an adjustment to a new policy landscape after the 1960s. Since 1973, the EU takes the lead in (General Agreement on Tariffs and Trade) GATT and World Trade

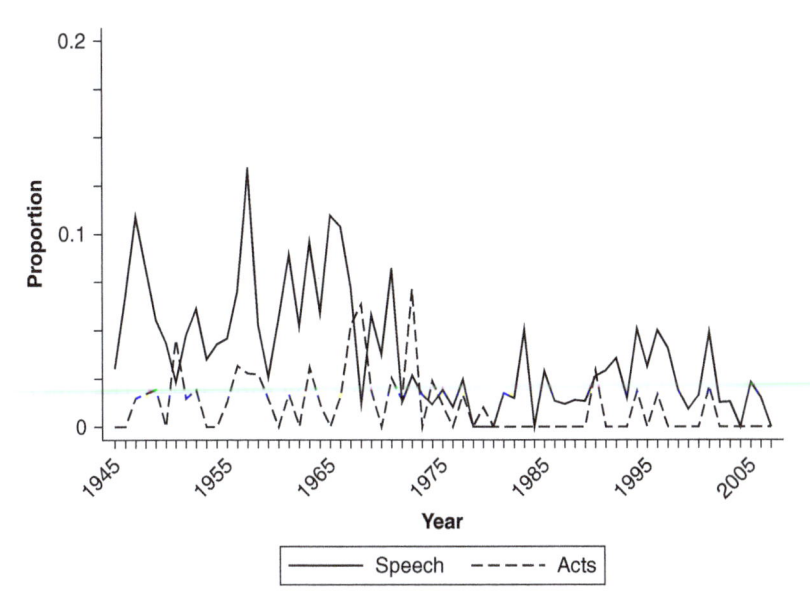

Figure 4.19 Focused adaptation in attention to foreign trade in speeches and laws, 1945–2008

Note: The mean for speeches is 3.8 and for laws 1.1 per cent with standard deviations of equal to 3 and 1.6 per cent respectively. The series have a Pearson correlation of 0.30 ($p = 0.02$).

Organization (WTO) negotiations on behalf of member states, which affects the UK.

Conclusion

This descriptive tour of different areas of public policy shows the nuances of each topic where a number of historical events and structural trends affect the policy agenda in a given area, whether it is entry into the EU or international events such as wars. It could be easy to sit back and say that each series shows the particularity of policy in each sector, but there is more to this underlying the series. After all, for every increase in attention to one policy area, there has to be a decrease in another or others, so the space has to be won and to reflect genuine problems as the government of the day sees them.[5] For each of these policy series, groups of civil servants and ministers argued for a place in the speech and the legislative programme, and the Prime Minister and leading ministers had to decide which topic should be given priority.

First, there are long-running changes in some of the lines of data that in part affect what is possible in other series. This is particularly the case with the economy and foreign policy. These are the classic functions of the state that demand a considerable amount of attention, even when there is no crisis. We expect patterns in these topics to be related to changes elsewhere. In the economy we find the large patterns of change from low to high to low (and to high at the end), which reflect how British politicians became preoccupied with economic problems (see discussion above).

The second big step change is the decline in attention to defence over the post-war period, which party reflects changes in Britain's status as a world power but also changes in the external environment itself. These were focused toward the end of the series as larger foreign policy problems receded, especially since the early 1990s. The end of the Cold War, partly caused by a new leadership in the Soviet Union under Michael Gorbachev, was seen to undermine the Eastern bloc states through regime change in the late 1980s and early 1990s. The decline of an external threat meant that less of the energy and resources of the state needed to be focused on preparing for an attack. Because of the way in which global politics was fractured by the East–West division, every local conflict was played out in terms of the larger Cold War. So that source of tension receded, though, of course, international conflicts and problems continued.

The third set of changes is the decline of some policy areas that were formerly important, such as agriculture, territorial issues and foreign trade, which reflect a series of structural changes in society and the economy. Thus agriculture is no longer an important policy topic as it once was, which is because there is such significant trade in inexpensive food across the world, that productivity gains have ensured its workforce has declined in relative size, and since 1973, key decisions have been transferred to Brussels. So what once required discussion in Parliament now becomes the subject of Council of Ministers decisions (while of course not forgetting Parliament's role implementing EU decisions in delegated legislation).

The fourth change has been the rise of new issues in the 1990s, such as crime, social welfare and civil rights. These have always been on the agenda but have gained prominence in recent years, perhaps because of skilful advocacy, media interest, greater interest by the electorate in the performance of public services and the weaker traction to be had from the more traditional topics, such as defence, agriculture and territorial affairs. It is, of course, hard to sustain the claim that the decline of these core issues created the space on the policy agenda for more recent ones. In particular, the movements are not contemporaneous with different directions in the policy agenda at different times. But such an account is plausible because of the slow-moving changes across the agenda that are as important as the bursts of attention we have highlighted (see Jennings et al. 2011b for longer treatment of this issue).

The key finding of this chapter is that agendas for each policy area experienced a series of trends, either upward or downward, which at times operated for long periods of time across successive governments. This is not a picture of stability as portrayed in some accounts of British politics, but one where the agenda shifts in relation to public problems and trends, often by large amounts. The key message is the change in importance of the leading issues over the period. There has been a decline of attention to some topics and the emergence of new ones, while the key topics of the macroeconomy and foreign affairs varied over time. Other domains have fluctuated as crises and problems hit them, and we do see some leaps of attention, particularly as a new government embarks on a series of policy reforms. Changes at the end of various series are intriguing, and indicate a particular approach to the policy agenda of governments elected since the early 1990s. Both the Major and the Blair governments recognised the importance of new issues, adapting their policy agenda to incorporate a wider range of topics, and thereby changed the landscape of British politics.

The implication for the study of agenda setting is that the claim of incrementalism is not supported by an examination of the data. There is too much change across the series to indicate that kind of pattern, except for a few series where there is a low level of interest, such as labour and employment, and even here there are strong movements in the data. The best defence is a form of disjointed incrementalism whereby incremental patterns happen over time but in a way that lead to long-term changes in the agenda, such as the slow declines in attention to public lands. There are some domains that illustrate what appears to be issue attention cycles, such as the environment, transport and banking. There are also changes that appear to be punctuations, such as with crime rising in the 1990s, or when foreign trade fell off a cliff in the 1970s, or New Labour's attention to government operations in 1997. But there are a large number of patterns across the series that show large trends and periods of change that do not seem to correspond to the three models of change. Instead, they seem to indicate important periods when attention shifted.

5
Policy Punctuations

In the last chapter, we described the policy agenda of British politics and government, using graphs and descriptive statistics. We conveyed both the complexity of what has happened to British decision-making since 1945, but also reported some of the broader trends. We explored how government responded to the problems and challenges of the day, such as on the economy and in foreign affairs. There were periods of stability, but also times of change, a pattern that is a key theme of this book. Some topics were subject to substantial shifts in attention, both upwards and downwards, such as on macroeconomic issues. A few topics did not receive much priority from British government at the start of the period, but became more important later on, such as topic two, civil rights and immigration; on the other hand, some topics secured a high level of interest from policy-makers at the start of the period but fell away over time, as was the case with topic 4, agriculture.

But it is hard to get a sense of the overall pattern of change and stability in the policy agenda with such a level of detail and 19 series to interrogate. Are there techniques that can uncover a more general pattern in the amount of stability and instability and help us to understand the balance of continuity and change in the British policy agenda? It is here that we turn to the stochastic process methods set out by Baumgartner and Jones in a series of publications (e.g. Jones and Baumgartner 2005a; Jones et al. 1998), which test the theory of punctuated equilibrium in public policy, discussed in Chapter 1. Using this method, it is possible to identify the large shifts in attention across the issue agenda in a way that is systematic and determines whether there are long periods of stability that are punctuated by periods of policy activism.

In this chapter we introduce the measurement strategy of Baumgartner and Jones, before offering some criticisms of their approach to analysing policy change. We present an alternative, setting out a typology of different kinds of large policy change that are expected. Then we interrogate the historical record to find out about the punctuations, using the executive agenda (the Speech from the Throne) and the legislative agenda (Acts of UK Parliament) once again.

Punctuated equilibrium

As we discussed in Chapter 1, Jones and Baumgartner offer a theoretical approach to agenda setting to explain why policy-making is subject to periods both of stability and change. The basic intuition behind their punctuated equilibrium theory of public policy is that the decision-making agenda is stable for extended periods of time, being locked-in through institutional arrangements, but at the same time is subject to occasional changes that are large in magnitude (Baumgartner and Jones 1993, 2009). This means that from time to time policy-making deviates from its long-established equilibrium as issues shift from being subjects of routine decision-making and matters of interest to experts and specialists to being a concern for the national political agenda and decision-makers at the top of government (True et al. 1999). Such changes in the prioritisation of issues or problems on the decision-making agenda in turn lead to changes in policy outputs and outcomes.

Baumgartner and Jones analyse the frequency distributions of policy change. The method is not sensitive to one particular event, but instead measures general patterns in the distribution of policy choices over time (Jones and Baumgartner 2005b). The argument is that the frequency of changes should adhere to a non-normal distribution because there are a large number of small changes and a few very large ones—the latter are identified as the punctuations. The stochastic process method requires the large number of observations that the Policy Agendas Project provides. As a result, there is now a considerable body of work that uses these data to demonstrate a disproportional and punctuated pattern of policy change, across a wide range of political systems, institutional arenas and time periods (e.g. Jennings and John 2009; John and Jennings 2010; Jones and Baumgartner 2005a, 2005b; Jones et al. 1998, 2009b). The attraction of this account is that it provides a clear test of whether the data series are punctuated or not. It provides a way of summarising a lot of data for a particular venue of decision-making (Jones et al. 2003, 2009a), and can be used to compare the extent of kurtosis—the measure of a punctuated series—across different decision-making venues and jurisdictions.

The problem with the stochastic process method is that it can highlight a large number of changes in the sequence of this kind of policy content data, which may not correspond to large changes in the policy agenda, partly from misclassification and because not every sudden change in attention is associated with the upswings in attention characterised in the punctuated equilibrium model (John and Bevan 2012). We argue that a better understanding of what punctuations are (and how many large changes in the data are actually punctuations) is needed in order to develop testable hypotheses concerning the mechanisms behind the punctuated equilibrium model.

We discuss the data in a later section of the chapter, but to summarise here we find some of the policy changes are procedural, that is to do with the coding system; and others are large changes that do not receive much attention in the media, leaving a much smaller subset of changes that are both large changes and attract attention in the media. Another difficulty is that the method measures fluctuations, but not necessarily long-term shifts in the policy agenda. The measurement of frequency distributions may capture short-term fluctuations in the data but not the long-term shifts in attention. In punctuated equilibrium, especially when compared to its natural counterpart of evolution in the natural world, we are interested in departures from a previous state of play, which change a policy area for good or at least for a significant period of time; we are less interested in the temporary leaps and lags in attention, which may be dramatic but do not lead to a change in the equilibrium, but where the policy or the level of attention to the policy returns back to where it was before. The aggregate approach provides no way of sorting out different kinds of changes, which we have categorised into procedural, non-salient and salient, where the latter change is closer to the idea type of a policy punctuation. This may be critically affected by the type of venue that is being measured, so with budgets it is easy to see whether a percentage increase or decrease sustains into the future, with other kinds of policy change, such as the speech and the law, the record of the policy might be one off, but the law or measure stays in the statute book in perpetuity being implemented.

Thus there is a danger that the stochastic process method does not capture the change points in the political system, when the agenda shifts. This is not surprising because it is essentially ahistorical. The method tends to enable an abstract characterisation of the amount of change and stability in the system, but does not identify the specific change points themselves, which can connect to the historical record. We need a method that is able to identify the change points and then to explain what are the factors that cause the agenda to shift.

Are speeches and laws punctuated?

To what extent are the policy activities and outputs of British political institutions subject to equilibrium or instability? As we discussed above, the punctuated equilibrium model implies a leptokurtic distribution of policy change, which can be measured with a kurtosis statistic (Jones and Baumgartner 2005a, 2005b).[1] When compared against the normal distribution, those with positive kurtosis (i.e. leptokurtosis) have a large, slender central peak to correspond to extended periods of incrementalism or stability, weak shoulders to reflect the relative lack of moderate change and fat tails that show the disproportionate occurrence of extreme infrequent disturbances (i.e. punctuations).

To analyse the distribution of change, we use the 'percentage-percentage' calculation method of the difference between agenda share in one year and the next (see Baumgartner et al. 2009a, p. 610).[2] The distribution of year-on-year percentage change in the content of policy agenda is presented in Figure 5.1 and Figure 5.2, while the kurtosis scores for each variable are reported in Table 5.1. If the value of the kurtosis statistic is greater than three the distribution exhibits positive kurtosis and can be said to be leptokurtic. In addition to calculation of the kurtosis scores for each agenda distribution, kurtosis is also tested for through the Shapiro-Wilk test, which considers whether the sample is drawn from a normal distribution (generating a W statistic for each series). The results of the Shapiro-Wilk test are consistent with the reported kurtosis scores and therefore provide validation of our measurement.

From inspection of the kurtosis scores, it is evident, first of all, that the patterns of change in both the legislative and executive agendas are leptokurtic distributions. The kurtosis score for the Speech from the Throne is equal to 8.15, indicating a non-normal distribution of change consistent with the punctuated equilibrium model. For Acts of Parliament, the kurtosis score is equal to 25.28, also suggesting that change in the legislative agenda is subject both to greater stability and to extreme disturbances. This is also consistent with the higher level of institutional friction associated with the legislative agenda.[3] In summary, this evidence indicates that the policy agendas of British

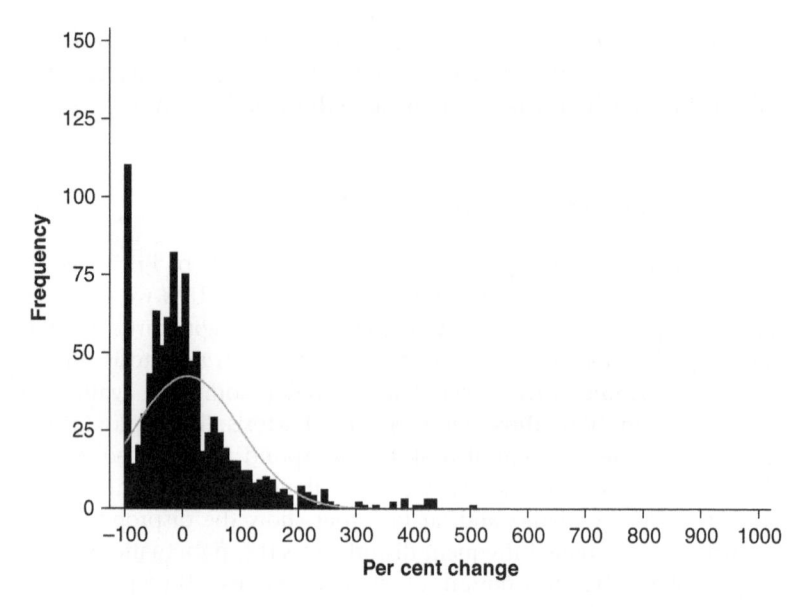

Figure 5.1 Frequency distribution of annual percentage change in the Speech from the Throne

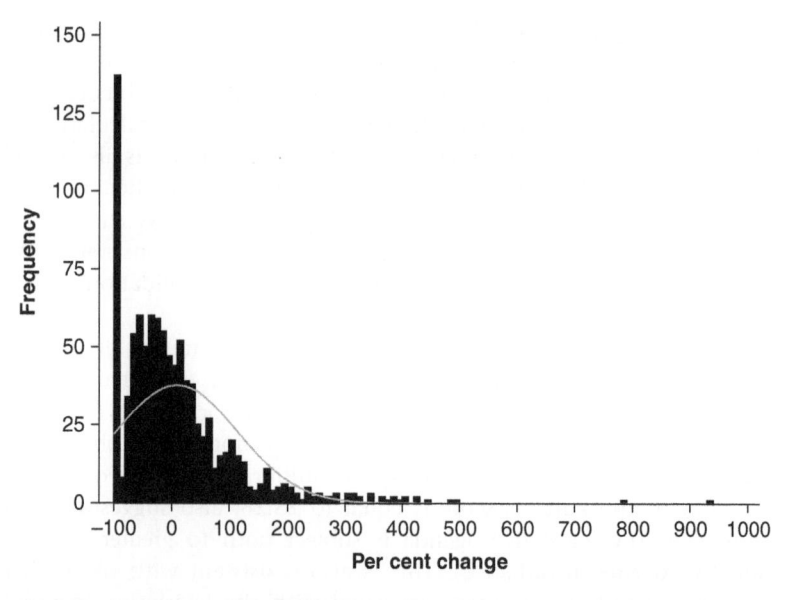

Figure 5.2 Frequency distribution of annual percentage change in Acts of Parliament

Table 5.1 Change in percentage attention to speeches and laws

Variable	Start	End	N	Obs.	Mean	SD	Kurtosis	Shapiro-Wilk W
Agendas Speech from the Throne	1945	2008	64	968	9.02	90.98	8.15	0.871
Acts of UK Parliament	1945	2008	63	994	10.66	111.82	25.28	0.785

government, both of the Speech from the Throne and Acts of Parliament, are subject to extended periods of stability and long-term equilibrium in decision-making, interspersed with occasional large-scale punctuations in policy attention.

An examination of the large changes[4]

One issue with the frequency distributions generated through the stochastic process method is that it is hard to know what the large changes in attention capture. Do they correlate with game-changing shifts in public policies that are implied in the punctuated equilibrium model? It is quite a straightforward task to list these large changes by looking at those shifts in attention that exceed 200 per cent. These are greater than the two standard deviations that are changes that are greater than most of—95 per cent of—the area under a normal distribution of (in this case) policy changes, so more than would be expected by chance. In Baumgartner and Jones' formulation, this area captures changes that would be expected under the incrementalist model—random shocks from the median—so by definition changes outside this area, above the two standard deviations, are policy punctuations, and there is only a 5 per cent chance that are the random shocks. Table 5.2 lists out these punctuations in the Speech from the Throne, in a simple list of years and major topic codes that apply. We calculate the change in attention by issue relative to its value in the previous parliamentary year.[5] For example, with this method a change from one act or line in the speech in 1950 to four acts in 1951 leads to a 300 per cent increase in legislative attention relative to the previous level of attention.

There are some 47 punctuations in the series, which shows the instability of the policy agenda. But with such a large number it seems implausible that each of these punctuations refers to major

Table 5.2 Policy punctuations in the Speech from the Throne, 1945–2008

Year	Topic	Proportion change (%)	Year	Topic	Proportion change (%)
1946	Gov't	574.60	1974	Energy	258.10
1947	Welfare	240.54	1976	Environment	215.38
1948	Banking	305.48	1977	Science	251.00
1951	Labour	202.44	1978	Civil	182.26
1952	Energy	261.76	1980	Energy	429.70
1954	Education	198.88	1980	Transport	217.82
1954	Transport	198.88	1982	Science	253.49
1955	Banking	319.81	1987	Education	212.98
1956	Gov't	213.82	1991	Civil	217.24
1957	Welfare	341.86	1991	Energy	322.99
1958	Education	262.11	1994	Health	230.77
1958	Housing	262.11	1994	Labour	230.77
1959	Transport	487.63	1995	Education	463.86
1959	Banking	389.69	1996	Environment	215.19
1961	Health	380.00	1997	Gov't	305.13
1963	Transport	213.04	1998	Welfare	560.48
1963	Housing	213.04	1998	Banking	277.42
1964	Civil rights	342.31	2000	Health	273.33
1964	Health	342.31	2000	Housing	220.00
1966	Welfare	215.63	2003	Civil	512.50
1969	Energy	251.14	2003	Labour	308.33
1970	Environment	255.56	2007	Labour	325.0
1970	Housing	211.11	2008	Defence	233.33
1972	Welfare	229.90			

game-changing events when policy monopolies shatter under the pressure of the emergence of new interests and institutional equilibrium. The punctuations are spread across the topics of the policy agenda, but not evenly, with 3 in the 1940s, 11 in the 1950s, 7 in the 1960s, 7 in the 1970s, 4 in the 1980s, 9 in the 1990s and 6 in the 2000s. Even taking into account that the data do not have all the years in the 1940s and 2000s, it is evident that the 1950s was an unusually active decade, which is not a common observation in British politics, which follows on from our earlier findings (John and Jennings 2010). The other highly punctuated decades are the 1990s and 2000s when the Conservative Party and then New Labour held power. So from the perspective of the overall distribution of change in the policy agenda, the decades of the 1950s and 1990/2000s are the more active periods in post-war Britain when it was more likely that the agenda was likely to experience large leaps compared with the 1960s, 1970s and 1980s.

It is also possible to examine variations across topics: that is, what kinds of topic experience the large shifts. The highest number of punctuations concern social welfare with five years in which there were greater than 200 per cent changes in attention, such as in 1947 when there were three items rising from a small base in the speech in the year before. The 1947 Speech from the Throne announced a major reform of the poor law and comprehensive system of assistance, and also a measure to care for children. In 1957 there were a series of measures on pensions. Similarly in 1996 there were policies announced on pensions and social security changes. In 1972 there was more of a set of unrelated policy changes, such as a social security reform, and an announcement of aspects of the EEC membership with a social policy dimension. Finally, we move to 1998, which is New Labour's programme of social security reforms, which reflect the preoccupations of the newly elected social democratic government, with the powerful Chancellor of the Exchequer, Gordon Brown, concerned with reform of the welfare state. There were measures to alter benefits for people with long-term illness or disabilities, and modernising benefits for widows. The government also introduced the Disability Rights Commission. So in this list of policy punctuations it is possible to observe different kinds of policy change, some more important than others, but also how each topic receives a lot of attention from policy-makers at once for a relatively short period of time, usually to introduce a package of measures.

There are a number of major policy topics that have four punctuations during the period between 1948 and 2008: civil rights, minority issues, immigration and civil liberties; health; labour and employment; education; community development, planning and housing; and banking, finance and domestic commerce. In community development, for example, in 1958 there was an expansion of attention including measures for compulsory purchase of land and a specialist building regulation for Scotland. These are hardly game-changing policies, and the increase also reflects that attention had declined the previous year. There is a second policy punctuation in 1963, which captures the building programme of the Conservative government and a plan to ameliorate pressures on the local tax rates, which does represent a surge in policy interest in a period before an election, and followed a white paper on housing policy in May of that year (HLG 117/181), which proposed an increase in the stock of housing. The next punctuation was in 1970 when the Heath government proposed changes to housing policy, making changes to the subsidy regime, which implemented the promises made in the Conservative election manifesto, and was part of the early reform policy of the new government. The final punctuation was under New Labour, which was a set of changes to homelessness policy and an announcement about new rights for leaseholders to purchase of freeholds.

The topics that have three punctuations are topic seven (environment), and eight (energy), ten (transport) and 20 (government operations). Remaining then is topic 17 (space), which contains two punctuations, and topic 16 (defence) which has one. With the exception of this last case, it seems that the main clustering of policy punctuations occurs in topics that have lower mean levels of attention so tend to be of less importance to British government. There was never a punctuation in policy-making attention for macroeconomic issues, for example, nor one for international affairs. It appears that governments maintain a high level of attention to these topics in most years so that any rise or fall in attention is generated from a high base leading to lower percentage changes. Topics that receive a lower level of attention will tend to experience larger percentage changes because it does not take that much of an absolute increase (i.e. a few lines in the speech or a few pieces of legislation) to create a policy punctuation from the low base. This can be accentuated if there is a higher level of attention two years previously, then a very low level once all the measures have gone through, and then a large rise again in the year in question. Thus policy punctuations can occur because of decreases in the policy content of the aggregate-level series as well as rises, which generate the percentage changes. Punctuations therefore represent intrusions of particular policy topics onto the agenda but often retreat soon after they emerge. For example, education may have received less attention in the early 1980s because of the Falklands War and labour issues, but the low average led to a punctuation once the reforms of the mid-1980s kicked in.

Punctuations in laws

Using the same approach, we examine policy punctuations in Acts of Parliament, which are reported in Table 5.3. This identifies 49 changes of more than 200 per cent over the period, which is a similar number to that found for the Speech from the Throne.

For Acts of Parliament, there is a different distribution of policy punctuations across the decades compared with the speeches. There are no punctuations in the 1940s, 10 in the 1950s, 10 in the 1960s, which then drop to 5 each in the 1970s and 1980s, rising to 11 in the

Table 5.3 Policy punctuations in Acts of UK Parliament, 1945–2008

Year	Topic	Proportion change (%)	Year	Topic	Proportion change (%)
1951	Banking	239.71	1982	Agriculture	217.31
1952	Education	226.92	1985	Labour	244.78
1952	Lands	226.92	1987	Transport	241.94
1953	Energy	256.16	1988	Environment	304.35
1953	Science	256.16	1989	Science	206.67
1954	International	403.45	1990	Defence	230.88
1954	Lands	277.59	1991	Social	491.30
1956	Defence	503.17	1991	Banking	417.39
1958	Labour	393.15	1992	Environment	243.28
1958	Education	294.52	1992	International	311.94
1961	Education	340.68	1993	Defence	226.83
1961	Social	230.51	1994	Lands	203.70
1963	Civil	209.28	1995	Education	440.00
1963	Defence	332.99	1995	Defence	350.00
1965	Labour	315.00	1997	Gov't	613.71
1965	Environment	315.00	1998	Gov't	254.29
1967	Welfare	568.42	2000	Economy	300.00
1968	Labour	623.81	2000	Labour	300.00
1968	Gov't	221.69	2002	Environment	308.70
1969	Social	375.47	2002	Energy	206.52
1970	Education	261.36	2003	Civil	263.16
1971	Science	456.96	2003	Social	263.16
1973	Civil	446.15	2003	Housing	384.21
1974	International	209.52	2004	International	442.86
1979	Lands	208.00			

1990s and 8 in the 2000s. There is much more variability across the decades with some not experiencing many large changes, whereas there is about one per year in the 1950s, 1960s and 1990s. Again, the 1950s are important, but here the number of punctuations declines in the 2000s, and it is the 1990s that is the decade when government moved to legislate very rapidly across the major topics in public policy. As before, the Thatcherite decade of the 1980s only has five punctuations. There is a slightly different distribution across the major topics, with quite a few topics having five punctuations over the period (labour and employment, education, social welfare, defence, public lands and water management). Here some of the core policy topics come into play such as defence, which does not appear as punctuated in the speeches, although social welfare appears again.

The topics of the environment and international affairs/foreign aid have four punctuations each, which again shows how laws can punctuate on core policy topics. Civil rights, minority issues, immigration and civil liberties and science (space, science, technology and communications) score three each. Even the economy is punctuated in 2000.

The classification of policy punctuations

The discussion about the occurrence of the greater than 200 per cent changes suggests that there is a lot going under the surface of these dots at the ends of a distribution figure. Some changes look like important programmes implemented by a newly elected government; others look like sets of reforms of the administrative machine that are linked together; others seem to be unconnected measures, and are often very minor revisions. Partly for these reasons, we claim that the measurement of punctuations by aggregate data analysis disguises a number of different processes that may get classified in the same way by the stochastic process method and the policy content coding system of the Policy Agendas Project. We think it is likely that there are different elements to punctuations, partly for reasons to do with coding and measurement, and partly due to different levels of intensity and importance.

Procedural punctuations

We proceed by first separating punctuations that occur due to procedural processes and the coding system from the rest. This method has the advantage of avoiding punctuations that we believe are not large policy changes even though their different elements might be important policies. Usually the expansion of the agenda implies one item dominates public attention, such as a war, or a major financial crisis. Out of chance that different, but related things needed doing at the same time,[6] government can attend to different problems within a major topic category. In spite of the activities not having much to do with each other, they get defined as part of the same policy punctuation as they occur in the same major topic category. Procedural punctuations do not come about from any formal aspect of policy-making. Rather they emerge from the exigencies of the coding system—or any other coding system—which requires that related issues be placed within the same major topic code. The coding procedure adds these related, minor topics together into their respective major topics, but does not establish whether the contents of the major topics are part of the same causal process. The research methodology needs a second step to do this, which can either be achieved by the analysis of more quantitative data, such as from the media, or by collecting and interpreting qualitative data.

If this argument is accepted, the appearance of these punctuations in the dataset is a misclassification, a type I error or a false positive, and they should be removed or analysed separately as they are large shifts in attention that do not match the agenda-altering definition of a policy punctuation whereby a policy change is associated with the expansion of other agendas. Of course, it is not possible to rule out that different expansions are an aspect of the same kind of interest, but expressing itself in different minor topic codes. And researchers must guard against the opposite problem of identifying large agenda changes as procedural punctuations, the type II error or false negative. One such idea is comprehensive health care reform, NHS, private insurance or doctors' pay/pensions. Something like that may appear procedural, as it occurs in multiple sub-topics, but in reality would be part of an overall system of reform.

Low- and high-salience punctuations

It is possible to have large changes in the policy agenda but for them to make little or no impact in the wider public arena. There may be reasons for changing legislation that involve compliance with international obligations or following EU decisions. Often a large amount of legislative time is taken up with revising legislation that wider publics and even many other policy-makers are not interested in because it has a technical nature, and it might involve ensuring compliance with previous Acts of Parliament. In this case, there might be punctuations in the data series, but they are low-salience punctuations and can be called as such. On the other hand, high-salience punctuations garner interest from wider publics and policy-makers alike leading to major changes in policy that are reported in the media. In this way, our categorisation of punctuations in laws reflects their importance, rather like other schemes, such as Mayhew's (1991) list of 'important laws'. Rather than a general sense of importance, however, we focus on the causal mechanisms analysts commonly associate with policy punctuations— their attention in the media and in other venues—so the cases resemble the endogenous processes identified by Jones and colleagues. For this reason, we treat data points differently in our data series, distinguishing between high- and low-salience punctuations through attention in the media. This categorisation, as well as procedural punctuations, is summarised in Table 5.4.

Table 5.4 Types of punctuations

Punctuation type	Description
Procedural punctuation	Attention to a single major topic through multiple minor topics following separate causal processes.
Low-salience punctuation	Attention to a single major topic through a single minor topic, but with limited or no attention by the media.
High-salience punctuation	Attention to a single major topic though a single minor topic with high levels of attention by the media.

Punctuations in the Speech from the Throne and Acts of Parliament

In this section, we calculate the change in attention by issue relative to the total number of acts and speeches in each year as well as the method of the per cent-per cent change implemented in the above sections.[7] For example, when the overall agenda space remains stable at 20 acts per year an increase from one act (a 5 per cent share of the agenda) to four acts (a 20 per cent share of the agenda) results in a 300 per cent increase in legislative attention relative to the total number of acts. By using both methods to identify punctuations we ensure not only a more robust result, but that punctuations based purely on expansions or contractions of the total number of acts in a given year, which affected the discussion of Table 5.1 and Table 5.2, are not included in our analyses. Finally, we identify a change as punctuated when both of these methods for identifying changes in attention are calculated to be greater than 200 per cent for an issue in a given year, which we justified before. While the word 'large' could be interpreted in many different ways: 200 per cent changes in the case of UK Acts of Parliament is a logical cut-off providing a fair and consistent sample of large changes to work with.[8]

A closer look at the punctuations

The discussion so far has listed out the punctuations, and has identified the different ones that appear in speeches and laws, which again points to the different character of theses series, and shows how government use the Speech from the Throne to draw attention to particular issues, whereas Acts of Parliament come in clusters to deal with particular issues. But so far we have not been able to explore the typology except to get a sense that the punctuations discussed so far vary in character. One way to look at the punctuations is to reduce them to a more manageable number as discussed above and take the Acts of Parliament as the sample. A complete list of punctuations using the combination of both identification methods is included in Table 5.5 that lists the issue that the policy punctuation related to, how many Acts of Parliament were associated with the punctuation, the starting year of the punctuation, the start and end date of the parliamentary year, and the type based on our typology discussed in the next section. The table contains 29 punctuations in acts.

Table 5.5 List of identified act punctuations by issue, 1945–2008

Year	Topic	Acts	Start date	End date	Type
1945	Agriculture	4	15-08-1945	12-11-1946	High-salience
1950	Environment	4	31-10-1950	06-11-1951	High-salience
1951	Commerce	6	06-11-1951	04-11-1952	High-salience
1953	Labour	3	03-11-1953	30-11-1954	Procedural
1953	Energy	4	03-11-1953	30-11-1954	High-salience
1953	Science	4	03-11-1953	30-11-1954	Low-salience
1956	Defence	4	05-11-1956	05-11-1957	Low-salience
1958	Education	3	28-10-1958	27-10-1959	Procedural
1958	Labour	4	28-10-1958	27-10-1959	High-salience
1961	Education	3	31-10-1961	30-10-1962	Procedural
1963	Civil	4	12-11-1963	03-11-1964	High-salience
1963	Defence	6	12-11-1963	03-11-1964	Low-salience
1966	Crime	12	21-04-1966	31-10-1967	High-salience
1967	Social	3	31-10-1967	30-10-1968	Procedural
1968	Labour	5	30-10-1968	28-10-1969	High-salience
1969	Social	3	28-10-1969	20-07-1970	Procedural
1970	Education	5	20-07-1970	02-11-1971	Low-salience
1971	Science	4	02-11-1971	31-10-1972	High-salience
1979	Transport	8	15-05-1979	20-11-1980	High-salience
1979	Lands	10	15-05-1979	20-11-1980	Low-salience
1979	Housing	7	15-05-1979	20-11-1980	Low-salience
1982	Agriculture	8	03-11-1982	22-06-1983	Low-salience
1983	Science	3	22-06-1983	06-11-1984	High-salience
1987	Transport	7	25-06-1987	22-11-1988	High-salience
1990	Defence	4	07-11-1990	31-10-1991	Procedural
1991	Commerce	6	31-10-1991	06-05-1992	High-salience
1991	Social	7	31-10-1991	06-05-1992	High-salience
1992	Foreign	5	06-05-1992	18-11-1993	Low-salience
1992	Environment	4	06-05-1992	18-11-1993	High-salience
1994	Lands	3	16-11-1994	15-11-1995	Procedural

Table 5.5 (Continued)

Year	Topic	Acts	Start date	End date	Type
1995	Education	5	15-11-1995	23-10-1996	Low-salience
1995	Defence	4	15-11-1995	23-10-1996	Procedural
1997	Gov't	14	14-05-1997	24-11-1998	High-salience
2002	Environment	3	13-11-2002	26-11-2003	Low-salience
2003	Housing	3	26-11-2003	23-11-2004	High-salience
2005	Health	5	17-05-2005	15-11-2006	High-salience

Applying the typology

The next step is to distinguish between the procedural punctuations and the rest. Here we identify eight punctuations out of the 29 that match the definition of procedural punctuations with Acts of Parliament passed on multiple unrelated issues, or minor topics, within a single major topic code.[9] These punctuations are listed in Table 5.5. The first is in 1953 and relates to disability benefits, pensions and banking industry work hours, followed by another in 1958, which contains legislation on art and education. The next is about education, museums and education (Scotland) in 1958. In 1967 there was legislation on family allowances and social work in Scotland, followed by 1969 legislation on milk for poor school children, council social services training and disability benefits. Arguably, this last measure could be about social policy, and the family allowances appear in histories of Labour's social policies (Thane 2000, p. 109), but these items had separate origins. In 1990 there was a set of legislation on war crimes, arms control, nuclear weapons and general military, though these measures were partially linked because of the end of the Cold War when it made sense to bundle items of legislation together. In 1994 there is another procedural punctuation on South Africa, Commonwealth development and Scottish Land Registers. The final one is in 1997 and is about chemical weapons, Hong Kong veterans reserve forces and another set of unrelated items.

These items are not unimportant. Indeed, far from it. It is significant that these laws are part of the same major topic code, for example, in drawing the public's attention to a policy issue like health or education. There are implications for interest groups and policy-makers in this field, say a department of health, or for a select committee, that a large number of items in a policy field occur at the same time. Nonetheless, we maintain the argument that there is a type difference between the procedural punctuations and ones where there are closer links between the policies creating the large shift in the policy agenda.

Next we turn to the low-salience punctuations that attract attention through a single initiative but that receive limited or no media attention. We offer a conservative account of low-salience punctuations in that the majority of the laws that comprise them should have no attention in the media. For the media, we use data from *The Times*, the newspaper of record for the period (see discussion in Chapter 3 and Chapter 8). To distinguish between low-salience punctuations and others, we examine salience in connection with all laws contained in the punctuations. If the majority of laws (greater than 50 per cent) comprising punctuations were not salient, then these punctuations are classified as low salience and a complete list is also contained in Table 5.3. This is a very conservative test in that many laws have a large number of mentions and only one mention puts the law into the salient camp. An example of the low-salience punctuations is education in 1970, which included the following acts: Education (Handicapped Children) Act 1970, Teaching Council (Scotland) Act 1970 and Welsh National Opera Company Act 1970, none of which received any mentions in *The Times*. The final calculation generates 11 low-salience punctuations. Given the small number of laws each year, it is surprising to find that so many do not receive a mention in the newspaper of record.

Table 5.6 contains the remaining 18 high-salience punctuations identified by attention to a single minor topic code and high levels of media attention identified by a majority of salient laws contained within each one. This represents a reasonable number of cases in the period 1945–2008 with one large event every four years on average. The table lists the year, the topic area and a brief summary of the policy issues.

There is a considerable diversity in these punctuations, which range across the decades and occur in most of the major topic areas. Some patterns stand out. Many represent attempts by Parliament to get to grips with regulation in a policy field, such as the 1971 reforms of the entertainment industry. These are classic examples of agenda expansion whereby several related areas simultaneously attract the attention of policy-makers or that regulation in one area precipitates a rethink in a related policy sub-field.

There were some changes that reflected the importance of public opinion and the media place on an issue, such as immigration in the early 1960s, which led to reform of nationality acts, and dominated politics for over a decade afterwards. Another example occurred in the late 1960s when the Labour government became preoccupied with labour market reforms, which reflected the increased public salience of employment matters and concerns about the state of industrial relations. The controversial *In Place of Strife* white paper (Department of Employment and

Table 5.6 High-salience punctuations in acts

Year	Topic	Summary
1945	Agriculture	Measures aimed at reviving agriculture post-war
1951	Environment	Regulation of water supply and management
1952	Commerce	Laws on consumer protection
1953	Energy	Measure on nuclear power and the utility industry
1958	Labour	Changes to the regulation of employment, such as wages councils
1963	Civil rights	Measures to regulate immigration
1966	Crime	A series of civil rights reform associated with Labour modernisation
1968	Labour	Welfare and employment reforms, for example, national insurance
1971	Science	Reforms of entertainment industry
1979	Transport	A range of reforms of transport, introducing more commercial principles
1983	Science	Reform of licensing and privatisation
1987	Transport	A range of transport measures, including the Channel Tunnel and seat belts
1991	Commerce	A range of measures to regulate commerce
1991	Social welfare	A number of measures to reform social security
1992	Environment	A range of environmental measures, several aimed at animal welfare
1997	Government	A whole range of institutional reforms associated with the new Labour administration
2003	Housing	Planning and housing measures
2005	Health	A series of related health service reforms

Productivity 1969) proposed a statutory basis for relationships between trades unions and employers, but the Labour government never implemented it. The environmental reforms of 1991 were a response to the large number of problems that came up for solution at that time, and that many of these regulatory changes were going through the EU. Also they were probably due to an increase in public concern about the environment from the late 1980s onwards.

Some punctuations have a partisan flavour, when a government in office puts its ideological stamp on a series of measures in a policy sector. The Labour government, which came into office in 1964 after a long period of Conservative rule, carried out a series of reforming measures in civil rights, and these created the observed policy punctuation. The Conservative administrations after 1979 were also highly partisan, wishing to introduce market forces into the public sector, for example, the 1980 reform of transport or the privatising reforms of the 1980s. New

Labour, when elected in 1997, carried out a series of constitutional reforms that reflected its reformist and modernising stance to government, such as referendums for devolution to Scotland and Wales. The conclusion to draw is that the selection of high-salience punctuations are indeed large policy changes that relate to periods of attention to particular policy issues, driven by external events and/or partisan preoccupations. Students of public policy and country specialists can use the typology to identify these high-salience punctuations and to observe their expression in laws.

The method does not replicate what standard histories of British politics do (e.g. Clarke 2004), which is to write about what are considered to be defining pieces of legislation, and to see them as symbolising and structuring politics and policy afterwards. Instead, it examines the expansion of attention to a major policy topic and its prioritisation at particular moments of time. Thus, a critic could examine the list in Table 5.5 and ask why the National Health Service Act 1948 that established comprehensive health care is not included. But the approach of the contemporary historian is different to the student of public policy: the former tends to focus on ground-breaking pieces of legislation, which may not take up a large amount of legislative time in any one year, whereas the latter is interested in the attention policy-makers pay to a particular topic. While the historical method can hone in on matters that automatically appear to be of importance, it can be prone to subjectivity in the sense of reproducing accepted wisdoms about British politics, whereas the aggregate method of collecting punctuations systematically find shifts in policy-making attention that do not appear so much in the historical record, and so alert the student of public policy to important changes that might not otherwise be visible. This echoes a traditional complaint from public policy scholars (e.g. Richardson and Jordan 1979) that other disciplines tend not to pay much attention to detailed or humdrum matters of decision-making preferring to concentrate on high politics. Our procedure for identifying policy punctuations finds a way of linking high and low politics through legislative attention.

Conclusions

Since the early 1990s public policy scholars have made considerable progress in understanding the character of the policy agenda, and they have successfully challenged the assumptions of an earlier generation of scholars who claimed that policy changes were largely incremental in character. As a result of the work of Jones, Baumgartner and their collaborators, most public policy researchers now believe that political systems regularly experience large-scale changes in attention to public policy even though there may be long periods of stability. Important in this enterprise is the analysis of aggregate measures of political attention. In support of this approach, this chapter used the method to throw more light on the main trends in policy-making in British politics by investigating the exact nature of these large changes and trying to understand the causal processes that comprise them. Like other scholars, we find the policy agendas series to be punctuated as measured through tests of normal distributions and leptokurtosis. The straightforward claim we make is that the aggregate measures subdivide into three different kinds of policy change, which reflect degrees of importance in the wider political system. Some of the punctuations in the data are combinations of activities that are not well connected together; others are large connected policy changes, but they are not salient to wider publics. Only the rest, the high-salience punctuations, with their upswings in media attention, resemble the policy changes as described by Baumgartner and Jones.

The typology works well in separating out different kinds of policy change. In particular, the procedure for identifying high-salience punctuations creates an important distinction between high-profile large policy changes and other kinds of policy change. This has a dual purpose. First, it guards against the problem of over-claiming from the policy agenda data that there are more policy punctuations—in the Baumgartner–Jones sense—than there really are. Second, the typology corrects for the selection bias that is present in many contemporary histories, which tend not to be much interested in public policy and focus on a few pieces of legislation rather than the shifts in attention across the wider political system and across many decision-making venues. In other words, by offering a leaner definition of high-salience policy punctuations public policy scholars can more effectively challenge conventional wisdom.

We have not sought to disguise the inherent messiness and complexity of policy-making. Once the analyst looks beyond the smooth representations of data series, decision-making is inherently differentiated and complex. We aim for generalisation and believe that the typology and the method we propose offer a valid distinction between different kinds of policy change. Nonetheless, there may be some overlap between the different kinds of punctuations, for example, elements of a low-salience punctuation that receive significant media attention, or procedural elements of a high-salience punctuation.

In terms of the models of agenda setting in the book, we have focused on an important candidate, that of punctuated equilibrium, and we have attended to how it is measured by Baumgartner and Jones. In our analysis, we have found that the aggregate method is likely to exaggerate the number of large policy changes existing in a series, such as in British politics since 1945, the one we use here, but also any other series by implication. In terms of representing the policy agenda, we cannot use the aggregate methods to say that the British policy agenda is characterised as according to the punctuated equilibrium model, even though punctuations have occurred in British policy-making. By reducing the incidence of punctuations, this indicates that other approaches to decision-making and other representations of the policy agenda have more traction. In the next chapter, we are able to turn directly to our preferred model of focused adaptation.

6
Structural Shifts in British Political Attention

In the previous two chapters, we outlined different ways of examining the policy agenda across time to illuminate aspects of post-war British politics and policy-making. But the methods used in these chapters have their limitations. Eyeballing time trends as we did in Chapter 4 does give a sense of how the agenda shifts and allows the reader to get a feel for the rise and fall in attention to issues across the period since 1945—or sections of it—but the eye can be distracted by specific ups and downs in the series that may not be helpful in characterising their fundamental substantive properties. Visual identification of time series data is also vulnerable to bias, either due to the shape of the series or from the researcher using their prior knowledge about what the important changes in the agenda are, such as from a significant partisan changes or external crises.

To understand these limitations better as well as to motivate an alternative approach to understanding change in the policy agenda over time, we must first define a set of terms. Consider a simple dynamic model of attention to macroeconomic policy in the Speech from the Throne between 1948 and 2008 that has been implicit in our discussions thus far. This model states that attention in the current speech is a function of attention in the last speech and some idiosyncratic component. Three parameters describe this relationship—the conditional mean, the sensitivity of current attention to that of last year's speech and the variance of the idiosyncratic component. This is the incrementalist model. A change in any of these parameters is described as a *structural* change as it relates to the structure of this simple autoregressive model that generates the observed values of attention to macroeconomic policy issues. The date on which this parameter changes is called a *change point* and the dynamics of political attention, the subject of this book, would be better understood if such points were uncovered. In the descriptive discussions that follow, our interest is in changes to a single parameter—the mean—of the agenda series we discuss. It implies an even simpler model in which the mean is the estimator of the expected value of the series. When the mean shifts, our expected value likewise shifts, and we are thus interested in change points even in this very simple case.

Chow (1960) developed a test for structural change. This involves, first, guessing a candidate change point on the basis of the researcher's own knowledge, dividing the series into two segments—before and after the candidate—and testing to see whether the parameters are statistically the same in the two segments, which is essentially the method deployed in Chapter 4. Hansen (2001, p. 118) notes that this approach can be difficult for two reasons. First, arbitrarily selecting the change point might lead a researcher to miss an honest one. Second, choosing a candidate change point on the basis of some feature in the time series may generate a false positive result; a change point may be identified where none exist. This is presumably the reason why Baumgartner and Jones believe that such speculation is fruitless as there are always a 'million stories in the budget' (Jones and Baumgartner 2005a, p.113) to talk about, or in our case here, different levels of attention in speeches and laws. To put it more technically, the problem is that the timing of the change point is endogenous to, or correlated with, the data in the series such that its relationship to the unmodelled idiosyncratic factors remains unobserved. It is thus important to find a way to respect the endogenous timing of the emergence of change points.

The previous chapter set out and discussed the punctuations—greater than expected changes in the policy agenda—as indicators of changes in the equilibrium. Because we suggested that leaps and lags of greater than 200 per cent could signify the key large changes in the series *a priori*, choosing to study them still ignores the endogeneity concern just discussed. The grand epoch-shifting breaks that are core to the punctuated equilibrium model may, if we are not careful, be artefacts of a statistical technique that generates false positive results. Consequently, we employ an alternative method that treats change point timing as endogenous and we compare results in the chapters that follow.

Many ways of estimating an unknown change point have been proposed (cf. Andrews and Ploberger 1994; Bai and Perron 2003; Chong 1995; Hansen 1997; Olshen and Venkatraman 2004; Quandt 1960). Like these, our approach in this chapter is to treat the periods of stability and change as endogenous, whereby some points of time are change points, but their identity reflects the overall pattern of change, a process of what we term focused adaptation in Chapter 1. To implement our different approach to change, we use a method that does identify crucial periods of policy change, but which neither has the limitations of regression-based models that assume stationarity of the time series' structural parameter of interest—the mean—nor the abstraction of plots of frequency distributions, nor the subjectivity of eyeballing.[1] Essentially, this approach models each series as a sequence of random variables, where each random variable represents a cluster of years with statistically equal means. These clusters represent periods of stability between estimated change points and they are drawn from a distribution that is a function of the probability of a change point in each year. This suggests that we can represent our estimates in a very intuitive way, namely, by showing the probability of observing structural change in the policy agenda series in a given year. As those probabilities grow, the chances that a structural break occurs in that year increase. The statistical model is discussed in more detail in the appendix to this chapter.

In terms of British politics, which we discuss in Chapters 1 and 2, we identify particular regimes when there was a structure to the agenda for a policy area, which can be identified through upswings and downswings as identified in the punctuated equilibrium model. Our approach then is historical, identifying the main periods in British public policy and linking them with agenda setting and prioritisation (Western and Kleykamp 2004, p. 354). In this way, we are able to understand periods of change in British politics and policy-making, and then time when the agenda shifted from one pattern to another. Using change point analysis, the chapter provides evidence of shifts in attention to a wide variety of issues and marshals that information into a new view of the policy landscape during this critical period of British history. These structural changes can help us to identify occasions of focused adaptation by British governments. That is, when attention to policy areas passes a change point in time, the government enters a new epoch of policy-making whereby attention is unlikely to return to its prior mean, breaking out of an issue attention cycle or pattern of incrementalism. The change is structural, relating to the mean that governs the series, rather than captured in its size, as in the case of punctuations.

We do this by estimating the probability of structural changes in various issue trends in the policy agenda and relating our estimated shifts to information from the qualitative record. By considering the change points to be random variables (see Barry and Hartigan 1993), it is possible to avoid assuming a specific location for a structural break.

We can thus discover the locations of important changes of emphasis. We use concentrations of change points to define epochs of instability in the British policy agenda. To that end, we begin by identifying structural breaks in various institutional venues, namely, the Speech from the Throne and Acts of Parliament (in later chapters we use change points on the public agenda, front-page stories in the media and budgets). The chapter then turns to a general discussion of epochs of change. Appendix 6A provides a description of the models we employ to estimate the change points discussed here.

Speeches from the Throne

Figure 6.1 displays years in which the probability of a change point in the individual agenda series was estimated to be 90 per cent or greater. We choose this threshold as it corresponds to conventional levels of statistical significance.[2] More change points in a time period indicate

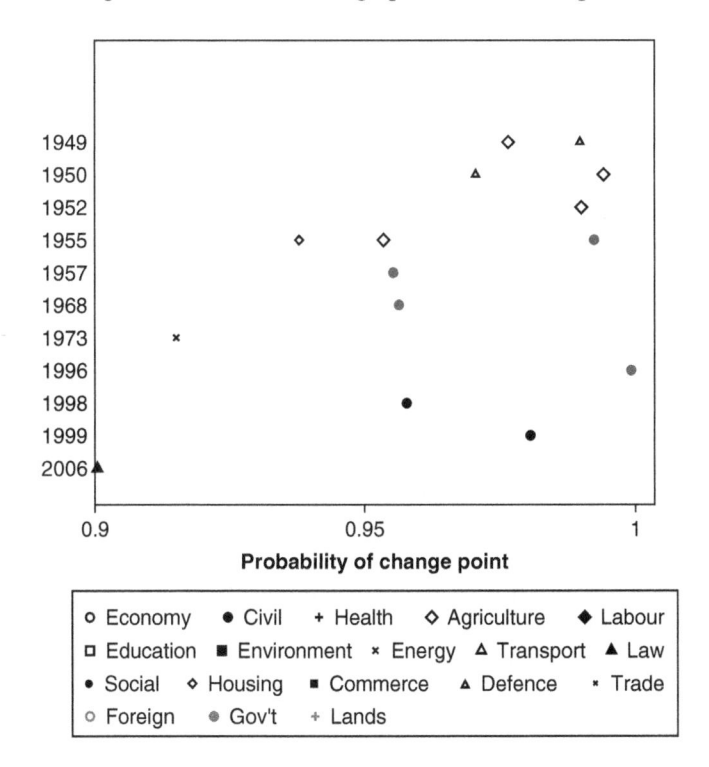

Figure 6.1 Likely change points, Speeches from the Throne, 1946–2008

agenda instability, and it is these periods on which we focus in this chapter.

The greatest number of structural breaks in the Speech from the Throne agenda occurs in the decades of the 1950s and the 1990s. In the 1950s, the change points that emerge relate to transport (1949, 1950, 1955), agriculture (1949, 1950, 1952), planning (1955) and then government (1955, 1957). The figures in Chapter 4 show the important changes in this early post-war period as it was a period of transition from the wartime economy, and a command state to a modern, complex, market economy managed by a more differentiated set of state functions. To achieve this transition, it needed the expansion of policies designed to support the infrastructure, such as building roads and housing, and it involved declining interest in agriculture once the post-war problems of food supply had been resolved. There were changes to the structure and organisation of the state at that time, such as to the financing of local government, which probably reflected the bedding down of the institutions of the welfare state. Successive years of economic growth gave the policy-makers opportunities to engage in significant level of public investment in infrastructure, such as roads and housing. Partly as a result, it was a period of high activity in these sectors. For example, Dudley and Richardson (2000) find significant policy changes and the impact of entrepreneurial ministers in transport policy in the 1950s.

Is the finding that 1950s was an age of policy activism surprising? Linking to the previous chapter, there are a number of punctuations in that period, which corresponds to our discussion of these changes in Chapter 4 the identification of policy punctuations in Chapter 5. Bulpitt and Burnham (1999), in their analysis of the stillborn experiment in market economics, Operation Robot, in 1952, identify the 1950s as one that historians compare with rather than analyse for its own sake. In fact, the 1950s was an age of innovation in its own right, which their case study illustrates. It is certainly interesting that the policy agenda the 1950s marked an important set of structural changes in attention that are not usually identified as important points in general histories of the period.

The surprise is that period of policy innovation in the 1960s did not see many change points in the policy agenda in the speech when it was a period of social change, economic insecurity and when the reforming Labour government 1964–1970 felt inclined to push through social measures (Fielding 2003). The only change point in attention was in the government operations topic, which is about the structures of the state rather than its policy initiatives. This agenda shift coincided with institutional reforms that Labour wanted to introduce in 1968, such as the reform of the House of Lords, regional government and changes in electoral law, which is consistent with the modernising agenda of this government and its commitment to liberal principles. It is interesting that such a probability of a change point took place late on in that government's period in office and this reflected the way in which the government became focused on a series of constitutional questions rather than the economic policy reforms of its early period. The two change points reflect first the upswing in attention to this topic then the lessening of interest once the announcement about reforms had passed.

The 1970s—in spite of the many policy challenges governments faced—did not show much structural instability in the policy agenda, making that period consistent more with issue attention cycles and incrementalist arguments. The only case was foreign trade in 1973. This was a period of large changes in the international economic system, such as the large oil price rise instigated by OPEC, and the beginnings of a more inflationary period. The pressures on the international system put pressure on policy-makers to respond with policy initiatives to address matters as trade imbalances in the level of the currency (Sachs et al. 1981). In the speeches of the early 1970s, such as 1971, there are references to difficulties of international trade, the objective of curbing inflation and the drive for exports, such as credit for shipbuilding. In 1972, we find the speech contains the declaration, 'It is My Government's intention to resume the maintenance of agreed margins round a fixed parity for sterling as soon as circumstances permit', which shows the worry about exchange rates and the pressure to have a flexible exchange rate. By 1973, the speech contained references to the need to sustain exports, a declaration to have a more liberal pattern of trade and an intention to reform the international commodity trade. In part, this interest reflected the pressures on international trade and international economic activity at the time; it also embodied the Conservative government's free trade and liberalising principles (Campbell 1993), and again the change point is later on in the government rather than just at the point of taking office, which shows how exogenous pressures were driving the policy-makers to act.

It is interesting too that the rest of the turbulent decade of the 1970s, and then the ideological 1980s, did not show change points in the speeches. In spite of the focus on policy problems by the Thatcher governments, they did not show a tendency to change their level of attention to the major policy topics—at least in the speeches. This is consistent with recent work on the Speech from the Throne by John and Jennings (2010) where the authors argue that 1979 was not a turning point in the policy agenda of British government but instead the changes occurred in the 1990s. This is consistent with a line of work that suggests that the Thatcher governments were preoccupied with a series of problems that had dogged their predecessors: the same problems of inflation, unemployment, poor economic performance and poor relationships with trades unions continued throughout the 1970s and 1980s (Hay and Farrall 2011). It was only when those policy problems had been solved or reduced, that government saw the attraction of focusing on new policy problems, which had emerged such as rising expectations for the NHS.

Unlike that article and also the conclusions of much of Chapter 4, however, we find here that the 1990s did not show any structural change in the attention mechanism that the speech represents, except just before the change in government in 1996. Whereas our eyeballing and diversity measures (John and Jennings 2010) of the policy agenda show the changes starting in the 1990s, in fact it was around the time the Blair government was elected that we see the change points once again. The period of New Labour was when the policy agenda shifted strongly. In fact, the 1996 change point represents a low point in constitutional reforms when attention dramatically fell. In the 1996 speech, there is the single earth-shattering phrase under the topic for government operations: 'Estimates for the public service will be laid before you.' Such a low level of attention to the topic reflected the Major government's unwillingness to address constitutional issues, perhaps paralysed by debates over Europe, but also from a disinclination to tinker with these structures that reflected the philosophy of the premier with his attachment to traditional English customs and practices. In this case, what the change point is telling us is that the policy agenda was ripe for expansion, and of course the modernising Labour government elected in 1997 was better suited to deliver that expansion than the Conservative Party. The eye can follow focused adaptation to that topic over the period where attention to government operations rose to just over 17 per cent in 1997 and 1998, just as we observed in Chapter 4 (Figure 4.4). Here the government promised legislation on regional development agencies, and then the intention to reform the funding of political parties, and announced the transition in Hong Kong and reforms of Parliament. In 1998, the speech contained promises on powers for Scotland and Wales, the modernising of local government, reform of the House of Lords and reform of London government. In fact, constitutional and institutional reform were very much a theme in that early period of New Labour, which did fade as time went on, but may have reflected the absence of reform under the Conservative Party prior to that period.

A similar kind of shift occurs in 1998–1999 in civil rights policy attention. This again is consistent with the reforming impetus of the Labour government at that time. As was noted in Chapter 4, there was little attention to this major topic for most of the period, so the attention of New Labour reflected a seachange in this policy domain, and again reflects the character of this reforming government. In 1998, for example, the speech promises to establish the disability rights commission. Then there was a promise of legislation on freedom of information. In 1999, there were signals of legislation on social exclusion and promise of a bill on racial discrimination. Under this topic too is legislation on asylum and immigration, which also increased in attention during this period due to the pressures of migration and public reaction to that (see Jennings 2009, 2010; John and Margetts 2009). Interestingly, the period of Labour in office does not include a change point for social welfare, education or health in spite of the rises in attention to these topics and the way in which these appeared to define Labour's period in office. So in terms of what is going on with the change points, there was a build-up of pressure for a change in the neglected topics in the landscape of policy problems, but attention to social policies may have reflected long-term trends and, while significant in terms of changes in the policy agenda overall, did not constitute change points.

The final change point is observed at the end of the time period, which is on crime. Here, rather than signalling the beginning of a period of policy activism, the change point indicates the end of a period of attention to crime that gradually rose during the 1990s, but did not prompt a change point in that period. It was only when Tony Blair stood down from office in 2007 that a new period of low activism began on law, crime and the family, which reflected the long-run trend in social conditions that reduced the level of crime (Farrall and Jennings 2012). The 2000s was an intense period of activism on crime, but at some stage it had to come to an end as background conditions did not require further intervention from government. The change of leadership to the less populist Gordon Brown may have also promoted a change in the policy agenda.

Acts of Parliament

The second part of this chapter examines Acts of Parliament and applies the same method of change points and their analysis. Figure 6.2

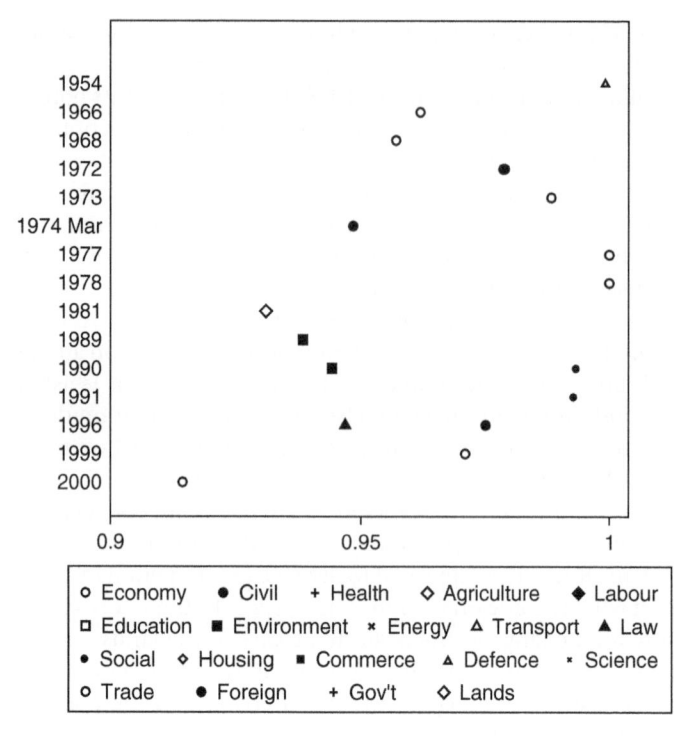

Figure 6.2 Likely change points in Acts of Parliament

summarises the change points for the acts in the same way as Figure 6.1 does for speeches.[3]

It might be thought that acts are a similar aspect of the policy agenda, but in fact they are not, as Chapter 4 shows. Although the Speech from the Throne contains legislative promises, it has other concerns, which are not about legislation but rather are promises of executive actions as well as general statements of policy intentions. Laws can advance through Parliament without having been in the Speech from the Throne. Indeed, for many of our domains, as Chapter 4 shows, we find that there is no correlation between speeches and laws and for that reason it is likely the change points will be different too. The period of the 1950s is not so much the period of activism in law as it was for speeches. But there is one exception. In 1954 there is a change point for transport. Although this is rather before the change points for speeches, it does reflect the changes to that policy topic in the 1950s discussed above and in Chapter 4.

The next structural shift in policy attention in acts occurs in the 1960s with foreign trade. More interestingly there is a further change point later in the Labour government, in 1968, perhaps because of the temporary solution of currency revaluation. After all, this was the year after the devaluation of the pound in November 1967, when Wilson famously said on a televisionbroadcast that 'It does not mean that the pound here in Britain, in your pocket or purse or in your bank, has been devalued.'[4] Showing the importance of this topic, 1973 is another structural shift in foreign trade, which matches the change point in the speeches noted above. All these change points reveal the instabilities of the British trading position at that time that was reflected in successive currency crises, and where the policy series take different directions.

The other change points are for the civil rights topic, which has change points in 1972 and 1974. This is the one period of instability for this topic before attention to it increased under New Labour in 1997. Key acts of that period were the Immigration Act 1971, the Representation of the People Act 1974 and the Pakistan Act 1974. This was a period when aspects of British citizenship were changing with new rules on immigration and changes to citizenship as a result of joining the EEC in 1973. Increases in migration, such as the flight of the Kenyan Asians from 1968 had put pressure on governments to introduce legislation that changed the terms of citizenship (Layton-Henry 1984).

In contrast to the speeches, the 1970s sees the economy as a key change point for acts, which happens later on in 1977–1978. This is just before 1979, which as we have discussed is thought to be an important moment of change in British politics, but where 1978 saw a large number of Acts of Parliament to deal with the economic crisis, such as the Price Commission Act 1977. In 1976, the government had to seek a loan from the IMF, and there were spending cuts to implement. Even though things had started to improve by 1977, there was still a change of policy to execute (see Holmes 1985, pp. 110–124).

In 1981, there is a shift in attention to territorial issues (the full title of the topic is public lands, water management, and colonial and territorial issues), which is when there was a large leap in attention to these issues. It partly reflects the final period of decolonisation, such as the Papua New Guinea, Western Samoa and Nauru (Miscellaneous Provisions) Act 1980 and the New Hebrides Act 1980, which came together in a set of linked demands for decolonisation (Fry 1983). But in the main it reflects a large number of acts that happen to come together at this time for this hybrid topic, which does not reflect large-scale changes (rather like the procedural punctuations highlighted in Chapter 5).

The next shift concerns the environment occurring in 1989–1990, which was an active policy area in the late 1980s and 1990s. As we discussed in Chapter 4, this was a period of activism from the EU when a lot of directives had to be turned into domestic legislation. For example, the Environmental Protection Act 1990 was mainly about implementing EU directives. There were, in addition, a number of other changes to legislation, but the two change points may be indicating that this was temporary change in attention to the issue rather than a change overall. It was a period of brief electoral prominence of the Green Party that did well in elections, but whose fortunes faded.

A similar kind of phenomenon may explain the change points in social welfare attention in 1990–1991 when there were a series of social security measures and related legislation that linked together as a burst of reform. These policies changed pensions and mortgage relief, and there was a reform of charity law. This represents the breaking of the logjam of legislation and the tendency for government to push through a set of related measures at the same time.

As with the speeches, 1996 is another interesting year with respect to the change points. There is a change point for law and crime that may have presaged the large expansion of legislation under New Labour. There was a large amount of legislation going through in 1996, such as the Offensive Weapons Act 1996 and the Sexual Offences (Conspiracy and Incitement) Act 1996 that aimed to tighten up the law, introduced by the populist Home Secretary Michael Howard. In fact, going back to Chapter 4, Figure 4.5, it is possible to see a leap of attention that goes from the Conservative to Labour governments in a straight line, nearly vertically upwards, such is the jump in attention to this topic.

The year 1996 also saw a shift in the mechanism of civil rights attention. This was a low point before the large expansion in civil rights legislation, as discussed with the speeches above. It may have been the case that the Conservative government had damped interest in this topic to such a low level that it created a natural turnout point as pressures built up—not unlike the period before a punctuation—but is better described as a focusing event in the process of focused adaptation.

Finally, attention to the economy shifts in 1999–2000, which is just before an upswing in the number of acts going through. The Labour government had been cautious in not wanting to embark on too much economic policy when entering office (sticking to the spending plans of the previous government), had a number of manifesto promises to implement, and wanted to gain a reputation for economic competence. In addition, the economy was doing well in this period so may not have needed attention; but in 2001 there was a need to put through a large amount of technical legislation at the time, particularly in relation to taxation. The change points therefore mark a reduction and then an expansion of legislative attention at this time.

Conclusion

In this chapter, we have used a statistical model to identify key points in the changes of the data series, which allows us to focus in statistical terms on the point in time when a policy agenda shows a likelihood of changing. In this way, we are able to understand the key points of change in the series and then link them to key policy changes that occurred in Britain at that time. We have done this for both speeches and laws, the two main series that have concerned this book up to date, and leave reporting of the other agendas (such as budgets, the media and public opinion) to a later point.

The great advantage of the Bayesian method is that it does not rely on prior intuitions to identify change points, which was the approach taken in Chapter 4. In fact, our approach is sympathetic with the stochastic process method of extracting the extreme values (i.e. punctuations) from the distributions of policy change that Jones and Baumgartner (2005a, 2005b) advocate. We suggest this method has a better chance of finding shifts in attention, whereas the changes in the punctuations series can reflect short-term changes that are subsequently reversed. The change points reflect the demarcation of two epochs, such as moving from a low average level of attention to a higher level or vice versa. What is central is that the change point emerges from the trends in the data series, so is an expression of adaptation and a piece of the focused adaptation claim we outlined in Chapter 1. A new epoch does not mean that a change in attention necessarily suggests that the substantive policy area has changed its approach, but it does indicate that the level of attention from policy-makers has adapted to the policy-making landscape in a significant way. Regimes can, of course, shift and then shift again, defining multiple epochs in our series, such as foreign trade in the 1960s, the economy in the 1970s, the environment in the late 1980s and early 1990s, social welfare in the 1990s and the economy at the end of the 1990s and start of the 2000s. Interestingly, the speeches are less volatile. The main examples are the government topic in the 1950s and the burst of interest in civil rights in the late 1990s. It seems that law-making does have these bursts of attention, and once the problem has been sorted out the policy agenda changes again. In this way, it might be thought that the Acts of Parliament show changes in the issue attention cycle rather than larger shifts. Speeches appear to embody these large changes in issue emphasis, such as the many changes in the 1950s, and then the reforms of New Labour from 1997. In this way, the method of testing for change points allows the political scientist or the historian to locate a particular era as one where consensus and post-war growth and consolidation led to series of important changes in the policy agenda. Then it identifies New Labour as bringing about an important partisan shift in the policy agenda, where the new government identified particular issues and wanted to introduce radical reforms, such as institutional reform and rights issues. Whereas the data show that there was gradually rising attention to crime, health and education, it was in relation to the areas of civil rights and government reform that New Labour made a distinctive mark. In this sense, the descriptive accounts in the preceding chapter and the change points of the current one tell the same story.

Appendix 6A: Our Approach to Change Point Modelling in British Policy Agendas

We used the bcp package for R (Erdman and Emerson 2007) that implements the Bayesian change point procedure proposed by Barry and Hartigan (1993) (hereafter BH). The Bayesian procedure allows for uncertainty in the form of a posterior probability distribution—the probability of a change point occurring in a year in the time series in our case. The method works well when irregular and variably sized changes are present in the time series are present as well as in the outliers (Barry and Hartigan 1993). In the following section, we briefly introduce the method and its application to a particular series in our dataset as an example.

Our application of the BH approach independently models each attention series as a sequence of discrete time random processes. That is, we have one model for macroeconomic attention in the Speech from the Throne, one for crime policy, as well as separate models for each of those categories in other institutional settings such as budgets and Acts of Parliament. Each time series is modelled as consisting of n random variables, $X_1, X_2, \ldots, X_n$. Each random variable is independent given the sequence of means μ_i with $X_{ij} \sim N(\mu_i, \sigma^2) = 1, 2, \ldots, n, j = 1, 2, \ldots, m$. μ_i is the mean of the normal distribution from which X_{ij}, the segment of the time series beginning in year i and ending in year j, is drawn. Barry and Hartigan (1993) assume that there exists an unknown partition ρ of the set $\{1, 2, \ldots, n\}$, which divides the sequence of data into contiguous blocks such that the sequence of means $\mu_1, \mu_2, \ldots, \mu_n$ is constant within blocks. The partition ρ is drawn from a product partition distribution $f(\rho)$. $f(p)$ is a function of p, the probability of a change point occurring in year i which is assumed to be independent in each year.

Since the approach is Bayesian, it imposes a prior distribution on each $\mu_i \sim N\left(\mu_0, \sigma_0^2/(j-i)\right)$. The choice of prior assigns smaller variance to clusters of years that are longer than to short ones. This is meant to bias us away from falsely considering as a change point small deviations from the mean. Such shifts would only provide relevant information about structural change when they persist for a long time. This also provides for more reasonable treatment of outliers and short, sharp shocks.

We follow the prior specification in Erdman and Emerson (2008, p. 2144). We must also specify tuning parameters p_0, the prior transition probability between segments and $w_0 = \sigma^2/(\sigma_0^2 + \sigma^2)$, the ratio of signal-to-error variance, which decreases as the incremental change in the variance of the series increases (Erdman and Emerson 2008, p. 2144). The parameters p_0 and w_0 are given a prior value of 0.2 to make the technique 'effective in situations where there aren't too many changes (p_0 small), and where the changes that do occur are of a reasonable size (w_0 small)' (Erdman and Emerson 2008, p. 2144, quoting Barry and Hartigan 1993, p. 312).

The likelihood function for the data series X given the model parameters is as follows:

$$f[X|\rho, \mu_0, \omega] \propto \int_0^\infty \frac{1}{\sigma^2} \prod_{i,j \in \rho} f_{i,j}(X_{ij}) d\sigma^2$$

where $f_{ij}(X_{ij})$ is the density for the observations X_{ij} for a given segment beginning in year i and ending in year j (Barry and Hartigan 1993; Erdman and Emerson 2007).

Estimates are based on between 50,000 and 100,000 draws from the posterior distribution for each topic series with 10–20 per cent burn-in exclusions. Substantial evidence of convergence is demonstrated for all models on the basis of Geweke (1992) and Heidelberger and Welch (1983). Longer runs and greater burn-in exclusions were based on the need for achieving numerical stability, but all estimates are based on at least 45,000 draws from the posterior distribution of the change point probabilities.

A sample analysis: attention to the macroeconomy in Acts of Parliament

The challenge of change point detection is to separate structural changes from random variation. Sometimes, systemic changes happen gradually over a long period of time; sometimes, they occur abruptly, either as temporary outliers interrupting the overall trend of the data, or permanently shifting the data mean and making the data plot look like a step function. To discern various forms of systemic changes, any method of change point detection should be sensitive enough to discover short, sharp deviations, while remaining resistant to temporary minor fluctuations. The BH method we described above works exceptionally well in these scenarios. Moreover, the BH analysis has a happy by-product—the posterior distribution of the probability of a change. Now we illustrate the technique by applying it to our series of the annual percentage of quasi-sentences in Acts of Parliament that mention the macroeconomy in the period 1946–2008. These issues cover inflation, prices, interest rates, unemployment rate, monetary supply, national budget and debt, taxation, industry policy, price control and stabilisation.

Figure 6.A1 is a simple scatter plot of the time series of macroeconomic mentions in Acts of Parliament in our sample. Visual observation suggests a minute increase in the mean over time. Fluctuations are small

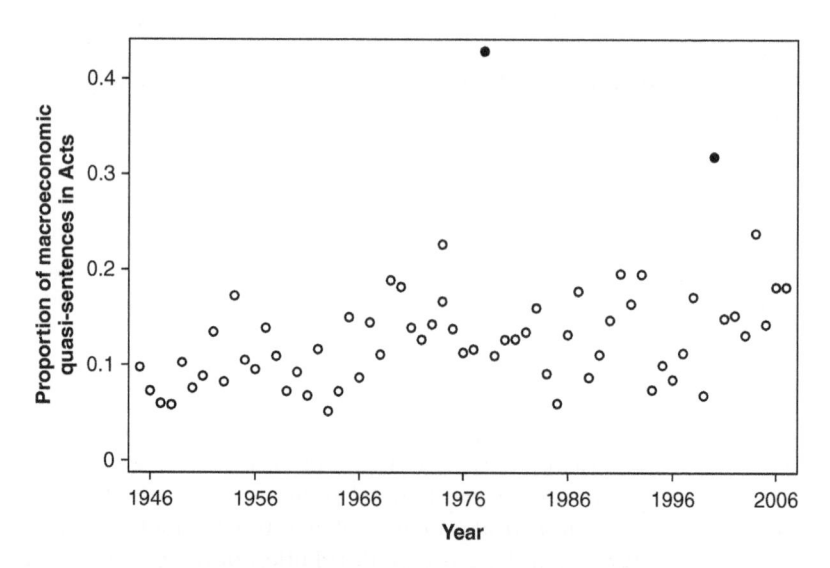

Figure 6.A1 Scatter plot of macroeconomic topics in Acts of Parliament

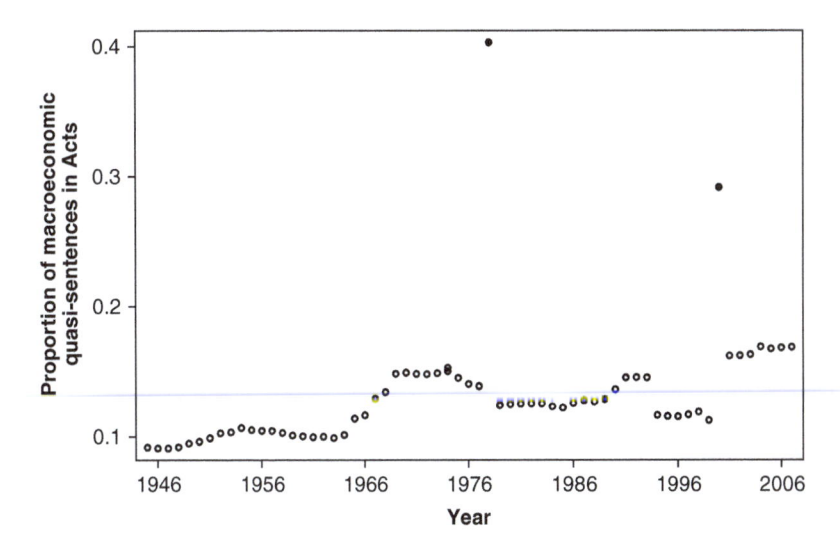

Figure 6.A2 The posterior mean and probabilities of a change point

and somewhat cyclical. Two outlying points in 1978 and 2000 interrupt the overall data trend. Thus, 'eyeballing' would direct attention to these outliers as well as potentially some other shifts in the 1950s through 1970s, but might also suggest that the mean remains stationary.

Figure 6.A2 shows the plots of the posterior means and probabilities of a change point in each year of the series. Overall, the top panel indicates a smooth upward trend with some fluctuations starting in the late 1960s in contrast to the slightly cyclical pattern of the underlying data. The outliers shift the mean upward, suggesting the existence of a change point in their vicinity, despite the somewhat lagged impact on the posterior mean between them.

Substantive speculation can be tested by the posterior probability of a change in the lower panel. Two periods of upward shock stand out— and they appear in proximity to our now familiar 1978 and 2000—with probability of a change close to one in five years of the series. Conventional levels of statistical significance (90–95 per cent) suggest the earlier structural change point is likely to have occurred between 1977–78 ($p \gg 1.0$). Our estimates suggest that the later change is likely to have occurred in 1999 ($p = 0.97$) or 2000 ($p = 0.91$).

7
Public Opinion and the Policy Agenda

In the next two chapters, we move away from analysing the formal agenda of the subjects that decision-makers focus on in government (Cobb and Elder 1983) and instead consider the wider, systemic agenda of those issues or problems that are defined by citizens and the media. These arenas share many characteristics with the policy agenda of government in their focus on the topics and decisions of the day, and can be categorised according to the policy content coding system of the Policy Agendas Project. However, these are separate from and different to the formal agenda of government in the sense that the priorities expressed in public opinion and the media neither have the sanction of the state nor have they passed through formal institutional processes of decision-making. Instead, they tend to reflect more general concerns of the public and media organisations that write or broadcast about issues in the news on a given day. That is not to say that these priorities are not connected to the formal agenda of decision-makers in government. In fact, these different agendas may all be seen as a part of one system reacting to the same international events and real-world changes and crises.

Earlier writers on agenda setting (Cobb and Elder 1983) argued that for an issue to make it onto the systemic political agenda it must be something that a wide range of people are attentive to at the same time, both agreeing that action is needed from government to solve it and that the problem falls within the capability and jurisdiction of decision-makers. In an older tradition of writing about public policy (e.g. Smith 1976), these venues were seen as inputs which affected the outputs in a causal model of decision-making linked to the pluralist or neo-pluralist models of influence over decisions, whereby power was seen to flow from society to politics. Scholars of public policy do not now subscribe to what is called the stages model of the policy process (John 2012, Chapter 2). It is also possible for government policy to influence these inputs, providing cues to the public and media agendas, and these agendas may interact over time, giving rise to complex chains of causation. However, there are reasons to expect a potential connection between the agenda of the public and media and other formal agendas.

In this chapter we consider the public agenda, which was an important feature of British democracy even before the development of mass opinion polls in the 1930s (Dicey 1917). In the British context, public opinion is a factor informing the everyday conduct of partisan politics and that links to the policy priorities of British government (e.g. Jennings and John 2009). For this reason, the public agenda is a potential factor in helping to understand why certain issues receive attention from policy-makers while others do not. For these reasons scholars have looked for links between public opinion and public policy. Others have highlighted how the public agenda responds both to changes in the content of media (McCombs and Shaw 1972) and to variation in real-world problems (Downs 1972; Wlezien 2005). For example, public concern about inflation and unemployment track their actual levels (Hudson 1994). Because of this, public opinion is seen as a crucial part of the agenda setting process. Kingdon (1995) considers public opinion to be one mechanism of problem recognition (i.e. the problem stream), in providing an indicator of problems in the policy process.

Signals of public opinion can take a range of forms: these can be brief or episodic, such as in protests or outcries due to crises or catalysing events, or instead be transmitted through more gradual shifts in opinion, with pressure slowly building for policy change. In this sense, public attention also exhibits characteristics of the issue attention cycle, remaining stable for long periods of time but on occasion undergoing sudden bursts of interest and then settling down again. Public opinion is also one of the main components of the punctuated equilibrium model (Baumgartner and Jones 1993), since it links the breakdown of an accepted issue definition (or policy image), through the mobilisation of popular support, to subsequent change in public policy. Of course, it is one thing for an issue to get attention—what Kingdon (1995, p. 3) calls the governmental agenda—but it is another for an issue to actually become part of the decision agenda (and indeed this is the point of the later chapter on implementation).

To understand the link between public opinion and the policy agenda in the context of British government, then, it is necessary to demonstrate (1) how the public agenda is interlinked with processes of problem recognition, and (2) how shifts in public opinion are linked with policy change. In both instances it is helpful to distinguish between processes that are characterised by long-term stability, and structural trends, and those subject to short-lived punctuated dynamics. In closing, the chapter examines patterns of correspondence between public opinion and the policy agenda in executive speeches, legislative outputs and budgetary expenditure, contrasting these with the level of congruence between the media and public agendas.

Problem recognition and the public agenda, 1960–2008

Across most parts of the agenda in Britain, fluctuations in the public's attention to issues can be linked to processes of problem recognition, often mediated through the political system, with mass media and political elites transmitting information to citizens about the emergence of new issues or events. On some topics, such as defence and foreign affairs, problem recognition is structured through the course of events. For example, in our data on the public agenda, plotted in Figures 7.1 and 7.2, increases in attention to the issues of foreign affairs and defence are evident in 1982 at the time of the Falklands conflict with Argentina, between 1990 and 1991 at the time of the Gulf War and in the late 1990s

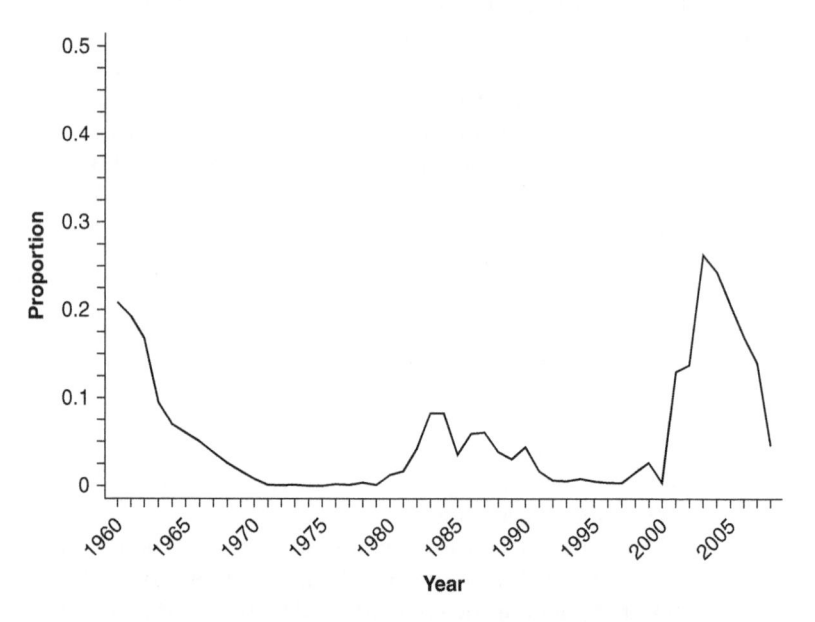

Figure 7.1 The public agenda and problem recognition: defence

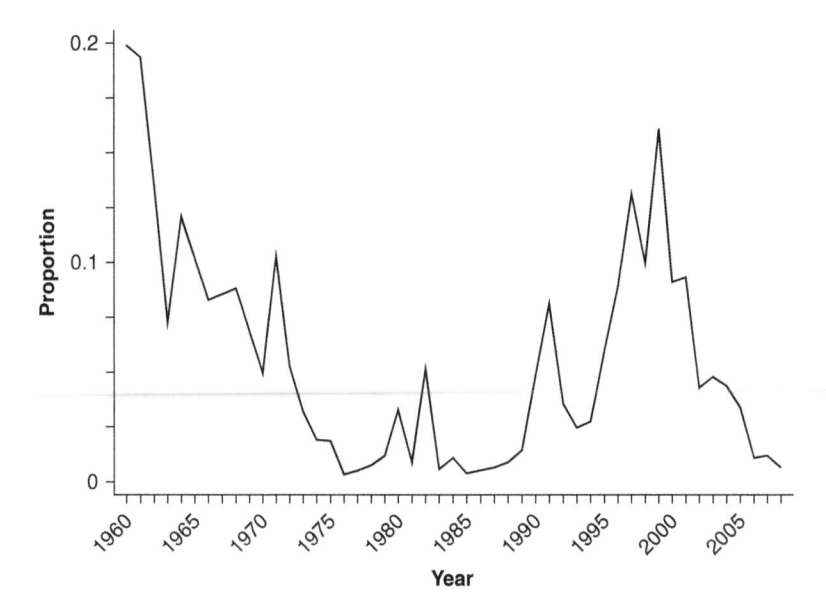

Figure 7.2 The public agenda and problem recognition: international affairs

with ongoing conflict in the Former Yugoslavia, with a further upturn in defence in 2001 following the 9/11 attacks, persisting until 2006 due to the British involvement in the Iraq and Afghanistan conflicts.[1] Earlier, during the 1960s, there was a much higher level of public attention to foreign affairs and defence due to a succession of events in the wider international environment: Britain's application to join the EEC in 1961, Cold War tensions throughout the 1960s (such as the events of the Cuban Missile Crisis in 1962) and the Vietnam conflict in the period 1964–1972 (the salience of these events is revealed in polling from the period, see King and Wybrow 2001, pp. 326–329).

In slight contrast to this emphasis on events, shifts in the public agenda can also be mediated through systematic trends. There is a clear link between the state of the British economy, measured using the headline indicators of inflation and the national rate of unemployment, and public concern about economic issues. This is also illustrated in Figure 7.3, with the rising salience of the economy during the 1960s and 1970s tracking rising prices (with the inflation rate peaking in 1975 and again in 1980), and kept at a high level during the 1980s due to the national rate of unemployment reaching 11 per cent in 1984, declining briefly with the economic recovery of the late 1980s, but increasing

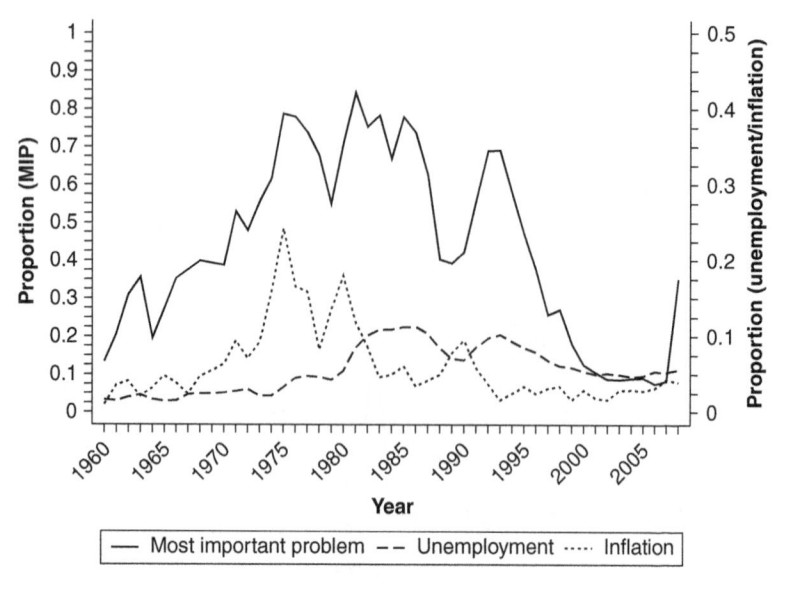

Figure 7.3 The public agenda and problem recognition: macroeconomics

again as a result of the ERM crisis of 1992 and the recession of the early 1990s. Together, the economy, foreign affairs and defence account for around 55 per cent of the public agenda throughout the period 1960–2008, suggesting that the public's recognition of the problem status of issues is a major factor in the agenda setting process.

Stability and change in the public agenda, 1960–2008

The attention of the public to issues tends to exhibit periods of incremental variation interspersed with occasional dramatic shifts that are consistent with punctuations and issue attention cycles. They may be the result of the uneven pattern of change in some input series (i.e. due to the sudden emergence of certain problems). In this light, it is possible to distinguish between (1) changes in public attention that are part of long-term systematic trends and stabilities, and (2) sudden and dramatic shocks to the public agenda that are indicative of periods in which the level of attention to an issue becomes self-reinforcing. The former pattern tends to be associated with long-term structural forces that push issues either on or off the public agenda, whereas the latter is often linked to exogenous shocks or to mobilisations of public opinion by organised interests or expert communities.

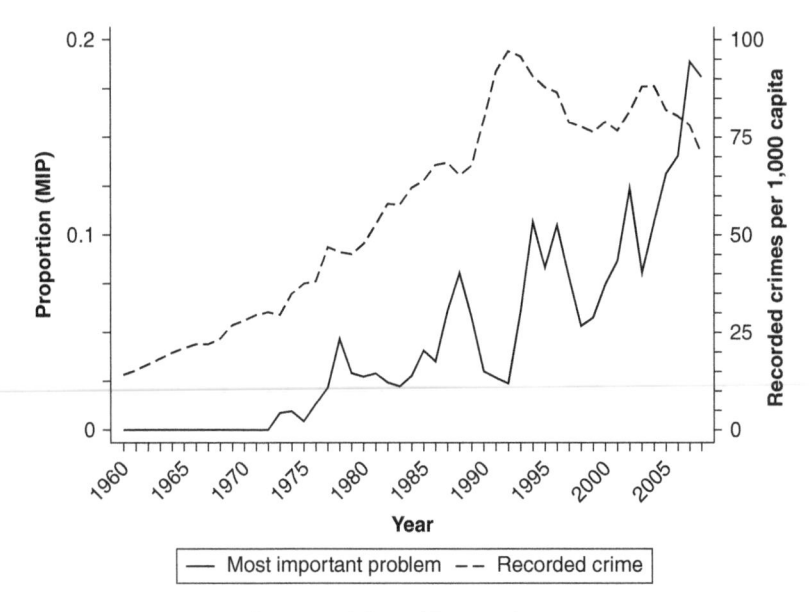

Figure 7.4 Long-term change and the public agenda: crime

Taking long-term patterns in public attention first, it is possible to link the rise of some issues to long-term social and economic trends. For example, the rise of the issue of crime on the public agenda since the 1960s, plotted in Figure 7.4, has tracked growth in the rate of crime (up to the 1990s at least, after which point crime rates started to fall), which itself has been linked to the state of the British economy and increasing politicisation of the issue of crime since the 1980s (see Farrall and Jennings 2012). Both health and education, plotted in Figures 7.5 and 7.6, observed increasing salience from the 1970s up until the early 2000s, reflecting a generational shift in expectations of standards in each of these domains. Green-Pedersen and Wilkerson (2006) link long-term upward trends in public expectations concerning health care to the combination of aging populations and rises in the cost of innovations in health technologies and services. While public attention to health and education has been in decline since the heights of the Blair years, this is indicative of longer-term structural dynamics, although mobilised from the mid-1990s by the policy agenda of New Labour.

Immigration is another example where long-term structural pressures have contributed to a rise of the issue up the public agenda, as shown in Figure 7.7. An increase in the numbers of Commonwealth immigrants

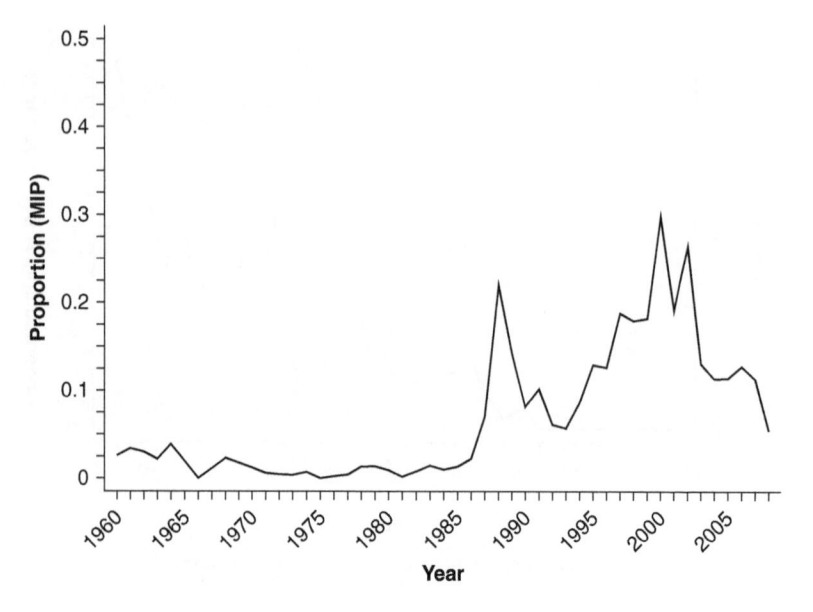

Figure 7.5 Long-term change and the public agenda: health

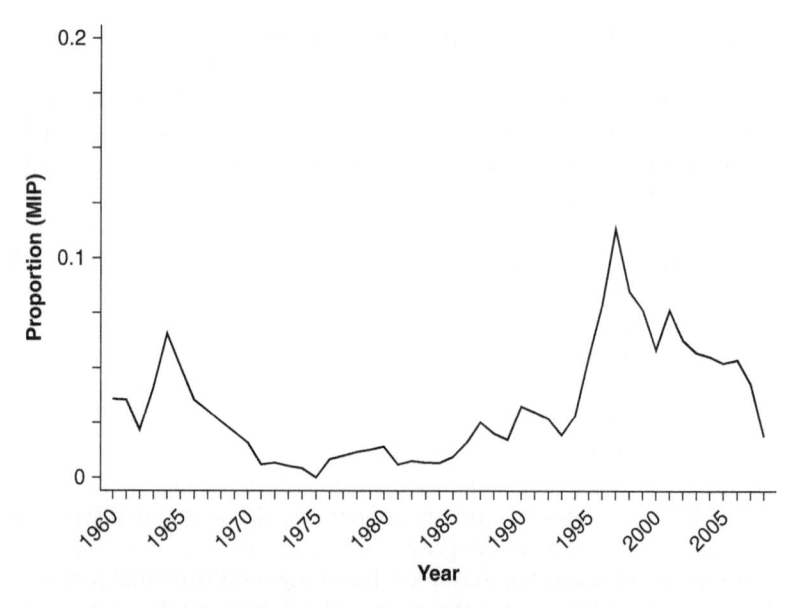

Figure 7.6 Long-term change and the public agenda: education

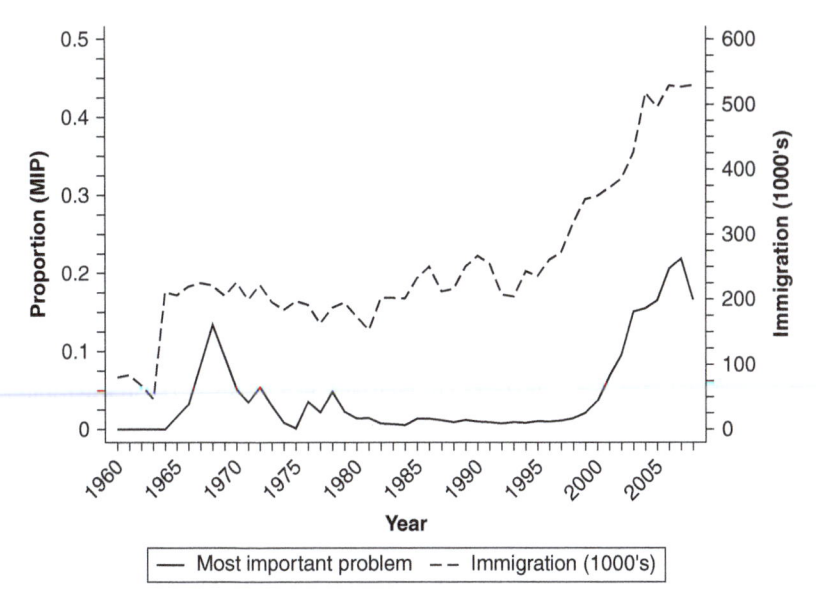

Figure 7.7 Long-term change and the public agenda: immigration

arriving in Britain in the 1960s preceded a series of waves of public concern about race relations and immigration, which have been reinforced through elite cues and political competition on the issue. The first spike in public attention to immigration coincided with Enoch Powell's inflammatory 'Rivers of Blood' speech in 1968, while the second wave of attention to the issues occurred around the time of the Race Relations Act 1976 and later escalated with opposition leader Margaret Thatcher's enunciation of public fear of being 'swamped' with immigrant cultures in an interview with Granada's *World in Action* in 1978. With continued growth in immigration numbers, combined with politicisation of the issue, race and immigration has surged up the public agenda since the 1990s. While the rise of immigration on the public agenda reflects certain demographic shifts, it therefore has also been linked to the cues provided by elites, with Enoch Powell attributed as having established a clear difference between the political parties in the public mind (Butler and Stokes 1974; Studlar 1978). Immigration is a complicated issue for the purpose of this analysis since it combines long-term trends with short-term instabilities, due to elite cues or other watershed moments that give rise to punctuated dynamics of change. For instance, toward the end of the 1990s a crisis in the management of Britain's asylum system, combined with emotive tabloid coverage of the topic, was followed by mounting public concern, which in turn was followed by intensive efforts on the part of government aimed at reducing the number of applications for asylum and speeding up the processing of cases (Jennings 2009, 2010).

Alongside topics where changes in public attention can be linked to long-term trends or structural pressures, it is also possible for public opinion to exhibit instabilities and sudden shifts in attention. These tend to be associated either with focusing events, elite cues or mobilisation through organised interests. The contours of the public agenda are most apparent in relation to labour and employment issues, the environment and energy, illustrated in Figures 7.8, 7.9 and 7.10. On the topic of labour and employment, where the share of the public agenda has, on occasion, exceeded 25 per cent, the period before 1990 appears to be captured by a series of issue attention cycles. The timing of attention spikes coincides with the protracted strike action during the Winter of Discontent in 1979 and the coal miners' strike action of 1984. The degree to which these large spikes in public attention track the number of days lost to labour disputes is striking, suggesting a high level of public attention to this issue. The drop in attention after Thatcher's exit from office

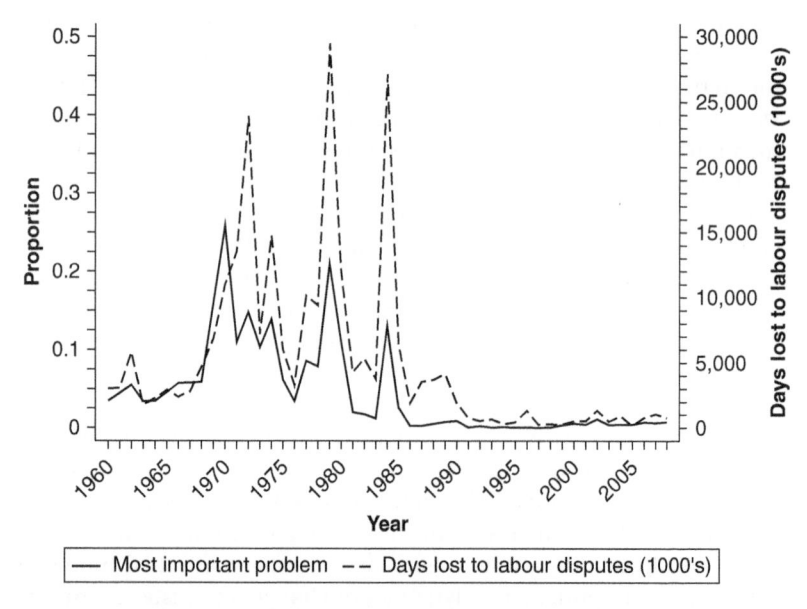

Figure 7.8 Patterns in the public agenda: labour and employment

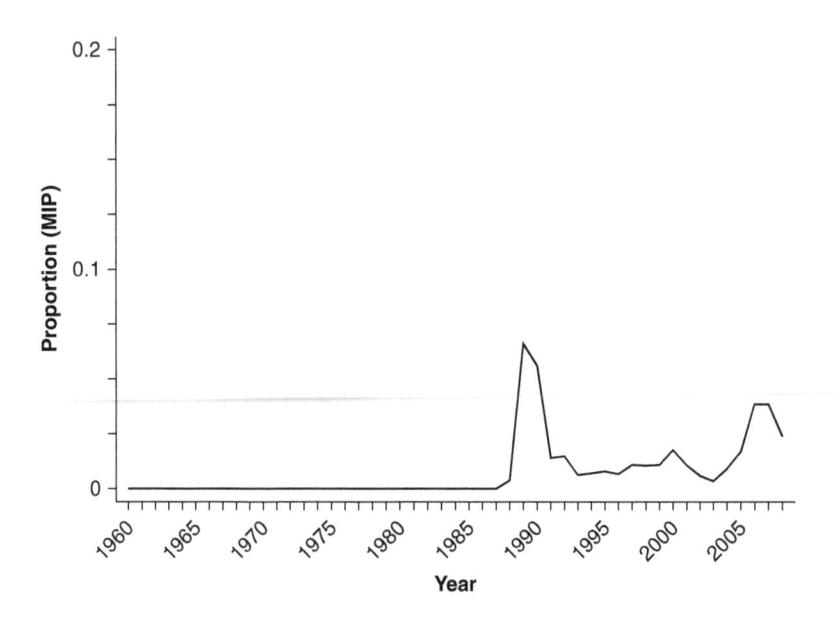

Figure 7.9 Patterns in the public agenda: environment

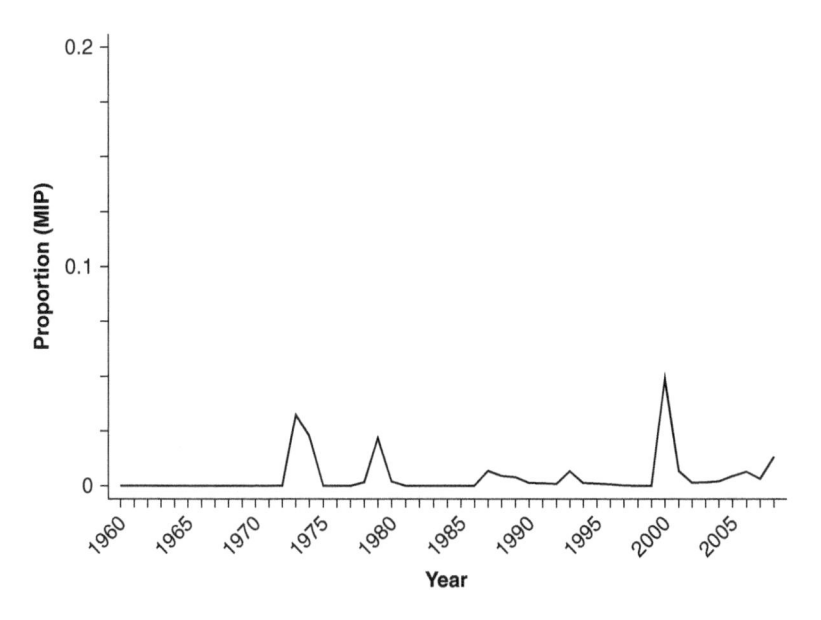

Figure 7.10 Patterns in the public agenda: energy

is consistent with adaptation. The pattern observed for energy is more consistent with issue attention cycles, where spikes in public attention are observed in 1974 at around the time of the OPEC oil crisis, in 1979 during the Winter of Discontent and the associated energy shortages and in 2000 at the time of the fuel protests during the first term of the Blair government. However, environmental issues achieved sudden prominence on the public agenda, consistent with punctuated equilibrium claims. The first punctuation in public attention to environmental issues occurred in 1989 at the height of the Green movement, due to a growing consciousness of ecological perils, such as acid rain and the Chernobyl nuclear accident. In similar fashion, growing concern about climate change since 2005 has been reinforced through the increasing influence of scientific evidence of global warming, with the issue now framed as an urgent societal risk.

Public opinion and the policy agenda, 1960–2008

While there is an extensive literature regarding the link between public opinion and public policy (for extensive reviews, see Manza and Cook 2002; Weakliem 2003; Wlezien and Soroka 2007), there is growing interest in the link between the issue priorities of the public (e.g. Bevan and Jennings 2010; Chaqués-Bonafont and Palau 2011; Jennings and John 2009; John *et al.* 2011; Jones and Baumgartner 2004; Jones *et al.* 2009). While it is possible that policy-makers and the public are responding simultaneously to the problem status of issues, it nevertheless is important that the policy agenda is congruent with the concerns of the public. We next turn to consider the degree to which variations in the public agenda are linked to subsequent changes in the policy agenda. In doing so, we draw on earlier work that has examined the interrelationship over time between public opinion and the policy agenda in Britain (see Bevan and Jennings 2010; Jennings and John 2009; John *et al.* 2011).

Our data enables us to examine the links between the policy agenda in the British context across the executive agenda (as presented in the Speech from the Throne) and the legislative outputs of government (in the form of Acts of Parliament). Our discussion focuses on a selection of the most prominent issues on the public agenda in Britain: macroeconomic issues, defence and foreign affairs, health, education, housing, labour and employment, crime and immigration (with the mean levels of issue importance between 1960 and 2008 shown in Figure 7.11). Table 7.1 supplies the descriptive statistics for these issues.

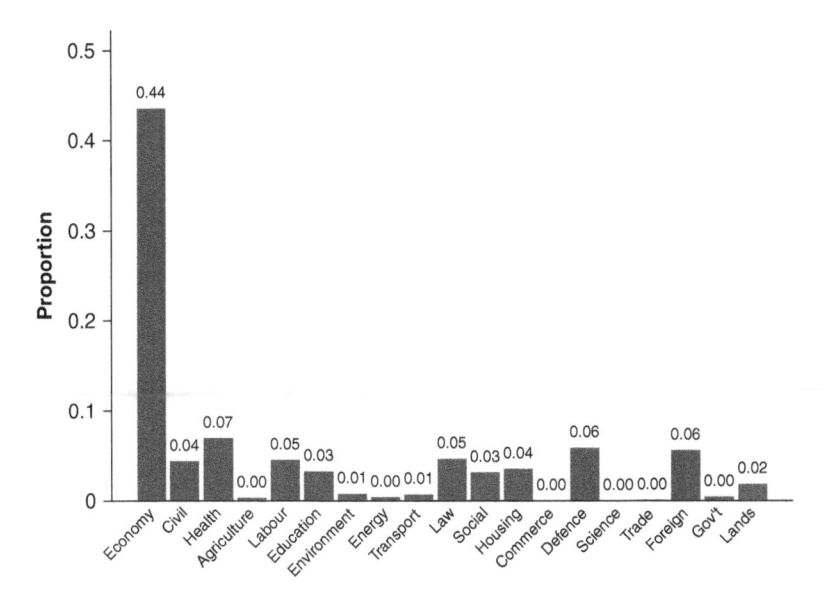

Figure 7.11 Mean levels of issue importance between 1960 and 2008

Table 7.1 Summary statistics of public opinion policy topic percentage by year, 1960–2008

Topic	Abbreviation	Mean (%)	Minimum (%)	Maximum (%)	SD	Kurtosis
1	Economy	43.78	7.54	84.30	24.07	1.74
2	Civil	4.13	0.00	21.91	5.61	5.30
3	Health	6.97	0.00	29.84	7.72	3.54
4	Agriculture	0.32	0.00	8.10	1.23	35.27
5	Labour	4.60	0.02	25.91	6.00	5.54
6	Education	3.29	0.00	11.34	2.60	3.40
7	Environment	0.74	0.00	6.61	1.43	10.04
8	Energy	0.39	0.00	4.90	0.92	15.14
10	Transport	0.72	0.00	5.08	1.21	7.06
12	Law	4.37	0.00	18.89	4.58	3.69
13	Social	3.16	0.00	9.67	2.40	3.54
14	Housing	3.55	0.34	15.22	3.33	5.72
15	Commerce	.	.	.	.	.
16	Defence	5.88	0.00	26.28	7.28	3.68
17	Science	.	.	.	.	.
18	Trade	0.08	0.00	0.32	0.09	2.97
19	Foreign	5.69	0.33	19.92	5.04	3.59
20	Gov't	0.42	0.00	6.96	1.09	28.67
21	Lands	1.88	0.00	11.17	2.81	6.01

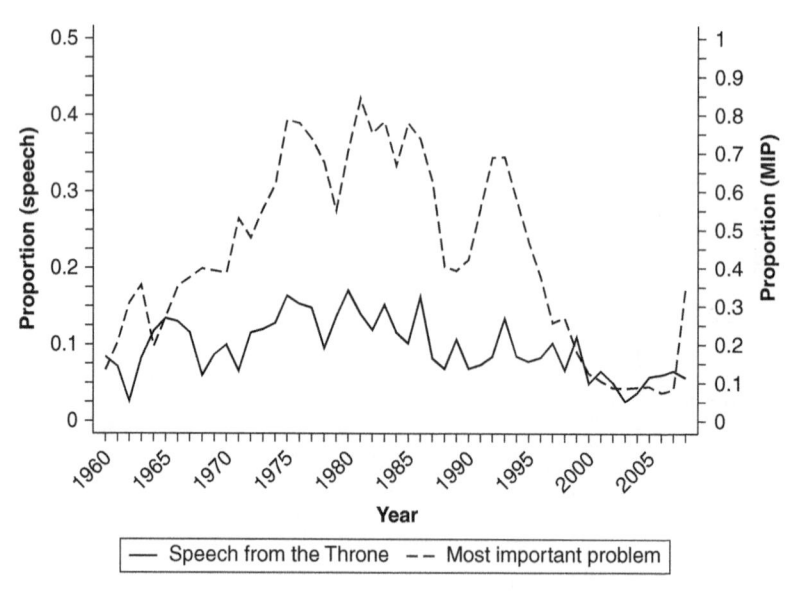

Figure 7.12 The policy–opinion link: macroeconomics

Taking macroeconomic issues as the first of these topics (see Figure 7.12), it is clear that the proportion of the executive agenda in the Speech from the Throne has tracked the level of public concern about the economy, rising from the 1960s onwards up until the mid-1980s (with occasional downturns in attention) and declining thereafter until the start of the global financial crisis in 2008. The degree of correspondence between public concern about the economy and the policy agenda is not quite as strong as for legislative outputs (not plotted here), although it remains suggestive of some common variation. Macroeconomic issues can, however, be contrasted with the pattern for foreign affairs and defence (Figures 7.13 and 7.14), where there is far less connection between attention to the issue in the Speech from the Throne compared with Acts of Parliament.

Turning next to four of the defining topics of the post-war British political consensus—health, education, welfare and housing (Figures 7.15, 7.16, 7.17 and 7.18)—each topic exhibits common variation over time between the proportion of attention to the issue on the public and the executive agenda (as seen in the speech). In the cases of both health and education, the level of spending accelerated around the time of the peak of its salience for public attention, for example,

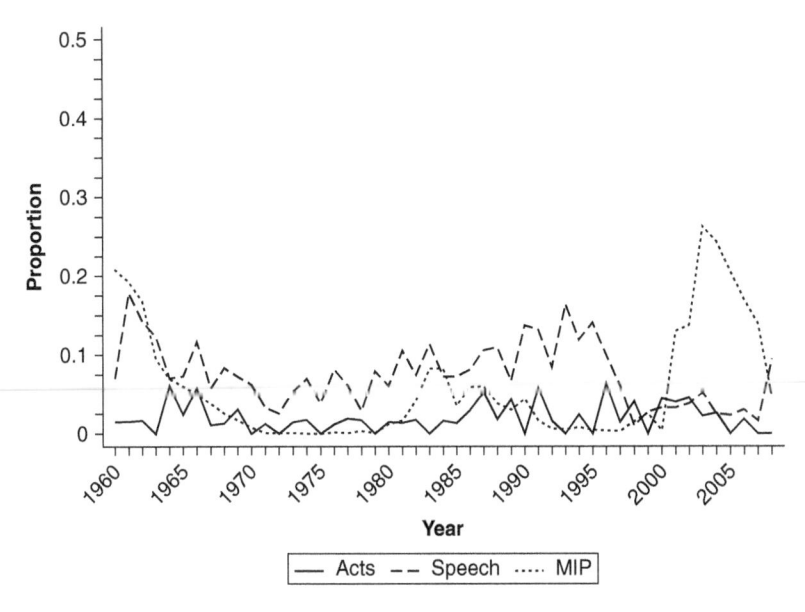

Figure 7.13 The policy–opinion link: defence

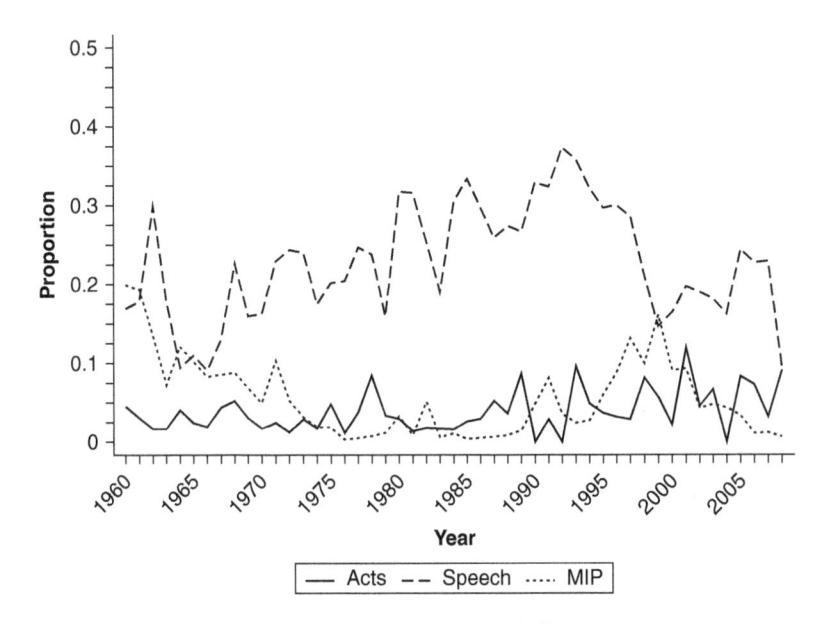

Figure 7.14 The policy–opinion link: international affairs

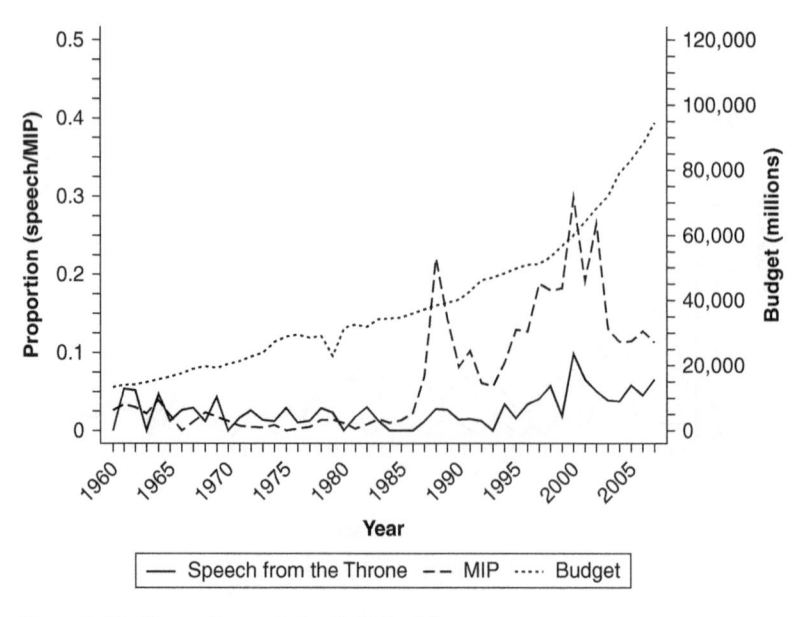

Figure 7.15 The policy–opinion link: health

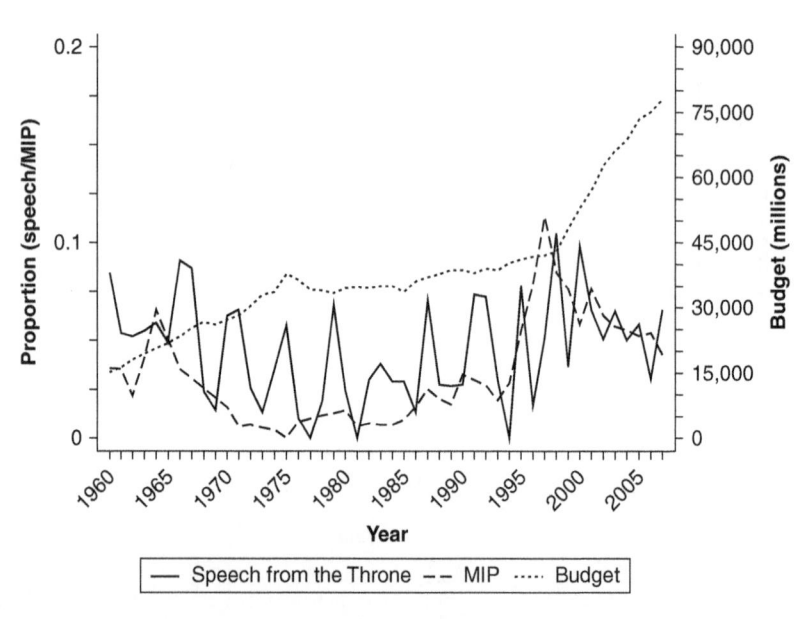

Figure 7.16 The policy–opinion link: education

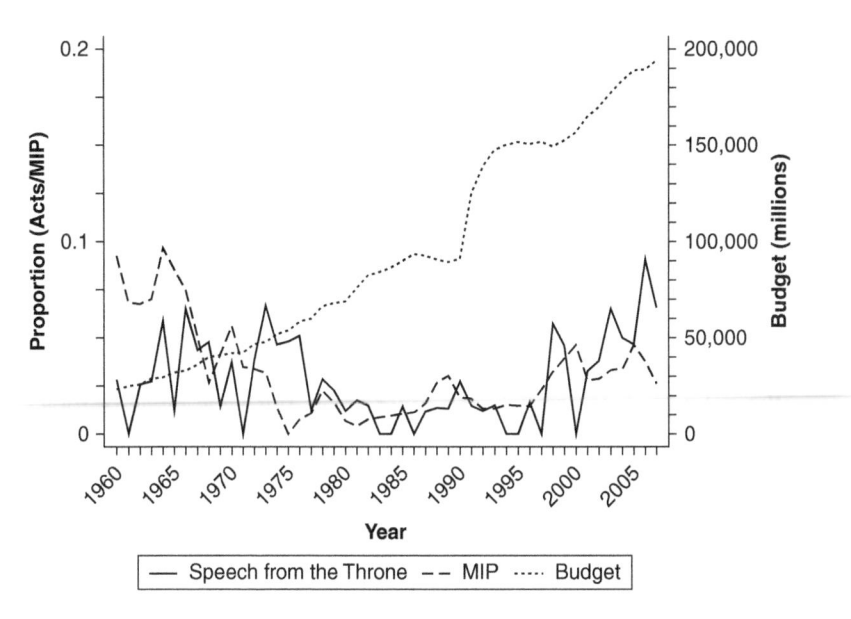

Figure 7.17 The policy–opinion link: welfare

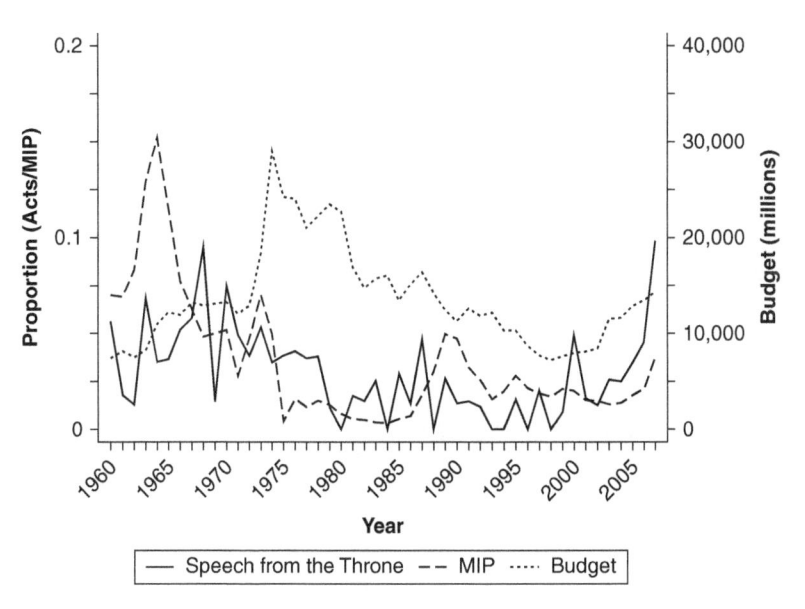

Figure 7.18 The policy–opinion link: housing

1998 for education and 1997 for health. Each of these step changes under New Labour marked a shift in policy-making. These trends can be contrasted with spending on welfare and housing, with the former increasing steadily over time but jumping as a result of the recession of the early 1990s and the latter experiencing a gradual decline in expenditure since the 1970s. Finally, the attention of British government to the issues of immigration (Figure 7.19) and law and crime (Figure 7.20) has often tracked public concern about these issues, with the issue of crime rising on the public agenda in particular since the 1990s and immigration attracting occasional interest in the 1960s and 1970s but coming to prominence from the early 2000s onwards. While public opinion and the policy agenda parallel each other across this wide range of topics, it is worth noting that in other work we find party effects on policy-making attention, even controlling for the level of public attention (Bevan and Jennings 2010; Jennings and John 2009; John et al. 2011; also see Chapter 4).

Public opinion and policy-making 1960–2008

Further to the observation of a relationship between public opinion and the policy agenda over time, it is also possible to determine whether

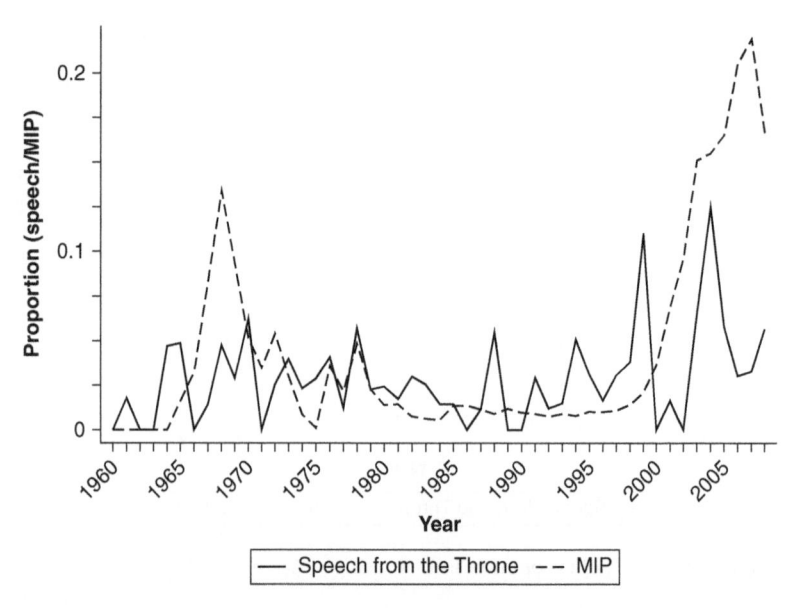

Figure 7.19 The policy–opinion link: immigration

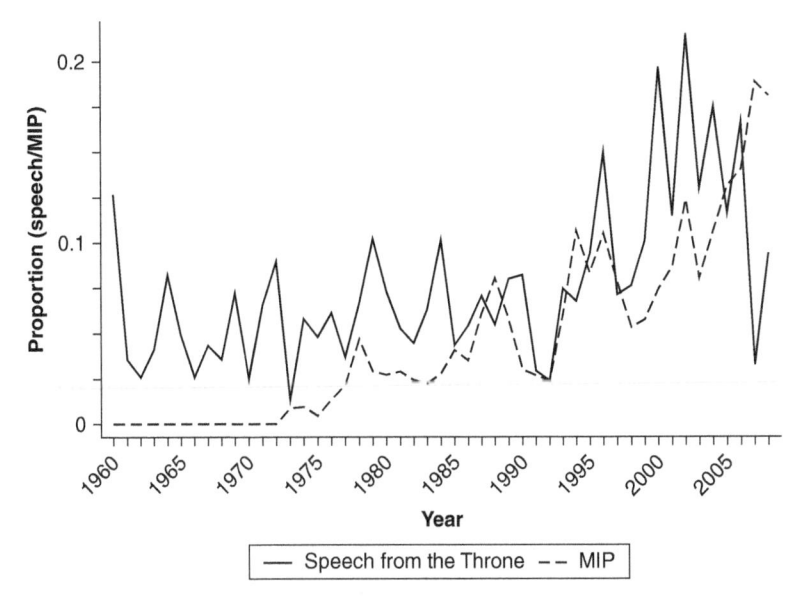

Figure 7.20 The policy–opinion link: law and crime

there is systematic variation in the link of policy agendas to public opinion. To assess this, the analysis that follows uses a method that tests the level of correspondence between the public agenda and policy agendas across all major topics on which there is observed public opinion and for a number of institutional venues (see Jones and Baumgartner 2004; Jones *et al.* 2009). The method tests across a number of policy agendas: the Speech from the Throne, Acts of UK Parliament and budgetary expenditure. We also test correspondence between public priorities and the media agenda. This enables us to test the degree to which there is a relationship between public opinion and the mass media.

Following Jones *et al.* (2009), the method constructs a correspondence matrix where each data point is the correlation between an issue's salience to the public and the proportion of the media or policy agenda dedicated to that issue over a given year. To estimate these correlations, matrices of priorities are constructed over time. For the public agenda, each cell indicates the proportion of MIP/MII responses ranking a given topic as the most important facing the nation in that year. For the corresponding matrix of policy agendas, each cell indicates the proportion of the policy-making activity on a given topic. The correspondence matrix is estimated as the degree of correspondence between public prioritisation of an issue and the proportion of the policy-making and media agenda assigned to that same issue.

The correlations indicate the direction, magnitude and statistical significance of the link between public opinion and the media or governing agenda. The results for the Speech from the Throne shows that the executive agenda is positively and significantly correlated with public opinion for macroeconomics, civil rights and immigration, health, labour and employment, education, environment, law and crime, and public lands and territorial issues.[2] In three cases—agriculture, defence and foreign trade—there is negative correspondence between public opinion and the policy agenda. This suggests that the executive attends to the issue less when it is of concern to the public. The strongest degree of correspondence is observed for macroeconomics, health, environment, and law and crime, suggesting these are issues on which the policy agenda most closely reflects public priorities.

Turning to the legislative agenda it is notable first of all that there are fewer statistically significant correlations.[3] Nevertheless, there is a positive and significant relationship between the public agenda and the legislative agenda for health, law and crime, and public lands and territorial issues. The link between public opinion and legislative agenda for agriculture, welfare and foreign trade is negative, however, suggesting that when the public is concerned about each of these topics, the government is less active in legislative attention.

For budgetary spending of UK government[4] there is a positive and significant correlation with the public agenda for health, education, environment, and law and crime, with the latter again observing the strongest degree of correspondence. Further to this, however, there are negative and significant correlations between public opinion and budgetary spending for agriculture, welfare and housing, suggesting there is an inverse relationship between public priorities and policy-making in this institutional setting. Finally, the set of correlations between public priorities and the media agenda[5] reveal a large number of issues on which there is positive and statistically significant correspondence: macroeconomics, civil rights and immigration, health, agriculture, education, environment, energy, transportation, law and crime, and housing. However, there is a negative relationship between public priorities and the media agenda, for foreign trade and defence and international affairs.

The general pattern is confirmed through inspection of the box plot of correlation coefficients (by topic) shown in Figure 7.21. There, the highest average level of linkage is observed for the media agenda and

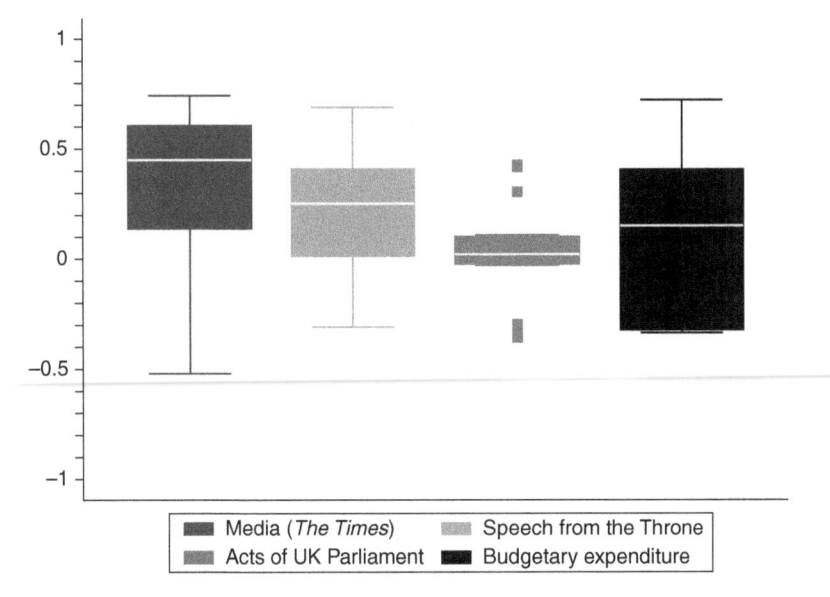

Figure 7.21 Average MIP-topic correlations, by policy-making arena (1960–2008)

the executive agenda (the Speech from the Throne), followed by the legislative agenda. This matches evidence from the comparative analysis in governing institutions (Bevan and Jennings 2010). Also of interest, for the purpose of this analysis, is the degree of correspondence between public priorities and the media and policy-making agenda for each topic. It is evident from the correlation coefficients, as reported in footnotes 2 to 4, that the most consistent pattern of positive correlations between public opinion and the policy agenda is observed for the health and law and crime topics, with a recurring pattern of linkage for education and environmental issues without legislative congruence. There is likewise a recurring pattern of a lack of linkage for agriculture, foreign trade, and defence and international affairs.

Structural shifts in public opinion

As described in Chapter 6, we can estimate change points in the public agenda, which indicate divisions among epochs in policy attention. In Figure 7.22, we report these important changes in the same way.[6] There are 31 occasions where there is a high likelihood of change points, which suggests that the public agenda is subject to change rather than

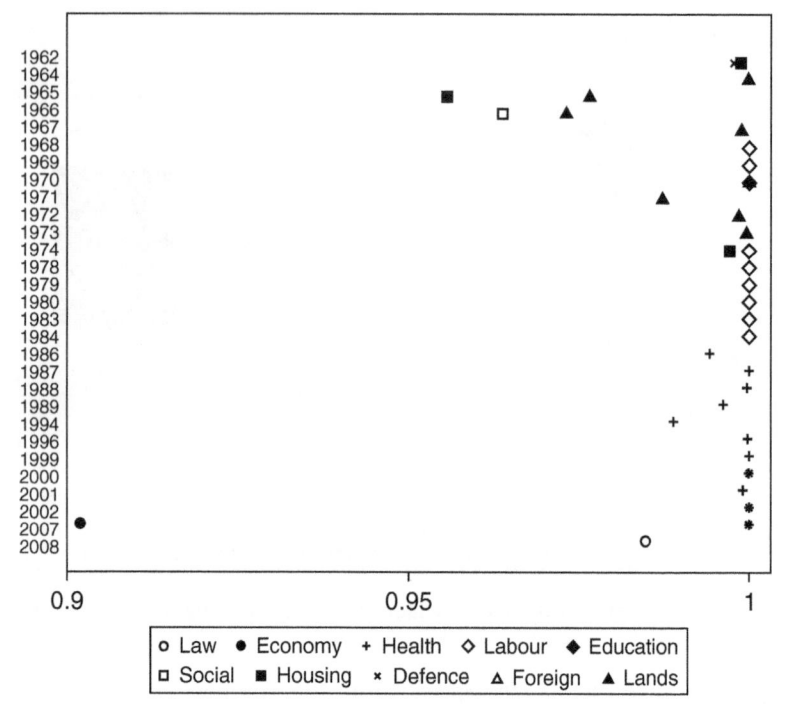

Figure 7.22 Likely change points in public opinion

remaining stable over time. There are a similar number of change points found during the early decades of the period, with eight in the 1960s, eight in the 1970s and seven in the 1980s, which then falls to four for both the 1990s and the 2000s.

The first change point on defence reflects the decline of public interest in the issue at the start of the series, which had been a concern during the 1950s due to conflicts, such as the Korean War and the Suez Crisis. The high likelihood of a structural shift on public opinion regarding territorial matters during the 1960s reflects the concern with colonial and Commonwealth affairs at the time. In the late 1960s, public concerns about international affairs associated with the Vietnam War resulted in two change points for that topic.

The change points in the public agenda on territorial issues in the early 1970s reflect the growth of concern with the troubles in Northern Ireland, while the shift in public attention to housing in 1974 occurred in the aftermath of the controversies on housing after the Housing Finance Act 1972. During the 1970s and 1980s there are a series of change points in public attention to labour and employment issues, which reflects the turbulence of the decade with successive industrial disputes (shown in Figure 7.8 earlier). What the change points indicate is instability in the public agenda—increasing as well as declining priorities—as the public reacted to outbreaks of industrial disputes and strike action. There was not a permanent or long-term shift in the prominence of this issue on the public agenda. As noted in connection with Figure 7.8, this period is characterised by a series of issue attention cycles that culminate in a structural shift, leaving labour policy as a low salience issue.

In the 1980s, a period of volatility in public attention to health began, with structural change probable at seven times between 1986 and 1999 and again in 2001. The issue became a matter of public concern in that period as exhibited in Figure 7.15, in particular in relation to the performance of the NHS and corresponding levels of government investment. From this it is apparent that levels of public attention to health fluctuated, as it remained a problem where there were still calls for policy solutions. The final sequence of change points relate to defence and foreign affairs, with three occurring in 2000, 2002 and 2007. This volatility reflects shifts in public concern about Britain's involvement in military conflicts, such as in Kosovo, Iraq and Afghanistan.

Overall, the change points identified for the public agenda demarcate periods of instability in public priorities, rather than indicate shifts that correspond to our claims about focused adaptation in the policy agenda series. They provide evidence of public opinion reacting to wider events, where concerns start to rise up the agenda, but also quickly decline in importance—a pattern consistent with issue attention cycles—whereas as the policy agenda of the Speech from the Throne and Acts of Parliament show fewer but more decisive changes in attention consistent with focused adaptation.

Conclusion

In this chapter, we have mapped the policy agenda as represented in public opinion and have found that it has many characteristics of the more general policy agenda. It tends to fluctuate in the same way, and exhibit patterns of stability and change. It is more volatile, which is as expected because the public agenda tends to react to the emergence of issues or problems on a day-to-day basis, rather than being a product of institutional processes of decision-making which are subject to greater friction and slower shifts in attention. The emergence of certain economic or social problems can take time to be recognised in public opinion, but be subject to dramatic and episodic shifts in attention as they become identified as the problem of the day.

We have also examined the pattern of change in public opinion and linked it to key events and trends of the post-war period. A relationship emerges between the public agenda and the priorities of policy-makers, although this varies across institutional venues. In all, the public agenda has a dynamic of its own as the public recognise issues as problems and attend to them. In the next chapter, we look at elite attention through the media.

8
The Media

Like it or loathe it, the media is an important part of the political process, whose value and influence continues to grow over time. Media attention measures both the events that occur in the world and salience. It is the salience of the media agenda that has the strongest agenda setting function as high levels of attention can propel issues beyond the 'threshold of attention' needed to cause real policy change (Jones and Baumgartner 2005a). Whether that salience is from the viewpoint of the public or the political elite is certainly a point for debate (see Bennett *et al.* 2007; Gandy 1982, for a discussion of the sources of news stories) but, regardless, the media matters for politics and tends to be closely tied to public opinion and other measures of public concern (Behr and Iyengar 1985; Entman 1989; Iyengar 1991; Iyengar and Kinder 2010; Jacoby 2000; Jasperson *et al.* 1998; McCombs 2004). To make a bold claim, media attention is likely just as important to politics as elections, and understanding how that attention is provided is fundamental to understanding British politics in the modern era.

The growing importance of the media is a very well supported claim. Numerous studies of politics have demonstrated the importance of the media in politics, particularly when it comes to the agenda setting process (see Baumgartner and Jones 1993; Birkland 1997; Cobb and Elder 1983; McCombs and Shaw 1972). Whether the media is used as a measure to control for events or as a measure of public concern, the place for the media in political studies is clear. Politicians do not work in a vacuum and it is their duty to respond to the world around them as well as their constituents, whose views are often summarised through media attention.

This chapter discusses in detail the patterns of attention contained in the UK Policy Agendas Project's media database, consisting of content-coded front-page headlines from *The Times* every Wednesday over the period 1960–2008. It starts by discussing the broad patterns of attention in the media dataset, including the number of policy versus non-policy stories and the amount of domestic versus international attention in the paper. It further focuses on media attention to different policy issues over time looking at both the broad pattern of attention to all issues and graphically analysing the relationship between media and government agendas for the issues of the economy and defence. We cannot answer the big question about the importance of the media in British politics, but we can examine an important element of it and how the attention of the media links to the big policy issues of the day.

Broad patterns of media attention

The media data gathered by the UK Policy Agendas Project exhibits several interesting and informative patterns of attention in relation to policy content and domestic versus international stories. These patterns of attention and the nature of the dataset covered in detail in Chapter 4 are particularly important as the constraints of an agenda have a large effect on outputs (Shepsle 1979). This section focuses on those basic patterns and discusses whether they are caused by changes in media attention or changes in our chosen source for the media agenda in Britain, *The Times*.

The Times, like all modern media outlets, contains a mix of both domestic and international stories. While the UK Policy Agendas Project has several international-focused major topic codes,[1] an additional level of domestic versus international headline coding proved particularly informative.[2] A large number of stories fitting domestic major topic codes, such as the performance of the US stock market (the topic of banking, finance and domestic commerce) or the prices set by OPEC (energy), were clearly focused overseas, but had a domestic impact on the UK. Similarly, many international stories focused on the place of the UK in world affairs, such as its involvement in the Iraq War (defence), while many others focused on purely international events, such as human rights abuses in mainland China (international affairs and foreign aid).[3] A quarterly comparison of the total number of stories with a domestic versus an international focus, according to this additional level of coding, is presented in Figure 8.1.

One clear and important aspect of media attention presented in this chapter is the absence of headlines for three-quarters in 1979 due to a strike that lasted from the end of 1978 to the end of 1979. Like many

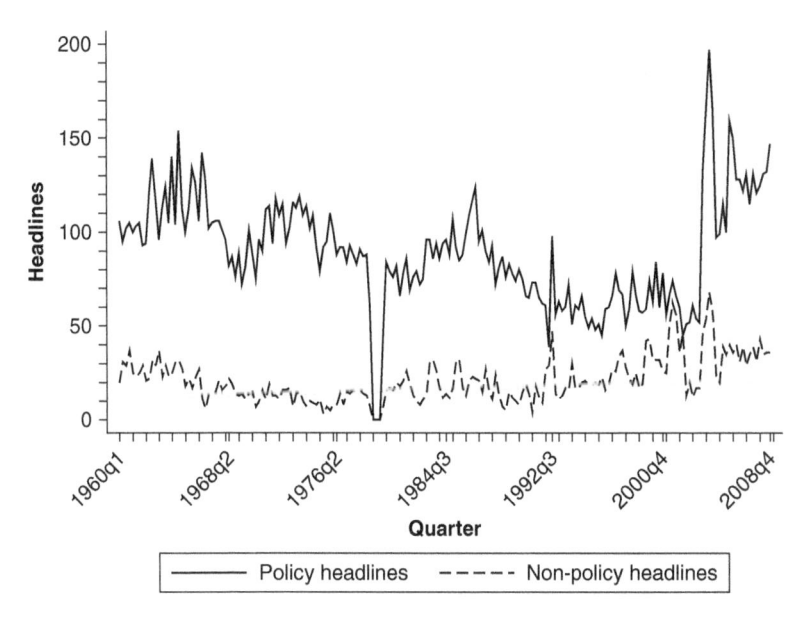

Figure 8.1 Quarterly *The Times* domestic and international headlines

British industries in the 1970s and 1980s, not even newspapers were free from collective bargaining with *The Times* itself reporting on strikes at several other papers up until its own. The details of this strike as well as other details concerning the data are presented in Chapter 3.

In Figure 8.1 it is clear that the main focus of *The Times* is on issues the UK is directly involved in both at home and abroad. However, with the change to a broadsheet format with a traditional front page in 1966, an increase in internationally focused stories occurred. This change was gradual and not immediate, from a low baseline in the pre-1966 period to a new and fairly steady high of roughly 100 stories in 1968. This represents an actual change in the content of the paper and is not an artefact of the sampling strategy for the pre-1966 period discussed in detail in Chapter 3. Furthermore, starting in the mid-1980s, the number of purely internationally focused stories begins to decline and declines further during the over-sampled tabloid period. There could be many reasons for this change, from a change in the focus of the paper, to less direct newspaper headlines. However, the decline of the British Empire reached a major turning point in the late 1970s with the granting of independence to the majority of the remaining British colonies, leading to a greater focus on international and world affairs rather than colonial

156 *Policy Agendas in British Politics*

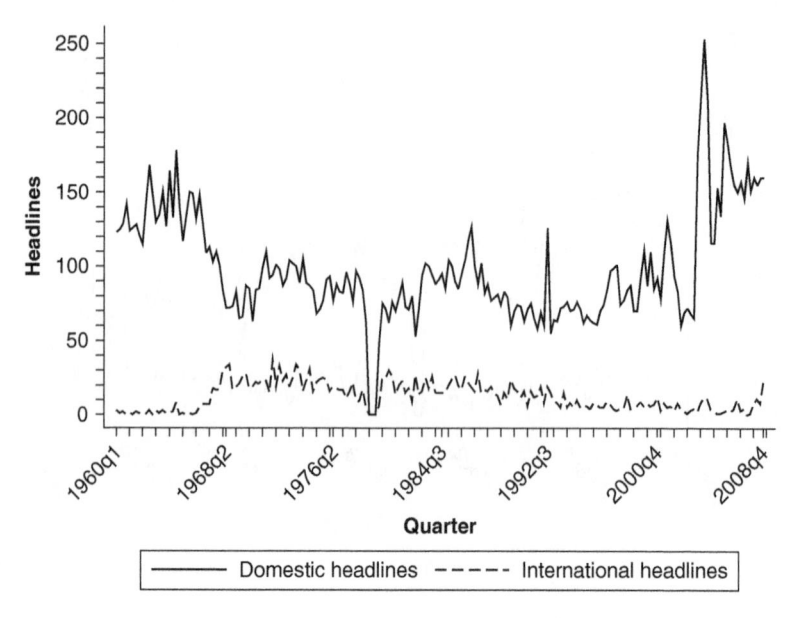

Figure 8.2 Quarterly *The Times* policy and non-policy headlines

affairs in government agendas. The change in the media agenda reflects these changes to British politics and is a likely explanation.

The media does not just focus on government and on policy. Many major headlines and front-page stories instead focus on events such as fires, extreme weather and, of course, entertainment and celebrities, and *The Times* is no different than any other media outlet in that regard. Figure 8.2 presents the number of policy and non-policy stories contained in *The Times* according to UK Policy Agendas Project major topic codes. The majority of policy stories do not relate to a particular piece of legislation, but instead focus on an issue area, such as health or social welfare, that is related to the policies to which government attends. Non-policy stories on the other hand cover sporting results, celebrity marriages and divorces, and other events that Parliament does not address.

In Figure 8.2 it is clear that the majority of the content in *The Times* concerns policy on some level, although the amount of attention to policy issues was on the decline until the start of the tabloid era. However, there were occasional spikes in the amount of policy content, such as in the mid-1980s with its high levels of attention to defence and international affairs and foreign aid. While the spike in the tabloid era is in part due to sampling, the increase is actually far too high to be due to the change in paper format alone and suggests that despite the name of the format change, *The Times* has become more policy oriented in recent years. This is further demonstrated by the lack of a similar increase in the number of non-policy stories with the change in format. Of course, this may be due to a restructuring of the paper, but nevertheless, the majority of front-page attention in the tabloid era remains focused on policy issues.

These core patterns of attention speak directly to the type of paper and the type of coverage *The Times* has exhibited over time. Importantly, each of the changes observed in Figures 8.1 and 8.2 represent changes in the focus of the media. While changes to the format of the paper may have facilitated these changes in focus, they do not appear to be directly responsible, and as such these shifts in attention are due to calculated choices either to serve the public or the key actors at *The Times*.

Media attention to policy

The share of the paper devoted to particular policy issues over time is another important pattern in media attention and the focus of the UK Policy Agendas Project coding. As a paper of record, *The Times* is viewed as reporting the news as it happens, but not all events are newsworthy and many issue areas are the purview of smaller and more specialised agendas (Carmines and Stimson 1989; Downs 1972; Jones and Baumgartner 2005a). Agricultural news, for instance, is unlikely to receive high levels of media attention except during a crisis like an outbreak of foot-and-mouth disease, which has a major impact on sheep and cattle. Other topics, such as wars and other defence-related issues, will likely always be high on the agenda as most news related to defence is salient. A different source for media attention would, of course, have a different pattern of attention, such as *The Financial Times*, which focuses more on business issues and economic affairs than the majority of papers. However, the similarity between the content of different national newspapers, especially on the front page, is marked (see Boydstun n.d.). Figure 8.3 presents the pattern of attention in *The Times* by policy-oriented major topic codes over time. While such an investigation does not confirm or deny *The Times* as a suitable source for media attention, it does allow for an assessment of the issues and how they are covered in the paper.

Many well-known events such as the labour disputes of the 1970s are quite evident from Figure 8.3, whereas others such as the outbreak

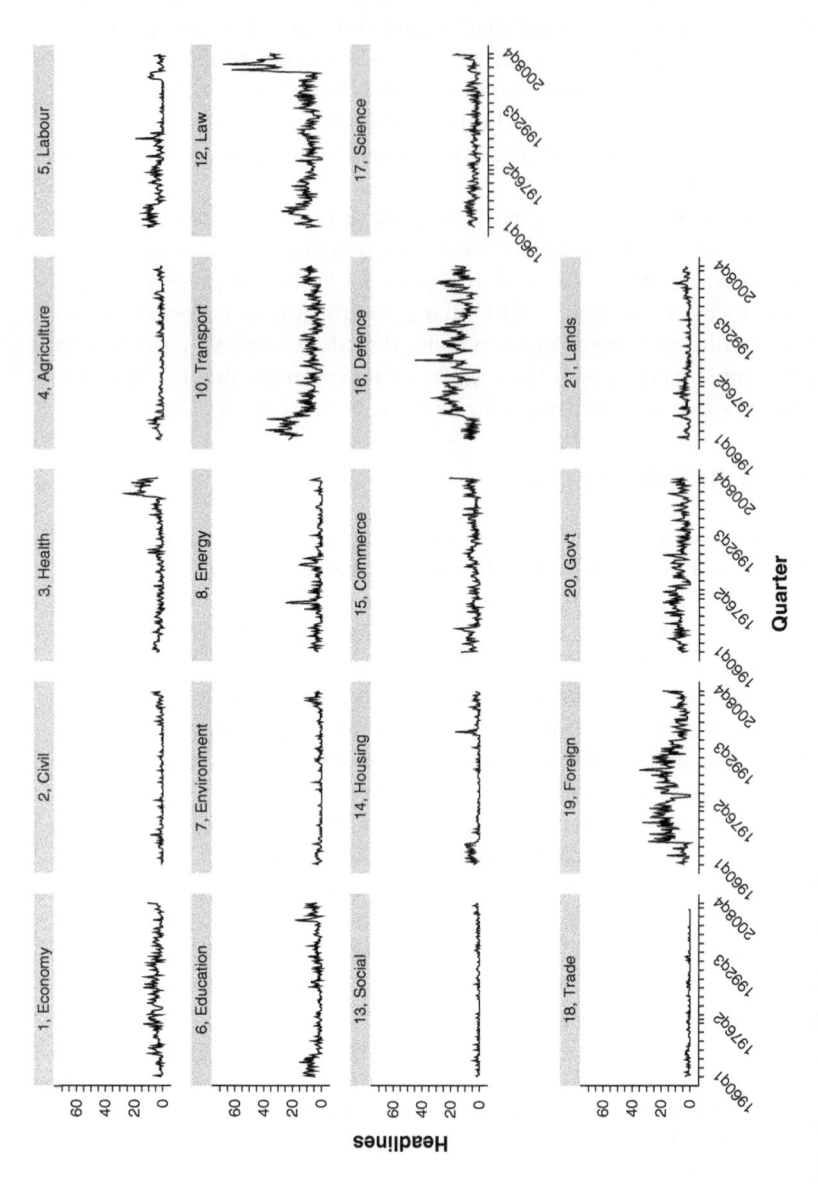

Figure 8.3 Quarterly *The Times* headlines by policy area

of foot-and-mouth disease in 2001, an agricultural issue, are less pronounced and clear. From Figure 8.3 it is also clear that certain issues—namely defence, international affairs/foreign aid and government operations—take up a large share of the media agenda. So do law, crime and family issues as well as transportation, which includes reports of road accidents, criminal driving offences and road safety in general. Other issue areas are not as well represented, but tend to be present in the media agenda following major events or movements, such as with concerns over environmental issues in the mid-2000s. As noted in Chapter 3, an over-sampling of the data proved necessary with the start of the tabloid era for *The Times* in 2003, but this over-sampling in the tabloid era appears to have only resulted in increased attention in two issue areas, namely health and law, crime and family issues. While investigating a proportional rather than count measure would help to control for the new format and other changes in the data, changes in the count and overall number of stories are just as telling and important. Furthermore, a count measure allows us to more directly observe the effect of over-sampling on the resulting data.

An additional way to consider these patterns of attention is to look at descriptive statistics by policy area, which tell an important story about volatility in attention. Table 8.1 presents summary statistics on news stories by policy topic for the entire 1960–2008 period, excluding the strike period so as to not unduly undercount attention, and to produce a meaningful minimum value for each issue.

Table 8.1 presents several interesting details about the media agenda in the consistently low levels of attention for social welfare and trade issues along with high levels of attention for defence and law and crime. Unlike Figure 8.3, the summary statistics presented in Table 8.1 allow a better view of some general patterns of attention. Most notably, with the exception of law and crime, each issue area has at least one quarter where there is no attention on the front page. Surprisingly, this includes no attention to the economy and defence. While such a pattern of attention is unexpected, it suggests that the media functions in a logical manner following what is newsworthy and not necessarily reporting on an issue area just because it has been consistently newsworthy in the past. While the economy and defence are often more newsworthy than issues such as social welfare and agriculture, the fact that these issues generally matter does not guarantee a place on the media agenda.

The kurtosis scores presented in Table 8.1 are also quite telling. Changes in attention to the important issue areas of the economy and defence are nearly normally distributed (indicated by a kurtosis score

Table 8.1 Summary statistics of media policy topic attention by quarter, 1960–2008

Topic	Abbreviation	Mean	Minimum	Maximum	SD	Kurtosis
1	Economy	4.08	0	14	2.99	3.49
2	Civil rights	1.15	0	9	1.47	8.06
3	Health	4.15	0	26	4.54	8.60
4	Agriculture	1.73	0	9	1.80	5.12
5	Labour	3.59	0	19	3.67	4.34
6	Education	3.25	0	17	3.19	5.80
7	Environment	1.26	0	10	1.72	9.46
8	Energy	2.75	0	25	3.37	17.12
10	Transport	9.12	0	39	7.41	5.41
12	Law	13.02	1	68	10.81	9.33
13	Social	0.69	0	4	0.89	4.43
14	Housing	1.67	0	17	2.46	12.25
15	Commerce	4.54	0	21	3.12	6.83
16	Defence	14.45	0	45	7.34	3.71
17	Science	4.16	0	17	2.74	5.70
18	Trade	0.61	0	3	0.83	3.94
19	Foreign	12.07	0	35	7.44	2.68
20	Gov't	6.89	0	19	3.92	3.31
21	Lands	2.17	0	12	2.26	7.58

of 3). This suggests that, despite the importance of these issues to politics, and the importance of media attention to these issues on policy, this particular input in the policy process does not appear to be punctuated. Other issues including those high in average attention, such as law and crime, and those that are generally quite low, such as civil rights and energy, are more volatile and appear to be more punctuated inputs. How this degree of volatility matters for policy-making is a difficult question, but it is evident that the media agenda is fluid and dynamic and varies both over time and by issue. If changes in the media agenda are linked to the policy agenda of government, then it is likely that greater volatility for an issue area is accompanied by corresponding volatility of policy, at least when the change in attention is greatest.

Attention to the economy and defence

Painted in broad strokes, the media policy agenda has a high degree of face validity and performs as expected with a few clear exceptions, such as the general pattern of a minimum of zero stories in at least one quarter for each issue. However, a more detailed look at attention to the economy and defence is necessary to understand better these important issues. An investigation of these two policy areas enables one of the most important trade-offs in politics to be highlighted, one that pits economic concerns against defence and national security. As Chapter 7 demonstrated in relation to public opinion, the economy and foreign affairs drive much of public concern and can even condition attention to other issues (Wlezien 2005). The same is true for the policy agenda of government not just in the UK, but also in comparative perspective (see Jennings et al. 2011b), with evidence that attention to an issue like the economy links to government attention to other issue areas. It is unlikely that the media is an exception to this general finding, making a clear understanding of media attention to these policy areas all the more important. Figure 8.4 starts this investigation with a graph of media attention, Speech from the Throne mentions and Acts of Parliament on the economy from 1960–2008, which depicts annual trends.

Figure 8.4 demonstrates media and government attention to the economy. Clearly, the economy is an important issue with generally steady levels of attention over time. The most notable exception is the

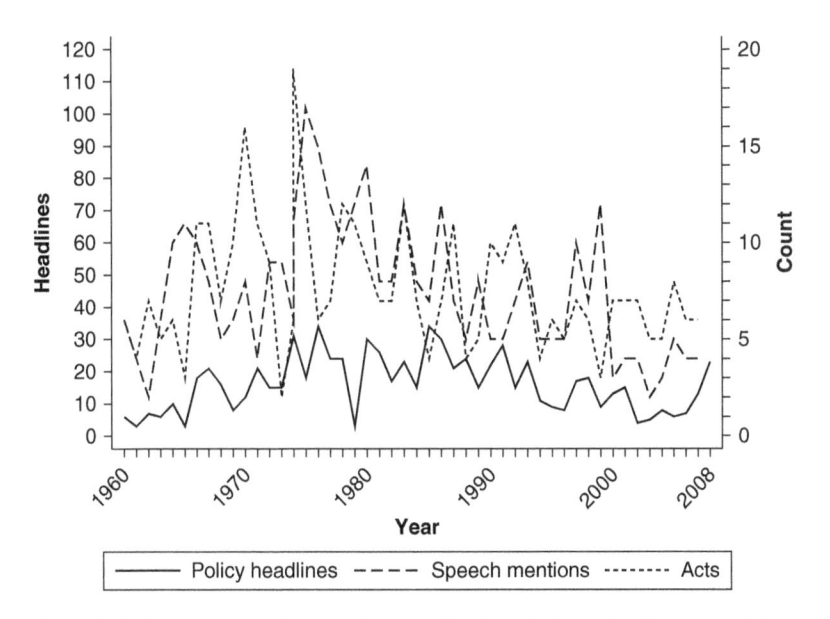

Figure 8.4 Yearly economic attention, media, Speech from the Throne and Acts of Parliament, 1960–2008

increased government attention to the economy in the mid-1970s, both through the Speech from the Throne and Acts of Parliament, with no similar increase in the media. The turbulent economic period of the 1970s is surprisingly unrepresented in the media agenda. While the volume of coverage was heavy, media attention primarily concerned other topics, for instance labour and employment, which focused on collective bargaining and more newsworthy stories concerning strikes. This anomaly highlights a common aspect of the media agenda, that the outcomes of policy decisions, and not always policies themselves, are the main focus of the media. The consequence of this deflection is not immediately clear, but can result in more temporary or incomplete solutions to political problems.

At the time of writing, the economy was a critical issue in politics, but just a few years prior defence had been a dominant concern with the aftermath of the terrorist attacks on the US and the debates and protests over the Iraq War. The salience of defence, while not a constant, is quite consistent over time. Figure 8.5 presents a graph of media attention, Speech from the Throne mentions and Acts of Parliament on defence in the period 1960–2008.

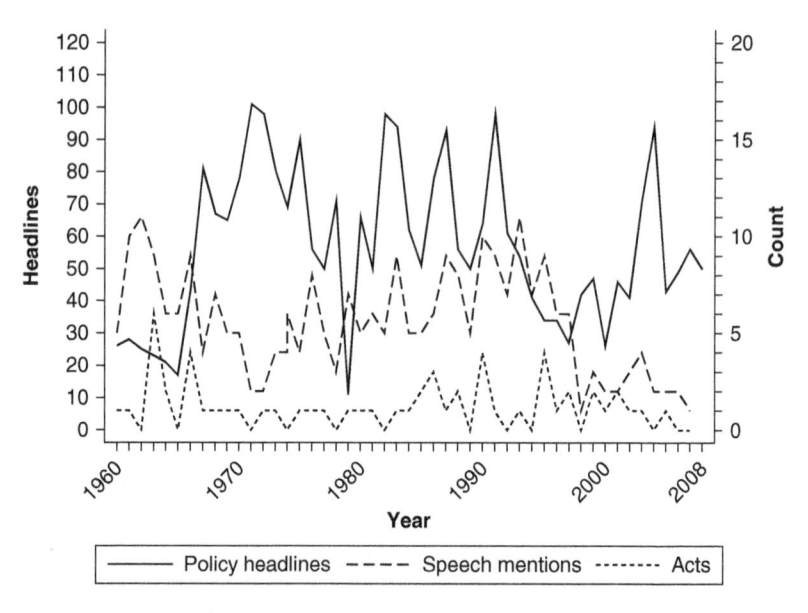

Figure 8.5 Yearly defence attention: media, Speech from the Throne and Acts of Parliament, 1960–2008

Here, the pattern of attention shows a higher degree of volatility in attention to defence than the economy for each of the executive, legislative and media agendas. The reasons for this volatility are likely due to the nature of national security and wars, which can rise and fall in importance quickly based on severity and external threats, public concern and the length of conflict. A closer investigation is consistent with some of this explanation. For example, attention to defence clearly increases for both the media agenda and the legislative agenda, Acts of Parliament, around the time of the Falklands War, but other spikes in attention for both occur over the entire time period likely due to the Cold War, the Gulf War, Kosovo and other important issues. While attention to defence stabilised in the early 2000s, the Al-Qaeda attacks on the US and the Iraq War lead to spikes in the media agenda and the executive agenda in the Speech from the Throne. Without a need for policy reform, however, no similar increase in Acts of Parliament for defence occurred during the 2000s.

This low level of legislative attention in the form of Acts of Parliament highlights one of the distinctive characteristics of British politics, that law-making is largely static unless a major reform is required. A lack of attention can be just as telling as a punctuation, and the absence of an expansion of the legislative agenda on defence during the course of the wars in Iraq and Afghanistan indicates that Parliament was not involved directly in managing combat operations. Executive and media attention to defence during this period signalled several different concerns, including the resolve of the government to stay the course and widespread public dissent over the Iraq War. However, policy-making was not legislative in nature, as the decision to go to or end a war is not determined by an Act of Parliament in the UK.

Structural shifts in the media agenda

As with the other chapters, we present information about the likely change points in the media agenda. We use the same methodology and techniques to analyse the series, which produces change points when the probability exceeds 90 per cent. We present results below in Figure 8.6 in the same way as previous chapters. These are for a shorter period than the change point analyses for speeches and laws, due to the shorter length of the media series.

From these, it is notable that 1965 emerges as an important change point. This is the year before *The Times* changed its format and precipitated an apparent structural shift in its editorial style and emphasis,

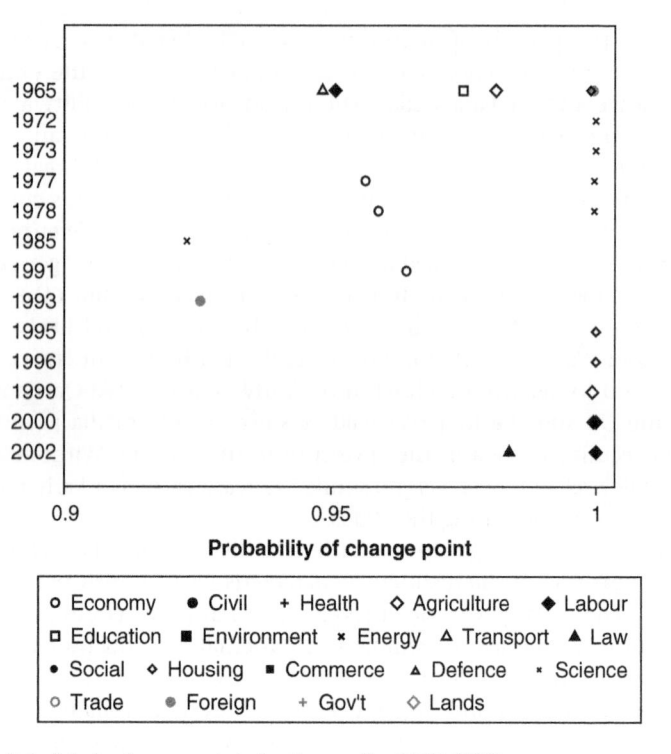

1965	△◆ □ ◇ ●
1972	×
1973	×
1977	○ ×
1978	○ ×
1985	×
1991	○
1993	●
1995	◇
1996	◇
1999	◇
2000	◆
2002	▲ ◆

0.9   0.95   1
Probability of change point

○ Economy	● Civil	+ Health	◇ Agriculture	◆ Labour
□ Education	■ Environment	× Energy	△ Transport	▲ Law
● Social	◇ Housing	■ Commerce	▲ Defence	× Science
○ Trade	● Foreign	+ Gov't	◇ Lands	

Figure 8.6 Likely change points for the media, 1960–2008

shown here by change points in the transport, employment, education, agriculture and housing series. These are domestic policy topics, which dropped in importance as attention to international affairs increased in this period, reflecting the outlook of the paper rather than changes in the emphasis of these issues.

What is also interesting is the stability in the 1960s overall, as contrasted with volatility during the 1970s that was due to industrial conflict and economic challenges. Energy, with an oil price shock, and the industrial conflicts with trade unions in these industries, is linked to agenda volatility, as there are change points in 1972 and 1973, 1977 and 1978. These leaps in attention may be observed for these years as large departures from the normal level of attention to energy. There is a further change point for energy in 1985, following the coal miners' strike of that year.

Similarly, there is a structural shift for the macroeconomy in 1977–1978 around the high point of the economic crisis of the 1970s after the

UK was forced to accept a loan from the IMF. However, the economic headlines continued to grow over the next five years, particularly with significant attention to unemployment, which grew rapidly during the early 1980s.

The 1990s has its share of structural instability, with 1993 marking a decline in attention to international affairs after the Gulf War and the end of the Cold War. The housing policy change point represents a recovery from the housing crash of 1992 and 1993, and reflects a rise of attention to this topic associated with rocketing house prices. There is another rise and fall in attention to the issue of housing again in 1996.

The year 2000, well into the first term of the Labour government, exhibits a structural adjustment in attention to employment at the start of the decade and another some years later. The late 1990s observed a low level of media interest in this issue, which changed in the early 2000s with a series of employment stories.

Finally, we see attention to crime precipitate a shift in 2002. There was a massive surge in crime stories in the media at that time, which is observable in the data, a lot of which relates to the reporting of crimes, but also to government policies, such as 'Blair "nationalises" police over muggings' (Baldwin et al. 2002).

Conclusion

The UK Policy Agendas Project media dataset focuses on *The Times* front-page headlines from 1960 to 2008 and as such captures the content of the salient media agenda. As the investigation of the broad patterns of media attention show changes in the format, this was unlikely the only cause behind changes in the paper's content. It is hard to say whether these changes were due to *The Times* looking to fulfil a public need for more international attention in the 1960s and a public desire for more non-policy stories over time, or is due to internal changes inside the paper from the editor-in-chief and other actors. However, as a result of these changes media salience also changed in a way that may have affected policy. The increasing focus of government and the media on international affairs over time, with the decline of the British Empire is one easily observable change. After all, while the British monarch may no longer be head of state for many former colonies, official state visits and other interactions are still quite common.

Changes in the format and general content of the paper are important, but the link of media salience to government is ultimately about attention to policy areas. As with public opinion in Chapter 7, media salience is far more selective on the issues it attends to than the government. Issue areas such as agriculture and housing are clearly important for the government and the public, but when the issues are stable, public concern is low. Without a crisis, new regulations just do not make good news. Media is as much about reporting the facts as selling papers, and attention to some issue areas are likely to only be high during a crisis. As this chapter demonstrates, even dominant issues do not always receive attention at every point in time, with every issue but law and order receiving a minimum of zero stories when considered quarterly.

More detailed investigations of media attention to the economy and defence demonstrate that even when it comes to the media, a crisis increases attention to these important issues. The attack on the World Trade Center and the Iraq War, for instance, led to noticeable increases in the number of defence stories, while the start of the most recent economic crisis led to a quick upward turn in attention to the economy at the end of the series. Many of these crises appear as change points in our series. Not surprisingly, at the level of the calendar year, media attention for these two core issues moved closely in parallel with the policy agenda for the Speech from the Throne and Acts of UK Parliament. This is especially true for the economy and for the relationship between the media agenda and the Speech from the Throne for the issue of defence. While this chapter does not try to investigate any sort of causality nor make any claims concerning the results, the media and, in particular, the media dataset used by the UK Policy Agendas Project, closely follows the government's executive and legislative agendas and helps to confirm the belief that the media has an important place in the policy process.

From the changes in the format of the printed newspaper, to steady levels of media attention on an issue and of course shifts in the media agenda, it is clear that the media matters for British politics and the policy agenda. While the exact effect of the media on government and agenda setting is something that is not yet known, numerous studies demonstrate the power of the media in politics (see Baumgartner and Jones 1993; Birkland 1997; Cobb and Elder 1983; McCombs and Shaw 1972). In this chapter we focused on the content of the media agenda in both terms of when and why it has changed. In doing so, we have provided insight into the relationship between the media and government in British politics, namely that more volatile agendas may be those most likely to lead to change in government agendas and that not all policy agendas are necessarily affected by attention to an issue area, such as Acts of Parliament during the time of the Iraq War.

Appendix 8A

Table 8.A1 UK Policy Agendas Project media dataset major topic codes

Topic	Abbreviation	Name
1	Economy	Macroeconomics
2	Civil	Civil rights, minority issues, immigration and civil liberties
3	Health	Health
4	Agriculture	Agriculture
5	Labour	Labour and employment
6	Education	Education
7	Environment	Environment
8	Energy	Energy
10	Transport	Transportation
12	Law	Law, crime and family issues
13	Social	Social welfare
14	Housing	Community development, planning and housing issues
15	Commerce	Banking, finance and domestic commerce
16	Defence	Defence
17	Science	Space, science, technology and communications
18	Trade	Foreign trade
19	Foreign	International affairs and foreign aid
20	Gov't	Government operations
21	Lands	Public lands, water management, colonial and territorial issues
24‡	Regional	Regional and local government administration
26‡	Weather	Weather and natural disasters
27‡	Fire	Fires, accidents and other man-made disasters
28‡	Arts	Arts, history, and culture and entertainment
29‡	Sport	Sports and recreation
30‡	Death	Deaths, death notices and obituaries
31‡	Church	Churches and religion
33‡	Parties	Political parties
34‡	Interest	Human interest
99‡	Other	Other, miscellaneous and uncodable

‡ Indicates a non-policy major topic.

9
Budgets and Policy Implementation

In traditional accounts of policy-making in Britain, political parties set out their proposals in election manifestos, and then the government of the day announces its policy programme in the Speech from the Throne (as described in Bara 2005; Herman 1974). The task of the other institutions of government—the civil service, agencies and local authorities—is to turn these proposals into concrete policy outputs (Smith 1976; Theodoulou and Kofinis 2004), a process that is termed policy implementation (Pressman and Wildavsky 1973; Youris 1990).

So far in this book, we have examined one kind of policy output, and that is Acts of Parliament, discussed in Chapters 4–6. As was observed, there is sometimes a link between the policy agenda laid out by government in the Speech from the Throne and the laws that are passed though Parliament. In this chapter we consider another kind of output of government, which forms another part of the agenda setting process. Here decisions are more concrete because significant costs and benefits are incurred from one policy choice over another. These trade-offs occur over decisions about the level of public finances that are associated with the different types of government activity, which use taxes and other revenues to deliver goods and services provided by the state for collective or individual benefit.

In the linear model of policy-making we expect implementation to reflect earlier commitments. So for the policy agenda, we expect the attention of government to a policy to be reflected in the Speech from the Throne, and then to be translated to legislation, and also to budgets, some of which may be implementing legislative provisions. By observing budgetary spending categorised by the policy content coding system of the Policy Agendas Project, it is possible to observe how the topics emphasised in the speech are reflected in the kinds of actions the state commissions and the policies that affect the citizens on the ground, whether it is health, law and crime, social welfare or other policies. To complete the circle, we would need to examine policy outcomes, which are the effects of all these decisions, such as analysing whether increased spending on crime actually reduces the rate of crime. That, however, is beyond the scope of this book.

We do not expect a one-to-one relationship between agenda setting and the policy outputs of government, due to the characteristics of different policies and the nature of agenda setting. As was shown in Chapter 4, there is a high level of variation as to whether attention to a topic in the Speech from the Throne leads to subsequent legislation. This is due partly to the nature of the speech. Certain policies may be announced that do not have specific legislation attached, and also that legislation may be passed for a range of practical reasons that are not covered in the annual statement of executive priorities. Similarly, with budgets there are policy choices that do not need to be highlighted in the Speech from the Throne; nor does all legislation require a large amount of public expenditure in order to be implemented. Further, budgets may be driven by factors outside the government's control. Policies typically suffer from drift, whereas the intentions of government are not implemented because of lack of clarity of the policy and the number of chains in the delivery process (Marsh and Rhodes 1992a; Pressman and Wildavsky 1973). We can also expect budgets to affect decision-making and policy agendas up the chain, for example, when there is a cost overrun that causes public debate and criticism. Just as much as central policy-makers are promoting their objectives, so too local agencies are seeking to influence policy objectives from the ground up (Mazmanian and Sabatier 1983; Sabatier 1986). In this way, budgets are both a connected and separate part of the policy agenda, showing some of the trends in British politics as revealed by our reviews of speeches and laws. Budgets also represent a distinctive venue for decision-making in its own right that is shaped by structural, demographic and technological changes driving costs in a policy sector, such as in health care.

For some of these reasons budgets have attracted the attention of public policy scholars seeking to understand decision-making in government. As we discussed in Chapter 1, budgeting has been subject to the foundational studies of incrementalism in decision-making in the US (Wildavsky 1984), and was the topic of Heclo and Wildavsky's (1974) classic book on policy networks in the UK Treasury and follow-up studies (Deakin and Parry 2000; Thain and Wright 1985). Budgets were also the focus of a school of thinking that emphasised that policy-making in the UK is inherited (Rose 1974; Rose and Davies 1994), as discussed in Chapter 2. Budgets have inspired incrementalist accounts of policy-making because they appear to be sticky and hard to change, where decisions are often made on the basis of spending in the previous time period. However, budgets have also been the focus of tests of punctuated equilibrium in public policy, both in the US (Jones and Baumgartner 2005a, 2005b; Jones et al. 1998) and in the UK (John and Margetts 2003; Soroka et al. 2006). Other accounts of public policy examining the linkage between public and party preferences in the UK have used budgets to examine the impact of placement on the left and the right on budgetary outcomes (Hofferbert and Budge 1992; McDonald and Budge 2005) or to test the relationship between public preferences and spending (Soroka and Wlezien 2005, 2010).

The chapter reviews trends in the budgets of British government as coded according to the policy content coding system of the Policy Agendas Project to reveal key trends in policy-making. The chapter first describes these trends, then compares them to the agendas of other institutional venues: the speeches and laws on the one hand, and the media on the other. We test for punctuated equilibrium in budgets, comparing the results with other agendas and report the change points once again. In this way, this chapter offers a reprise of the themes explored in the book through the specific lens of government spending and is a fitting precursor to the reflection on change and stability in the policy agenda of British government that is offered in the conclusion.

Trends in budgets

As was explained in Chapter 3, our data on budget agendas are drawn from official reports of spending by British government and coded according to the policy agendas topics. These data series do not cover all the major topics because of the lack of data for some areas of government activity or where a particular major topic does not have a category of functional spending associated with it (such as is the case for environment and energy). However, most of the core functions of the state are included in our analysis. We are limited by the sources of the budgets and only have good data from 1951. The descriptive statistics that support the following graphs can be seen in Table 9.1. The table has a column of kurtosis scores, which becomes useful in the section on punctuations later in the chapter.

Decision-making about budgets reflects bargaining across government in an annual cycle that is managed by the Treasury. The budgets run

Table 9.1 Summary statistics of budgetary expenditure in billions by policy topic, 1951–2007

Topic	Abbreviation	Mean	Min	Max	SD	Kurtosis
1	Economy	16.28	0.47	36.84	10.15	2.19
2	Civil	.	.	.	.	.
3	Health	34.26	9.92	94.55	21.57	3.34
4	Agriculture	4.93	3.07	9.37	1.40	5.70
5	Labour	.	.	.	.	.
6	Education	34.19	9.85	77.98	16.80	3.40
7	Environment	6.15	3.10	12.82	3.03	2.53
8	Energy	.	.	.	.	.
10	Transport	10.41	4.00	17.75	3.88	2.05
12	Law	11.89	2.21	31.71	8.58	2.67
13	Social	82.04	15.24	194.12	57.05	1.93
14	Housing	12.90	5.78	29.01	5.63	3.90
15	Commerce	.	.	.	.	.
16	Defence	29.03	24.05	35.71	3.16	2.20
17	Science	.	.	.	.	.
18	Trade	.	.	.	.	.
19	Foreign	.	.	.	.	.
20	Gov't	.	.	.	.	.
21	Lands	16.28	0.47	36.84	10.15	2.19

from 31 March to the same period the following year (for simplicity we have linked the main year of the budget to other years in our series). The final budget is announced in a budget statement in March before the year begins. But much has been decided long before. At the beginning of the financial year, departments submit funding requests to the Treasury and these get published in the *Central Government Supply Estimates (Budget Year-Following Year): Main Supply Estimates*. The government then can publish *Supplementary Estimates* in the winter and spring, which can change the figures in light of new forecasts and contingencies. The government then issues a *Pre-Budget Report* in December that contains most of the decisions. Parliament then approves the budget.

Since the 1960s there have been attempts to introduce a longer time horizon for budgeting, which governments try to adhere to. The latest of such attempts is seen in the *Comprehensive Spending Review* that is still in place at the time of writing. At regular intervals, government plans expenditure up to three years in advance. Nevertheless, in practice the budget still follows an annual cycle and fluctuates accordingly, although the planning process can also introduce longer-term changes. We observe both of these scenarios in the series that follow. In general, the executive exerts strong control over its public funding and budget decisions do not involve the legislature as much in other countries. This results in a process in which informal negotiations tend to inform the formal authorisation, which was the finding of Heclo and Wildavsky (1974). Other countries have a more open process with significantly more involvement by the legislature (see Gray et al. 2000).

In spite of these strong central controls, the government has to acknowledge that some spending items are affected by demand rather than planning, as is recognised by the distinction between the departmental expenditure limits (DELs) and the annually managed expenditure (AME). The AME is driven by entitlements that the government has to honour, such as social security payments. Other budgets may be driven by cost overruns, unanticipated expenditure (famously in defence) and political considerations. These calculations may cause ministers to approve annual changes.

Figure 9.1 plots the budget for macroeconomic issues, and compares it with that topic's inclusion in the Speech from the Throne. The eye is immediately drawn to the variation in the data with a large amount of economic activity associated with the post-war period and how this was offloaded quickly. At 6.3 per cent, the mean share of spending is

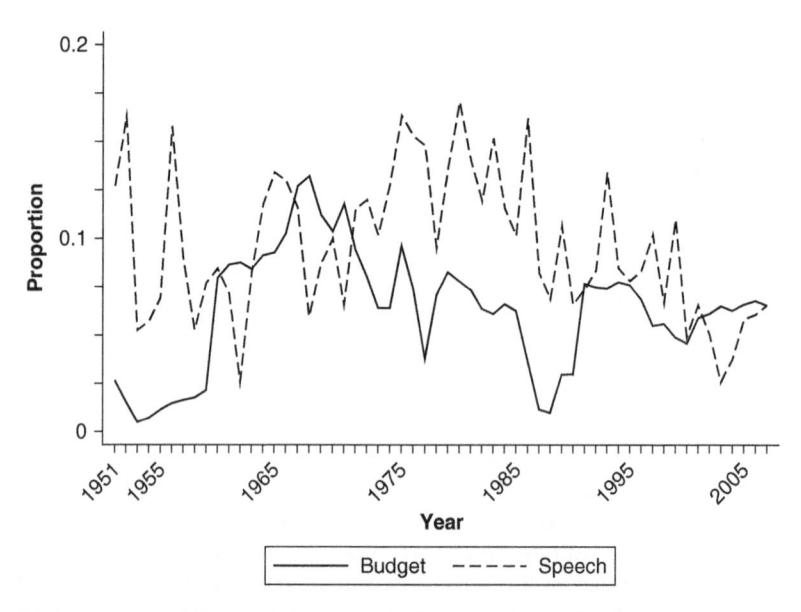

Figure 9.1 Percentage of public expenditure and the Speech from the Throne on the macroeconomy, 1951–2007

large for a non-social policy issue and has a moderate standard deviation of 3.1 per cent. Spending starts to rise from the 1950s up until the early 1970s and might be thought to reflect the age of corporatism and state ownership of key economic enterprises, following the nationalisation programme of the Atlee government. What is also observable is the later long decline of expenditure on the macroeconomy, which falls to very low levels during the height of the privatisation era of the Conservative government elected in 1979. There then appears to be a rise shortly before New Labour entered office in 1997. Overall, Labour tends to spend more on the economy on average 7.5 per cent of the budget compared with 5.5 for the Conservatives (t = 2.4). There is no correlation between attention to the issue in the Speech from the Throne and the budget ($p = 0.58$), even though the series appear to track each other for periods of time, such as from 1975 to 1990.

Following the order of topics presented in Chapter 4, we next consider defence and international affairs is not traditionally a spending domain (aside from spending on international development, which historically was quite low despite rising in recent years). The percentages of the budget and the speech apportioned to defence are shown in Figure 9.2.

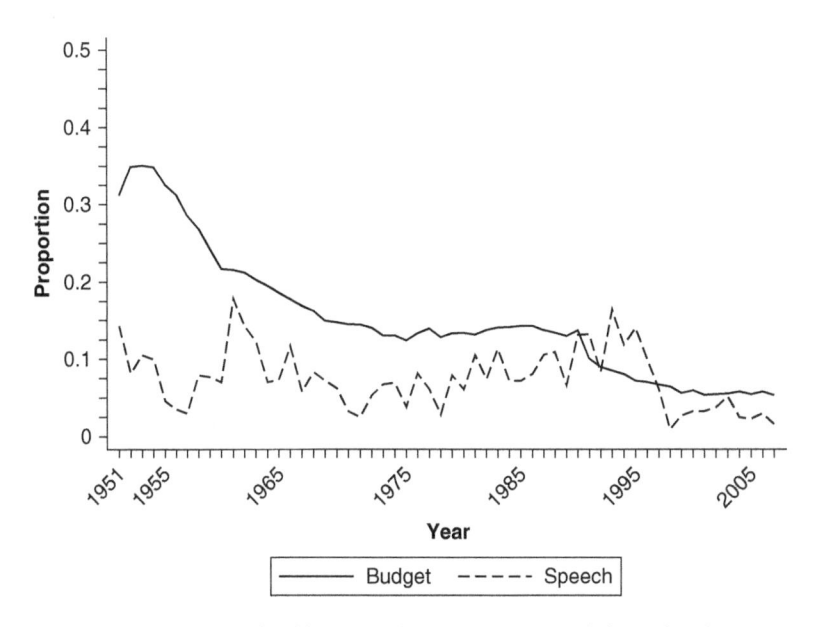

Figure 9.2 Percentage of public expenditure and the Speech from the Throne on defence

The pattern is consistent over the post-war period whereby there was a decline in the percentage of expenditure on defence after the Second World War, then an increase in relative defence expenditure around the time of the Korean War, which then fell at a stable rate from the 1950s to the late 1990s. In 1990 there is another fall in defence spending associated with the end of the Cold War and this downward trend continues afterwards. This reduction in the proportion of government spending allocated to defence may reflect a decline in Britain's international commitments, but has occurred despite military operations in conflicts in Northern Ireland, the Falklands, Kuwait, Bosnia, Kosovo, and more recently Iraq and Afghanistan.[1] There is no significant correlation between government attention to defence in the Speech from the Throne and budgets (0.24, $p=0.06$). For some periods attention to defence is rising in the speech while at the same time falling in budgets for periods of time, such as in 1994 and 1995. The mean of 15.2 per cent of overall spending across the domains is sizable and also has a large standard deviation of 8.3 per cent. On average, Conservative governments tend to spend more on defence (18.2 per cent in contrast to 10.7 per cent for Labour ($t=3.7$)), which supports the established view from the literature (Hogwood 1992, p. 445). The trend of reducing the proportion of spending allocated to defence is observed over a long time period, but it appears that 1989 and 1990 were critical years when expenditure fell more dramatically than others (see discussion in Crawford et al. 2009, p. 25).

Government expenditure on law and crime is plotted in Figure 9.3. While attention to law and crime in the Speech from the Throne oscillates, albeit from a low base, spending grows steadily as a proportion of the government budget, up until 1990, and there are no large rises (or falls). The average is a relatively low proportion of total government spending at 4.2 per cent, but this increases to nearly 5.0 per cent at end of the period in 2007, having started at a low base of 2.5 per cent in 1945. So there is a gradual increase in spending on law and crime except for a sharp fall in the proportion of government spending in 1991. There is a relatively low standard deviation of 1.3 per cent. Even though the series exhibit distinctive patterns their trends are headed in the same direction and there is a correlation of 0.57 ($p = 0.000$). There is no difference between Labour and Conservatives in the proportion of overall spending on law and order when in government.

As with the structure of Chapter 4, we next consider the budgets of other major spending domains, taking health first. Figure 9.4 shows the high levels of spending on health (with a mean of 13.1 per cent) compared with lower levels of attention in the Speech from the Throne.

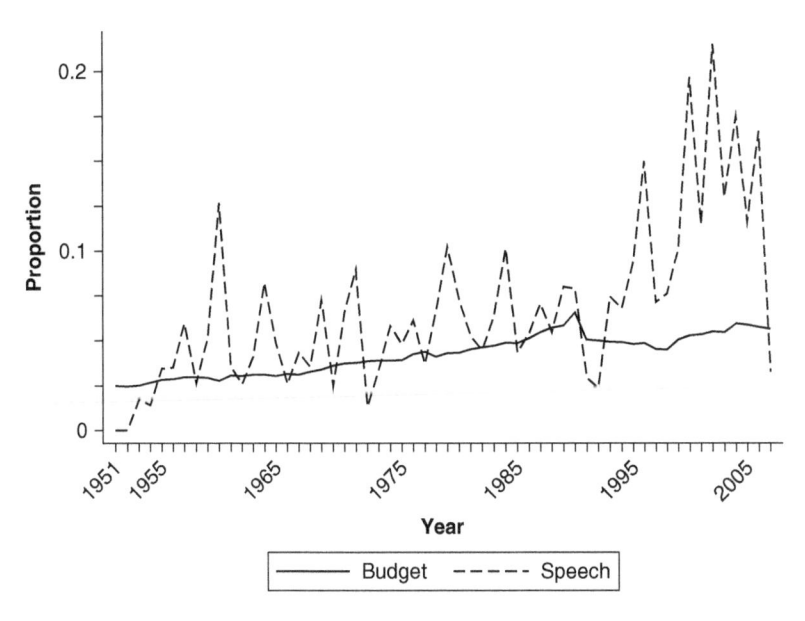

Figure 9.3 Percentage of public expenditure and the Speech from the Throne on law and crime

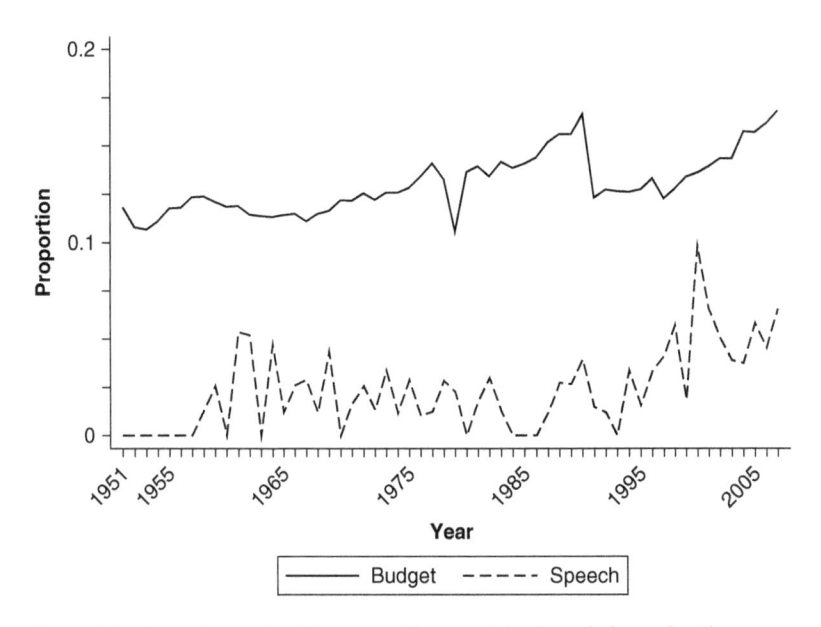

Figure 9.4 Percentage of public expenditure and the Speech from the Throne on health

As a share of the policy agenda, the British government did not tend to give particular emphasis to health, at least until the mid-1990s. The share of spending on health tends to be quite stable, with a standard deviation of 1.5 per cent. In the period since 1980, both attention to health and spending have risen, consistent with the growing importance and cost of modern health care, as well as an ageing population. There is a correlation of 0.34 ($p = 0.008$) between speeches and health spending. There is no difference between the political parties in how much they spend on health.

Another major spending domain, education, is plotted in Figure 9.5. As is the case with health, British government spends a high proportion of its total spending on education with an average of 13.9 per cent of expenditure and—like health—gives it much less proportion of attention in the Speech from the Throne. There is more variation in education spending with a standard deviation of 2.0, which might reflect population trends and where there are cyclical factors. However, spending on education is much more stable than the policy agenda of the Speech from the Throne. Education budgets came under strong pressure from the mid-1970s and was a target for expenditure cuts,

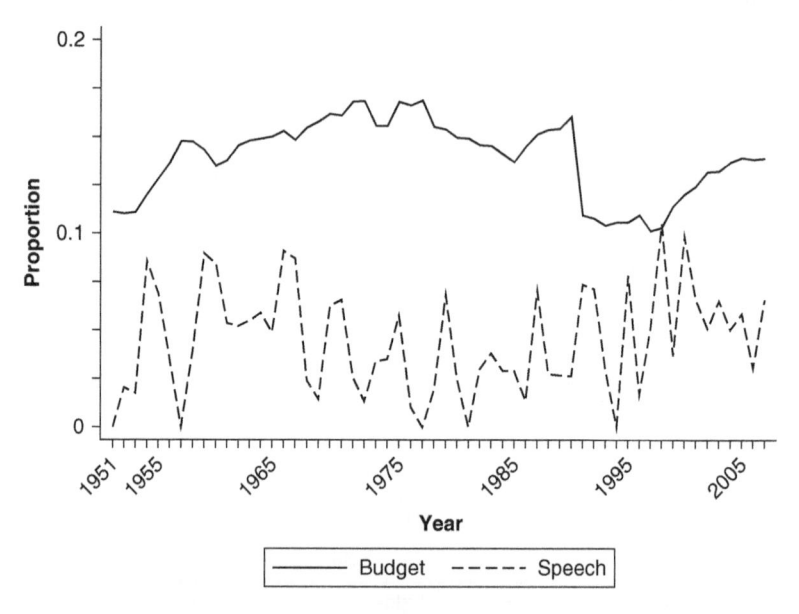

Figure 9.5 Percentage of public expenditure and the Speech from the Throne on education

but simultaneous demographic changes put less pressure on education budgets as the baby boom of the 1960s left primary and secondary education, and governments reduced the relative share of spending despite rising attention to education issues as reflected in the Speech from the Throne. There are some changes in spending priorities such as a drop in 1991, which is not reversed, not even under New Labour. This happened at the same time as there was another rise in demand for education spending from another baby boom. With these considerations affecting speeches and budgets, it is not surprising there is no correlation between the two agendas. In fact, the Labour government elected in 1997 did tend to give greater emphasis to the issue of education when first elected, but the increase in spending occurred later (having committed itself to remain within the public spending limits of the previous Conservative government for its first two years in office) while the level of attention in the Speech from the Throne dropped off. So there is some truth in Tony Blair's speech about 'education, education, education', even if this was not reflected in the prioritisation of the issue in spending until later on during the party's time in office.

Social welfare is another topic that represents a large proportion of total government spending but tends to receive a much lower level of attention in the policy agenda of the Speech from the Throne. The two series are plotted in Figure 9.6.

At an average 29.3 per cent of total functional expenditure over the post-war period, social welfare is the largest spending item of British government, which varies over time at a standard deviation of 7.2 per cent. There was pressure on the welfare budget during the early post-war period, but this fell away by the 1950s. There is then a steady rise from the 1960s, which increased further in the 1970s and 1980s, which reflects new entitlements, more recognition of disabilities, the changing structure of the population and the shifting availability of work. These external demands on spending might be the reason there is no correlation between the speech and the laws ($p = -0.08$). High levels of unemployment in the 1980s contributed to continued growth of the welfare bill despite rhetoric of the Thatcher government about restricting benefits. Even though New Labour assigned a greater share of attention in its policy agenda to social welfare than its predecessor and regarded the topic as important (Annesley 2001), the proportion of spending on social welfare fell under Labour in 1997, as the unemployment rate declined after the recession of the early 1990s. However, even with a decrease New Labour on average spent 35.6 per cent of the budget on social welfare compared with 27.8 before 1997 ($t = 3.5$). Overall there

178 Policy Agendas in British Politics

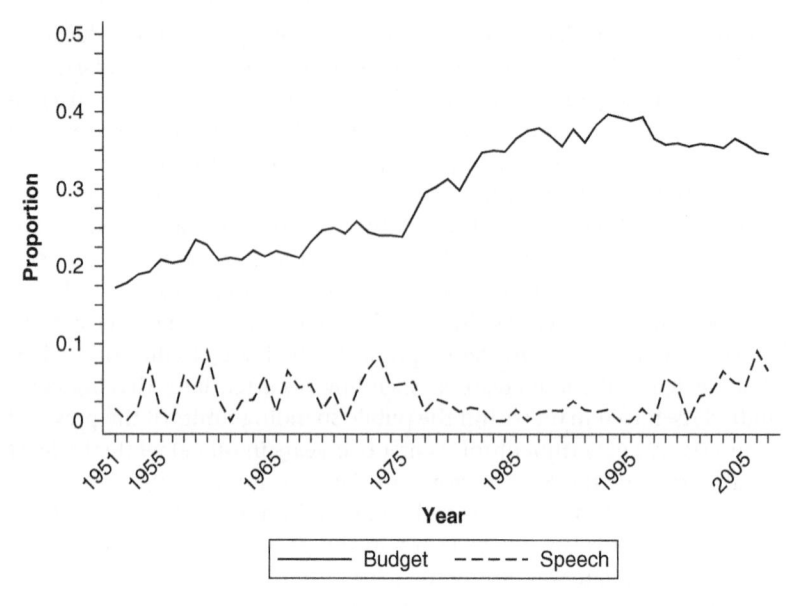

Figure 9.6 Percentage of public expenditure and the Speech from the Throne on social welfare

is no difference between the political parties on welfare (t = 0.35), so this is another policy domain where New Labour has brought a distinctive approach, even in the context of reducing its share of expenditure.

Housing is another topic with potentially high levels of spending, although not as high as other policy domains—see Figure 9.7. The average is 6.3 per cent, which has a moderate amount of variation at 3.1 percentage points. There is a strong connection between the budget and the speech with a correlation of 0.37 ($p = 0.047$). As such, this policy domain provides an example of how the policy priorities expressed in the speech are linked to spending decisions.

There is a distinct set of trends over time. After an early post-war dip, spending on housing grew as a proportion of total government expenditure during the 1960s, which was a period when the parties competed over the delivery of public housing. The peak of its share of spending was under the Labour government between 1974 and 1979; followed by a rapid fall that predated the election of the Conservative government in 1979. There was no recovery in levels of spending on housing and it flattened out over the period when New Labour was in office. There is no difference between the political parties in the average proportion of spending (t = 0.6), even for a policy domain that can be used to

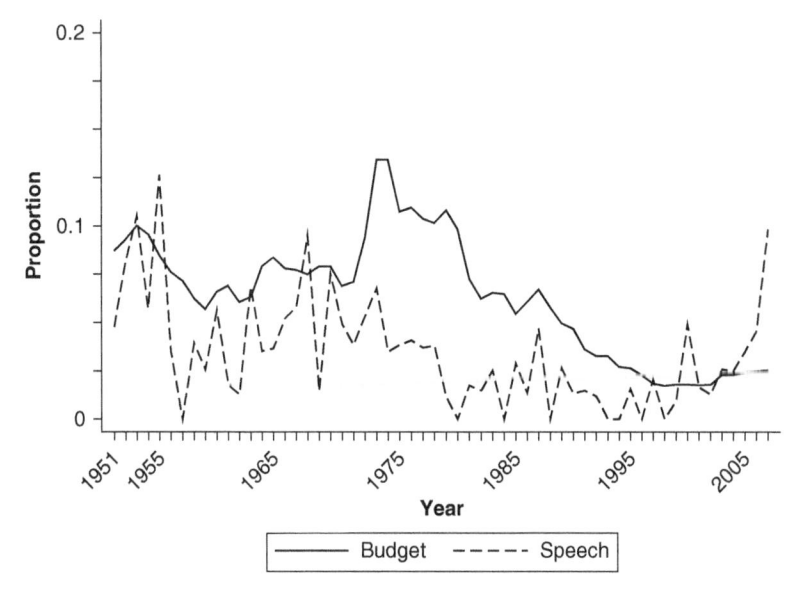

Figure 9.7 Percentage of public expenditure and the Speech from the Throne on community development, planning and housing issues

remedy inequality and provide for disadvantaged groups, which could be expected to appeal to Labour. Both the growth and contraction of the proportion of spending on housing reflected consensus between the parties for distinct periods of time, first with a wider political consensus about the desirability support for housing in the immediate post-war period and a further consensus that government should leave more housing provision to the private market.

Next are the more infrastructure-related and environmental topics. Transport is plotted in Figure 9.8, though we only have data on spending for part of the period (up to 1989) making generalisation harder than for the other domains. Transport is less important as a spending item than other functions of government, representing 6.4 per cent of total functional expenditure, and experiences a small amount of variation with a standard deviation of 2.4 per cent. It is a topic that benefited from the growth in the state and the economy in the post-war period which entailed a high level of investment in transport from the late 1950s and into the 1960s; but it has suffered in more parlous times as pressure on government spending increased. The high capital element to transport spending means it can be a target for cuts in times of fiscal retrenchment. Over the entire post-war period, there is no difference in

180 Policy Agendas in British Politics

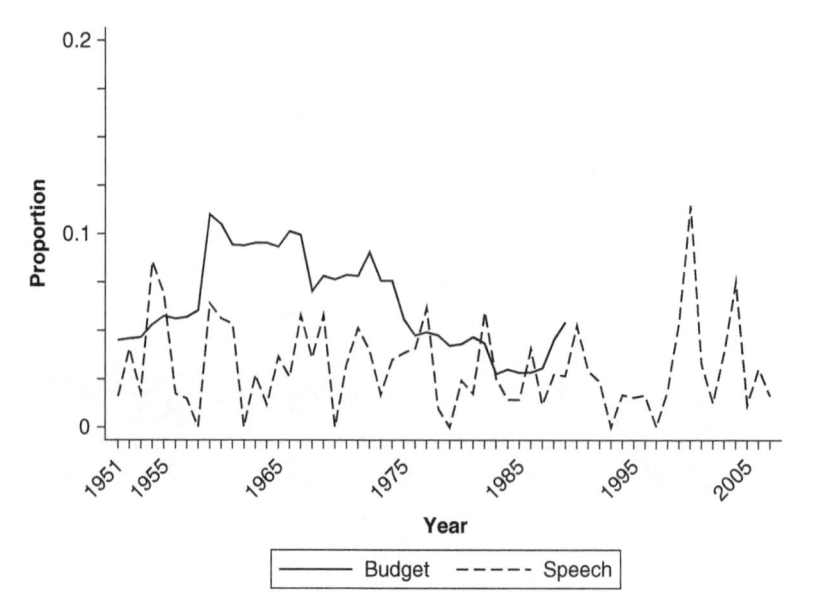

Figure 9.8 Percentage of public expenditure and the Speech from the Throne on transport, 1951–1989

the proportion of spending on transport between the political parties, and there is no correlation between attention to transport in the speech and the proportion of spending ($p = 0.15$).

Spending on agriculture is shown in Figure 9.9, plotted against attention to the issue in the Speech from the Throne. Exhibiting a similar trend to the policy agenda in the speech, government spending on agriculture has undergone substantial change over the period, starting from a high of about 10 per cent of total expenditure across the domains and falling to 1.5 per cent at the end of the period where we have the data, which makes the average of 3.3 per cent deceptive, and the standard deviation of 1.9 per cent more revealing. Spending on agriculture started to fall well before Britain joined the EU, as concern about self-sufficiency in production and the importance of the agriculture sector also declined. There is no party effect ($t = 1.0$), which may reflect the low salience of the issue, which is in contrast with other countries. There is a strong correlation between speeches and budgets of 0.36 ($p = 0.02$), which reflects the parallel decline in attention to agriculture over the period in both institutional agendas.

For these spending domains it is therefore possible to observe how British government adjusted its allocation of the overall budget pie.

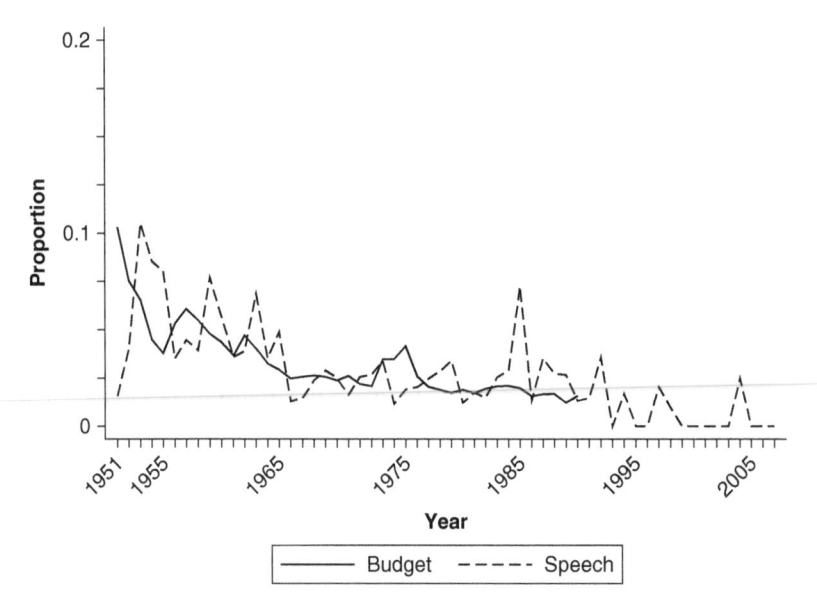

Figure 9.9 Percentage of public expenditure and the Speech from the Throne on agriculture, 1951–1989

While there is less variability across the series than for the policy agenda of the Speech from the Throne, it is possible also to observe the trends in spending over time. These trends tend to correspond to the policy agenda expressed in the speech for many but not all issues (that is defence, law and crime, health, housing and agriculture), although other considerations and pressures influence all of these agendas. There are some differences in spending according to party control of government, but these are small in number and the results may be to do with the coincidence of long periods of office for parties in government and structural shifts in the agenda. With this caveat in mind, there is a higher proportion of expenditure under Labour for the economy and government operations, and higher spending under the Conservatives for housing, but not much else, and even these differences do not represent the classic characterisation of the issues that parties of the left and right tend to attend to (Budge and Farlie 1983). The conclusion to draw is that the allocation of government spending to major budget items tend to be driven by long-term trends, such as increased dependence on social security due to unemployment, the rising cost of health care due to technological change and an ageing population, and declining international commitments creating less pressure on defence spending.

Where there have been decisions to change the proportion of spending, as with law and crime, both political parties have converged to a consensus in following a long-term trend rather than distinguish themselves on relative commitments to the policy domain, such as to defence, social spending or law and order.

Budgets and the wider policy agenda

As the previous two chapters discussed, we expect the policy agenda of government in different institutional agendas to be interconnected. In this section we explore the relationship of budgets to both speeches and laws. We also show figures about media attention to give a wider context. The public agenda series is driven by the dominant influence of attention to the economy that makes comparison with other issues quite hard, so we do not present the information here (but see Chapter 7 for a discussion of the correlations). In the analysis that follows we plot the level of spending on a particular topic and compare it against attention in the media, as well as legislation on the topic. We discuss the topics in the same order as before.

Figure 9.10 plots the proportion of spending on the macroeconomy. As other chapters have noted, the agendas in different institutional

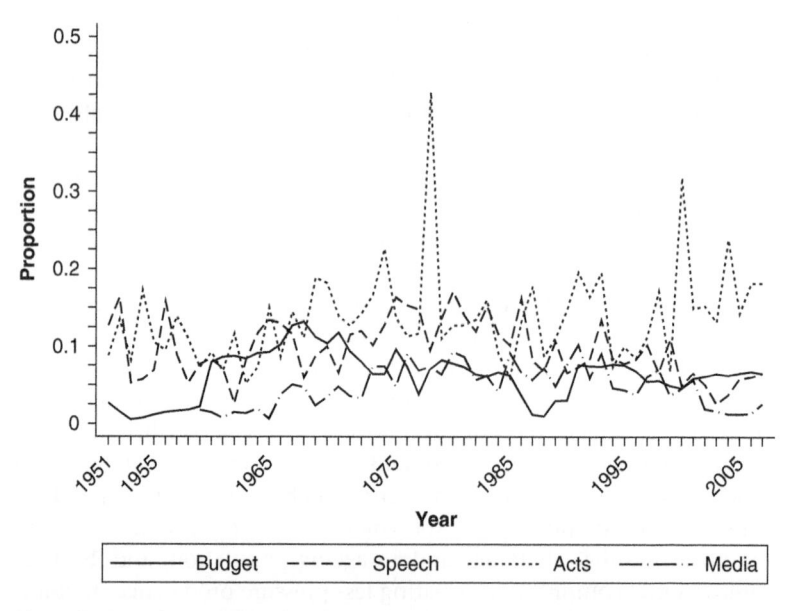

Figure 9.10 Policy agendas for the macroeconomy, 1951–2007

venues tend to move together, and this figure depicts a similar pattern overall, with a fall in the initial period after the Second World War, then a gradual rise and fall in attention to the economy. This is consistent with the general picture that we have observed elsewhere (Jennings *et al.* 2011a; John and Jennings 2010). However, it is clear that budgets have a slightly different trajectory where the changes are more pronounced in the immediate post-war period followed by a decline from 1975 to 1987. This suggests that while the attention of policy-makers to the economy increased over the 1970s and 1980s, attention to spending in the domain fell, perhaps as a result of a shift in the tools of government away from direct economic interventions (with the wave of nationalisations after the war contrasted with the wave of privatisations in the 1980s and 1990s).

The policy agenda for defence is shown in Figure 9.11. What is striking here is the gradual downward trend in defence spending as a proportion of total government expenditure when compared with the other defence policy agenda series, such as Acts of Parliament or the Speech from the Throne. The other series are either quite stable or subject to leaps in attention at specific points in time, especially for the media agenda, such as in the early 1980s (linked to the Falklands War), the early 1990s (the Persian Gulf War), and the mid-2000s (the Iraq and Afghanistan wars)

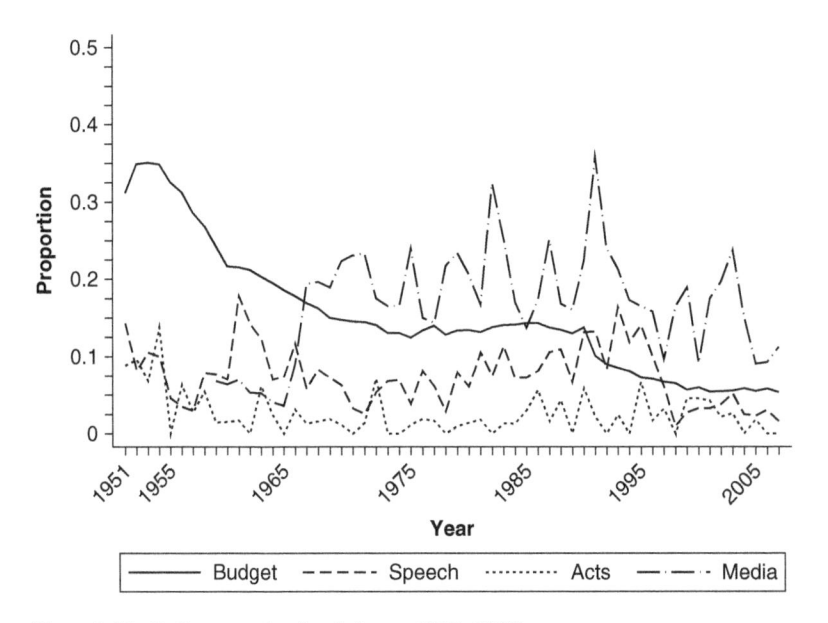

Figure 9.11 Policy agendas for defence, 1951–2007

that are not matched by changes in the defence budgets. This long-term decline in defence spending is the accumulation of decisions taken over many decades by Britain's policy-makers on the proportion of government spending allocated to defence, and may be seen as an expression of focused adaption to changes in priorities. This is only partly reflected by trends in the level of attention in the executive, legislative and media agendas.

The policy and media agendas for the issue of law and crime are plotted in Figure 9.12. What is striking is the way in which most of the agendas are stable up to the early 1990s, whereas the proportion of government spending on this topic rises steadily right across the period (albeit at a gradual rate). The major shift in the agenda occurred in the mid-1990s with the introduction of a large number of legislative measures on crime and a rise in the interest of the media (signalling an increase in societal and political attention to the issue of crime over this period, as discussed in Farrall and Jennings 2012). This increase in legislative attention dissipates after the first few years of New Labour (while remaining at quite a high level), but the number of media stories is subject to pronounced growth in 2004 and the years after. In comparison, government spending on law and crime has remained stable in

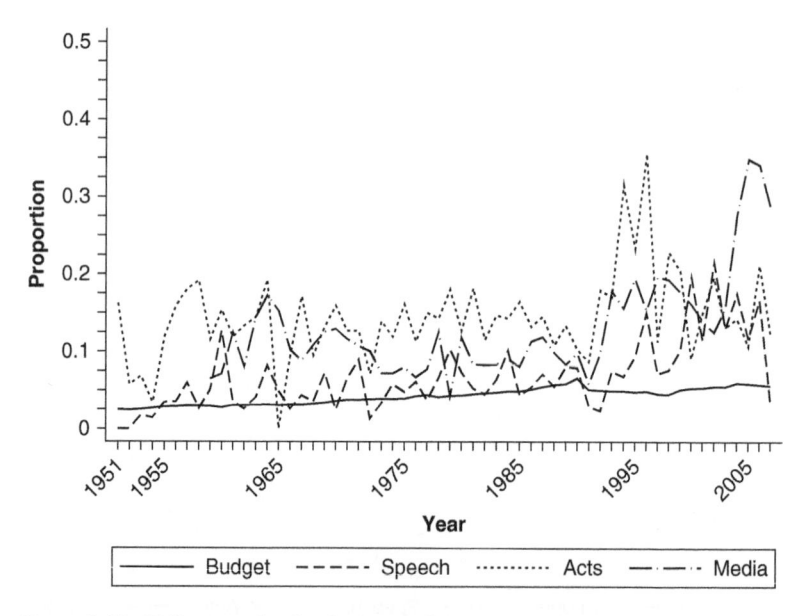

Figure 9.12 Policy agendas for the law and crime, 1951–2007

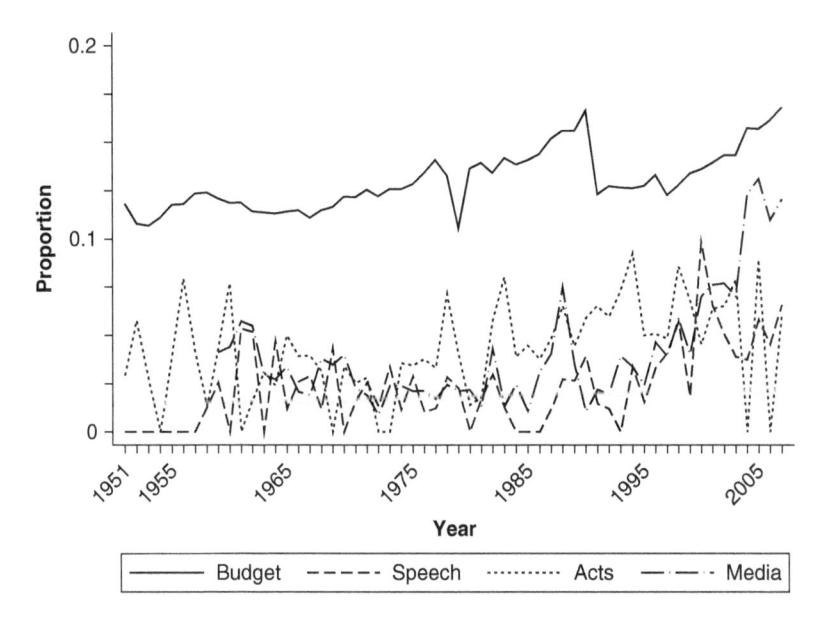

Figure 9.13 Policy agendas for health, 1951–2007

relative terms since 1990. The policy agenda was included in speeches and budgets, but did not appear to be connected to budget increases.

Figure 9.13 presents the proportion of the policy and media agendas assigned to the issue of health. While health is a major item of government spending, always equal to more than 10 per cent of total expenditure, attention to the issue in the other agendas usually amounts to less than 5 per cent of the agenda, at least prior to 1985. In the late 1980s there is a shift to increased attention to health for all the series—speeches, acts and media—as well as with budgets in spite of the dip in relative spending on health in 1991. It appears that this trend started well before New Labour took office (although it was vocal in emphasising the issue when in opposition under Blair and his predecessor John Smith), with inter-party competition over health that rose in prominence on the agenda as the 1990s proceeded. This reflected the emergence of distinct policy problems in the health domain, such as rising patient waiting lists and under-investment in the NHS. It was only in 1997, however, that spending on health started to rise in its share of total government expenditure. In part this reflects more general trends for attention to health in different venues to rise in a similar pattern across nations (Green-Pedersen and Wilkerson 2006).

186 *Policy Agendas in British Politics*

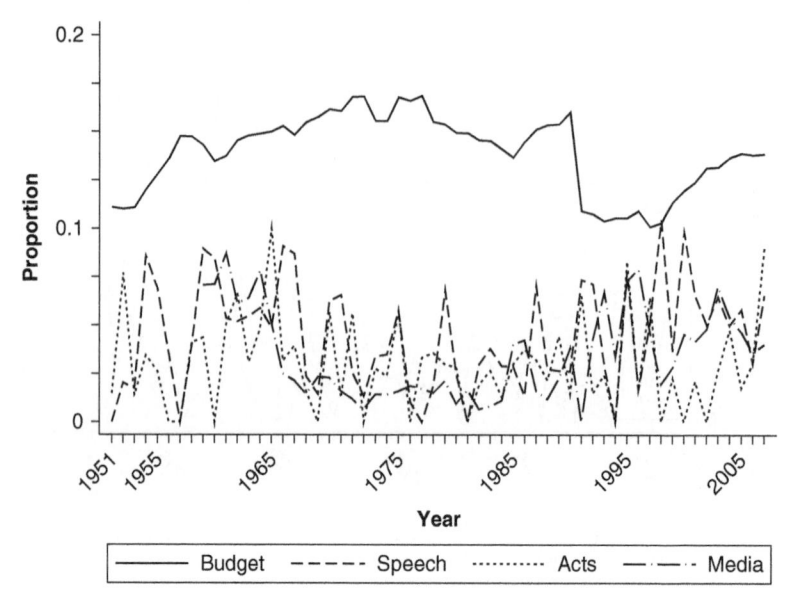

Figure 9.14 Policy agendas for education, 1951–2007

Education (Figure 9.14) shows another interesting pattern where different parts of the policy and media agenda move together over time, although the trend for spending appears quite distinct. There is a high point in the Speech from the Throne in the late 1950s leading up to the reforms of secondary education in the mid-1960s, after which attention declined and remained relatively stable until the 1990s. There was increasing attention of the policy and media agenda from the early 1990s as we have discussed. The proportion of spending on education is linked to these trends to the extent that there is a rise following the reforms of the 1960s; but education became less of a spending priority from the mid-1970s while attention in the other institutional venues increased. This downward trend in spending on education was not reversed until Labour took office in 1997.

Social welfare is the next major spending item, and this is reported in Figure 9.15. Similar to health and education, there is much less attention to this topic in speeches, acts and media than as a proportion of total spending. In fact, compared to the budgets of these large spending domains, the other agendas do not exhibit a clear trend. This is a domain where large changes are caused by pressures on these transfer budgets and efforts by core policy-makers to contain them, both of which may

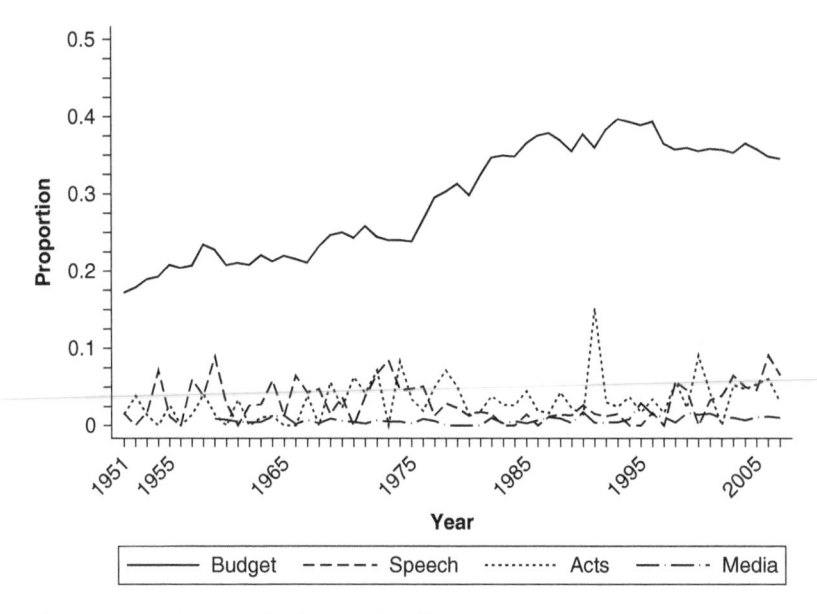

Figure 9.15 Policy agendas for social welfare, 1951–2007

be occurring independent of the policy agenda in other institutional venues and away from the attention of the media.

Housing, on the other hand (Figure 9.16), presents a complex picture where it is not clear (from visual inspection of the data at least) how the agendas relate to one another. This possibly could be due to the coding system's aggregation of specific policies within the housing major topic, as private and public housing issues might give rise to distinct patterns. It does appear that after the mid-1970s there has been much less attention to this topic in spite of it appearing on the legislative agenda on a regular basis, and a low level of interest from the media despite a spike in attention in 1997. Nonetheless, the long-term decline in spending on housing is unmistakable and a clear trend that covers the Labour government of 1974–1979, the Conservative government of 1979–1997 and extends to the New Labour government after 1997.

We now move to the infrastructure and environmental topics that tend to receive a lower proportion of attention and overall spending of government than other topics. Figure 9.17 plots the policy and media agendas for transport. Here, it is difficult to discern a clear pattern of correspondence between the agendas. The downward trend in government spending on transport, which is observable from the late 1960s, is

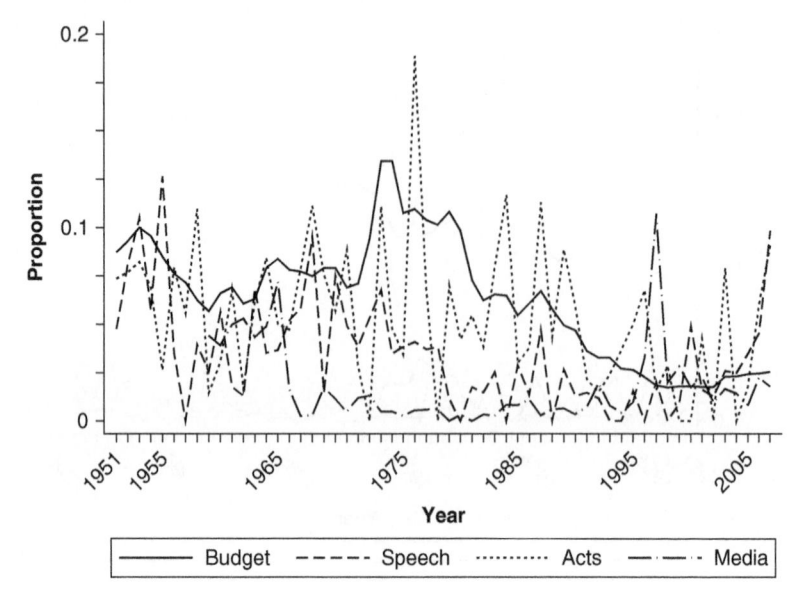

Figure 9.16 Policy agendas for community development, planning and housing issues, 1951–2007

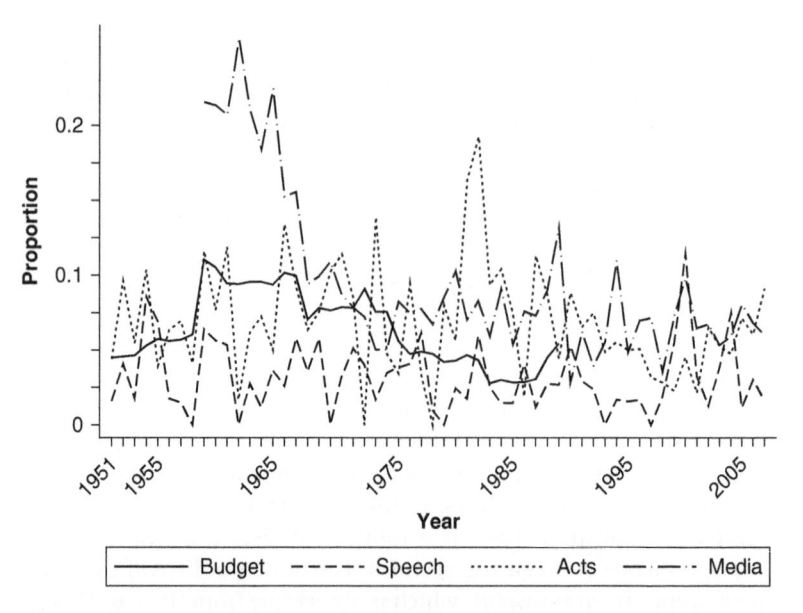

Figure 9.17 Policy agendas for transport, 1951–2007

countered by an increase in attention to transport in legislation. For the media agenda, the pattern of front-page headlines about transport has a number of peaks, having started out at high levels of salience in the 1960s. Whereas transport is an issue that can become prominent on the media agenda, spending in this domain has a more secular pattern.

Finally, we turn to the issue of agriculture, the agendas for which are shown in Figure 9.18. This topic exhibits a striking decline in attention across each of the agendas, most of all for budgets and speeches, but this trend is evident for all the institutional venues over the period 1945–1996. There are occasional periods of heightened attention to agriculture, with bursts of activity through Acts of Parliament, and the topic attracts higher levels of attention from the media in the mid-1980s and mid-1990s associated with food and health scares such as the BSE crisis. The overall trend is downward and then flat, however.

Policy punctuations in budgets

In Chapter 5 we discussed the presence of policy punctuations in the Speech from the Throne and Acts of Parliament, and the subsequent chapters on the media and public agenda reported the degree of kurtosis of those wider agendas. We can likewise examine the properties of the budget series, which is particularly appropriate given the work on

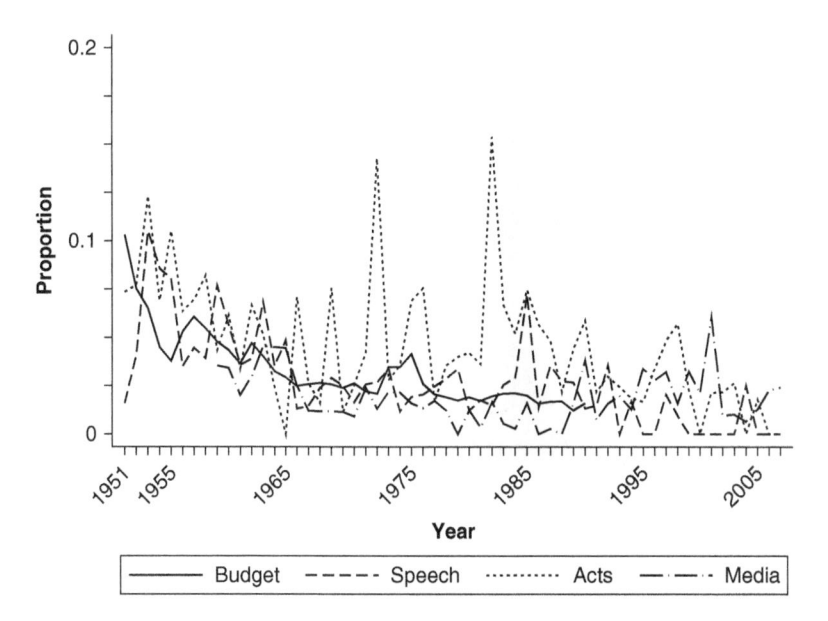

Figure 9.18 Policy agendas for agriculture, 1951–2007

patterns of policy change in budgeting in the US, the UK and other countries (e.g. Jones *et al.* 2009a). To do so, we use stochastic process methods to assess the distribution of year-on-year change in the budget categories of British government used here, for the period 1945–2007. This amounts to 637 observations that indicate the percentage change in the budget from one year to the next. The mean of 3.3 for the distribution of changes indicates that budgets increase over time with a standard deviation of 26.2, which is high. Overall, the distribution of budget change has a high kurtosis score of 58.8, consistent with a large amount of work on budgeting, not least earlier work on budgets in Britain (John and Margetts 2003; Soroka *et al.* 2006). This figure is also much higher than the kurtosis score of the change distributions of 8.8 for the Speech from the Throne and 25.6 for Acts of Parliament. The finding of leptokurtosis indicates the coexistence of an unusual number of large changes (outliers) with extended periods of stability, consistent with previous work on the policy agenda of British government (John and Jennings 2010). It is also possible to examine this pattern of change in attention with the frequency distribution plotted in Figure 9.19. This ordering of the degree of leptokurtosis across the agendas (Jones *et al.*

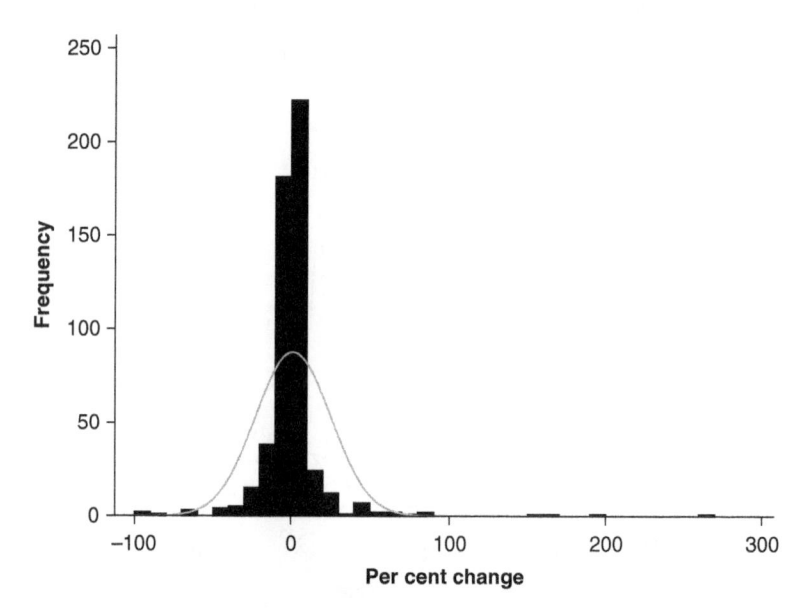

Figure 9.19 Frequency distribution of annual percentage changes in the Speech from the Throne and Acts of Parliament

2003) is consistent with Jones and Baumgartner's (2005a, 2005b) theory of disproportionate information-processing and institutional friction, which suggests there will be a higher frequency of large changes in policy (i.e. policy punctuations) the greater the institutional and cognitive resistance to change in decision-making. It is important to be cautious testing this claim in the UK context where it is relatively easy for national government to adjust spending. Budgets are passed through procedural legislation in the House of Commons, where the second chamber cannot challenge finance legislation. This is in contrast to other topics of legislation that can be more difficult to get past the second chamber and have been increasingly amended by the House of Lords. The provisions of budgets are rarely amended by the Opposition, reflecting the strength of the executive under the Westminster system.

As before it is useful to examine these periods of extreme policy change (i.e. policy punctuations) by identifying the shifts in attention, both negative and positive, which are greater than 200 per cent changes. These are reported in Table 9.2. For the budget series, there are only three major punctuations, all observed in macroeconomic issues.

In 1960, there is a large increase in attention to macroeconomic issues that reflects the rapid increase in importance of industrial policy at that time. During this period, British government increased the national debt so was increasing interest payments. The second and third punctuations were increases in attention to macroeconomic issues occurring after a long period of decreased attention to the economy, which had declined owing to sales of nationalised industries and other ways in which the Conservative government had reduced direct support to the British economy. These punctuations may therefore be considered as representing a correction back to levels at the start of the 1980s.

Structural changes

In earlier chapters we reported and discussed the likely change points that can be identified in each agenda, and budgets can be analysed and

Table 9.2 Policy punctuations in UK budgets, 1951–2007

Year	Topic	Proportion change (%)
1960	Economy	309.0
1989	Economy	204.9
1991	Economy	269.6

192 *Policy Agendas in British Politics*

Figure 9.20 Likely change points in budgetary expenditure

discussed in the same way. The summary of the method was presented in Chapter 5 and the results for change points in budgets are reported in Figure 9.20.

There are 14 change points in the budget series overall, compared to 15 possible shifts in speeches and 17 for laws, which puts it in the same range. However, because there are a smaller number of topics for the budget series, this represents a higher proportion of the possible number of change points in the series. As before, we observe change points right across the topics from the 1950s to the 2000s, but in fact there is only one change point in the 1950s for the economy and none in the 1960s. The changes appear in the 1970s, and then through the 1980s, with three change points found to occur in 1990 in the final year of the Thatcher government. So over time there has been a greater tendency for budgets to exhibit a probability of change, which may reflect the relative stability of public finances in the early post-war period of gradual growth, and then the more difficult decisions governments faced in the 1970s.

The change point in 1959 reflects some of the large changes in spending on the economy that were happening in that period, which had fallen to a very low proportion of total government expenditure in

1953 and 1954, and then had started to rise, reflecting a new interest of policy-makers in industrial policy. 1959 was the point at which spending on macroeconomic issues tipped from 2 per cent of total expenditure to 8 per cent in 1960. This is also one of the three greater than 200 per cent changes—a policy punctuation—in the budget series as discussed above.

The next change point in the budget series occurred in 1973 and relates to community development and housing, and is due to a large increase in spending in that year. This was caused by the housing reforms of the Conservative government, which were designed to target public resources to where they were needed, enacted through measures contained in the controversial Housing Finance Act 1972, even though the legislation was criticised at the time for penalising the poor (Campbell 1993, pp. 378–379). There was an expansion of expenditure on housing subsidies, partly as a result of charging market rents which meant that more public money had to be given to pay for them (Balchin 2002, p. 30). The second change point is in 1974 in the same domain and captures the drop in spending on housing to its previous level. The fiscal pressures of the 1970s led policy-makers to pursue large cutbacks in support for public housing that continued during the long period of Conservative government from 1979 to 1997. Just a year after the Conservative government in 1973 had sought to increase public investment in housing and community development, Labour returned spending on housing its previous level, marking the start of a long period of decline in spending on housing that has never been reversed.

The 1970s also saw a change point for social welfare in 1976, which was also when public finances were more constrained as for housing. However, as Figure 9.7 shows, 1975 marked the point when the share of public spending on social welfare increased rather than decreased. It is not clear why this year was important, as many of the reasons for the upswing were to do with long-term changes to the labour market and to the structure of the population. Clark and Dilnot (2002, p. 10) argue that it reflects 'huge increases in the numbers dependent on benefits—both because of a huge increase in unemployment (and non-employment more generally) and because of changes in the demographic structure, such as the increasing numbers of low-income lone parents'. One crucial factor is therefore that the unemployment rate started to rise around this time (continuing into the 1980s at high levels). The tipping point may have been induced by the favourable stance of the Labour government in its concordat with the trade unions, what was called the Social Contract agreed in 1975, whereby trade unions exchanged wage restraint in exchange for more employment protection, as introduced by the Employment Protection Act 1975, and also more generous benefits (Donoughue 2005, p. 177). At the same time the government improved benefits. The State Earnings Related Pension Scheme, which was a generous state supported benefit for pensions, was implemented under terms of the Social Security Pensions Act 1975, so may have contributed to the change, although the measure was only implemented in 1978. In later years, government would seek to control the rise in security spending with tighter controls over payments and means-tested benefits, but this only happened in the 1980s and did not contain the rising share of expenditure that welfare took up.

The 1978–1979 period marks a shift in health policy, which had a dip in prioritisation and then returned to a higher and rising proportion of spending after that period (as shown in Figure 9.5). Health was subject to strong cuts in the late 1970s, particularly in relation to capital spending (Greener 2008, p. 126; also see Bevan et al. 1980, p. 1, who note that the cuts in heath were not as acute as in education and housing). Rather than marking a turning point, the change points in health indicate a brief reversal of the trend of growth in health spending as a proportion of total expenditure.

There is a change point in housing spending in 1980. As we commented above, the early 1970s had seen the first turning point in expenditure on housing, followed by another later in the decade, but it appears that the early 1980s marked an acceleration in the decline of expenditure associated with the policy agenda of the Conservative government elected in 1979, which sought to increased private ownership of housing, such as in key legislation of the same year, the Housing Act 1980. This was the point where the cessation of government investment in council housing contributed to the fall in expenditure under this topic. Whereas housing took up about 5.5 per cent of general government expenditure (GGE) in the 1950s and 1960s, it had fallen to near zero by the end of the 1980s and only recovered to 1 per cent in the 1990s and 2000s (Clark and Dilnot 2002, p. 15).

The end of the 1980s identifies a change point in spending on law and crime in 1989, where the proportion of spending increased before it dropped a few years later in 1993. This may have reflected the end of a long period of growth in spending in the 1980s when policing received favourable treatment under the Conservative government elected in 1979. The change may have represented a correction, although expenditure continued to grow at a fast rate after this relative change in priorities. As Crawford et al. (2009, p. 27) note, 'Over the whole period 1978–79 to 2007–08 spending on POS as a share of national income fluctuated around a very gradual upward trend, increasing from 1.5 per cent in 1978–79 to 2.4 per cent in 2008–09.'

There are three change points in 1990, indicating that this was an important year for public spending, and may have reflected some shift in priorities with the change in Prime Minister and the end of the Cold War. With regard to the latter, there is a change point in defence spending in 1990. Although there was a rise in the percentage of expenditure on defence in 1990, there was also a large drop in 1991 and then in 1992 as the spending cuts started to bite following the *Options for Change* review of 1990 (HC Deb 25 July 1990, c 470–488 and *Statement on the Defence Estimates 1991: Britain's Defence for the 1990s*, Cm 1559, July 1991), which sought to restructure the armed forces and to reduce spending in the light of the reduced level of external threats, and reduced need for armed forces in West Germany. This seems a clear example of an external event prompting a shift in budgeting priorities, although within a context of a long-term trend of reductions in the share of spending allocated to defence.

The second change point in 1990 is identified for macroeconomic issues, and marks a period just before a long period of decline in spending on the economy, which parallels the long-term decline in attention to the economy from the 1990s onwards (up until 2008). This change point is still quite early in time and identified before the housing crash in 1991–1992 and the crisis of Britain's exit from the ERM in 1992, but it may have been that the economic signals were on their way after the long economic crisis of the 1960s–1980s was receding.

The third change point is observed for law and order, and represents the downswing we discussed above whereby spending rose in 1989, but then fell in subsequent years.

The final change point concerns health spending in 2003, which represents an acceleration of expenditure at that point in time. The Labour government first elected in 1997 had already increased expenditure on health faster than other areas, but it had commissioned the Wanless review, reported in 2002, to review its spending priorities. The review recommended large increases in spending on health based on predicted increases in demand, which the government subsequently delivered.

Conclusions

This chapter on budgeting has reviewed a different aspect of decision-making to that of a presentation of a programme in the Speech from the Throne or the passing of legislation, and one that is more detached from the worlds of public opinion and the media agenda. Budgetary decisions occur further down the implementation chain where there are particular pressures and constraints that affect prioritisation between issues, which are not as acute as for speeches and laws (i.e. while government finances are scarce there is less of a shortage of space in the Queen's Speech and in legislative timetabling). Budgets reflect particular considerations, such as the pressure of employment on social security, that are not so obviously connected to the formal agenda of decision-making. Or they may represent choices taken by the political and bureaucratic elite to manage change in a policy sector, which is again separate from media or parliamentary concern and such factors may not trouble speeches and legislation. The pressure to contain growth in spending on social security might be part of this pattern. Defence fits this too with the political wish to reduce spending over time, but where the end of the Cold War provided the political elite an opportunity to reduce commitments more rapidly. Health shows how successive governments have faced rising costs as a result of growing public expectations about service quality, an ageing population and growing costs of providing health care, which have been hard to contain.

In spite of these internal factors in the budgeting process, which tend to focus attention on decision-making in each discrete policy domain, there are close connections between budgeting and the wider policy and media agendas. The issues that British governments emphasise in the Speech from the Throne do tend to correspond to their subsequent spending decisions as we showed for defence, law and crime, health, housing and agriculture. Visual inspections of the series illustrate how they co-vary together over time, with media, speeches, acts and budgets trending together, at least for periods of time. For the economy, represented in Figure 9.10, we see this pattern of growth and decline of the series from 1960 to 2005, which can be observed across each of the agendas, although the decline in spending occurs earlier than the other venues. Whereas there is no detectable pattern for government operations for most of the post-war period, there is a shift late on where all the agendas rise together reflecting the increased attention of the New Labour government to constitutional affairs. There is a similar rise in the series for law and crime occurring from the mid-1990s, rather than 1997 as might have been expected. Health is subject to increased prominence on the agenda from the early 1980s after a stable pattern before then. There is even the similar pattern for education with an upswing at the end of the series from the early 1990s, but with expenditure following this trend in the 2000s rather than earlier. Just as some of these issues were rising on one agenda, they fell at the same time in another venue, such as for housing and agriculture. In other sectors there was more of a mixed story, with no close link for defence and social welfare, and no pattern for transport. One of the key messages of this chapter is that the link between budgets and the rest of the agenda both varies according to policy domain but also is contingent on a time period when the agenda started to shift, and where such changes were felt and fed back through all the institutional venues.

With such important changes occurring in each of the policy agendas it is not surprising that there are important moments of change in the agenda that do not tend to reflect the importance of last year's budget, but points in time when the trends become apparent and there is a turning point in the focus of government attention. In that sense, the strong pattern of change across the agendas presents a challenge to long-held wisdoms about budgeting in Britain and accounts of decision-making elsewhere. The claim in the work of Heclo and Wildavsky (1974), and later in Rose and Davies (1994) that budgets are constrained by the weight of past decisions and inheritance before policy choice is belied by these large changes, in particular in the role of the centre in driving relative choices in budgeting decisions, whether it is the impact of the spending cuts of the mid-1970s, the decision to contain spending in the 1990s, the defence review or the decisions to increase spending on health in the 2000s. Here were clear choices made by the political and administrative elites to change the course of public expenditure that shifted the balance of the budgetary agenda. In this way, we see budget changes reflecting those strategic priorities as decision-makers were responding to changed conditions, which can sometime lead to change points when the structure of prioritisation changes.

It is hard to detect partisan influences with the budget data presented here and our measures of it. Such an analysis would require a powerful set of statistical procedures and a need to implement strong assumptions about the data. Even then it could not resolve the counterfactual of what would have happened to spending on each issue if another party had been in power for the same period. Our best judgement is that the main partisan difference in the agenda is found in 1997 rather than at other points in time, and even that was not the case for all the series, but more spending for crime ($t = 4.5$), social welfare ($t = 2.4$), health ($t = 3.9$) and less spending for housing ($t = 6.6$), education ($t = 2.7$) and defence ($t = 4.6$). We need to be cautious in some assumptions because such differences may be attributed to long-term shifts across the agendas (especially those due to long-term structural shifts or changes) rather than the precise date that a party entered Downing Street. Nevertheless, it is remarkable how in many areas New Labour had a distinctive spending pattern to the rest of the series. Some of these trends can, however, be dated to earlier in the 1990s, which suggests that the key turning point in British politics and public policy of this era might come somewhere between the ejection of Margaret Thatcher from Downing Street and the election of Tony Blair (see John and Jennings 2010).

The method of testing for change points enables us to identify key moments of change, which sometime link to partisan concerns such as with health spending in 2003, and housing spending in the early 1970s and in the early 1980s (ironically both for Conservative governments), others reflected change and turning points, either from the pressure to increase expenditure, or to contain it, which would have been faced by either party when in power. So we observe key points in our series that reveal times when new parties in power wished to put their stamp on government, but more often when a combination of circumstances forced a change in direction in spending, either ending the post-war consensus over public policy or responding to upward pressures. These are not the result of the processes of punctuated equilibrium, but the result of responses to structural changes, captured by our concept of focused adaptation, where governments both moved with the times, but also changed course when the opportunities presented themselves. Such considerations take us to the larger conclusions of this book, which are addressed in the final chapter.

10
Conclusion

In this book, we have mapped out the policy agenda in Britain since 1945. Using the measurement strategy outlined in Chapter 3, we have established the topics of public policy that core decision-makers in British government decided to focus on. We know whether these policy topics appeared in policy programmes as communicated in the Speech from the Throne, were the subject of legislation in Parliament and were supported by budgetary decisions. We also understand the extent to which the public considered those same issues to be important, and the level of attention given to them in the national media. On this basis, we can depict the changes in the policy agenda across the different institutional venues of agenda setting in British politics. With these data we have gathered and analysed, we are able to understand why particular topics came into prominence at different points in time and why certain items declined or rose in importance over the long term.

One important contribution of the book is the effective application of the coding system of the Policy Agendas Project to key institutional venues of decision-making in British politics, as shown in the figures displayed in Chapter 4 for the Speech from the Throne and Acts of Parliament, and in Chapter 9 for budgets. We argue that the information that we present in the book is an accurate representation of the policies decision-makers in British government paid attention to. This concerns internal validity: the proportion of attention allocated to topics like defence, health, education and so on approximates to the priority governments actually devoted to those issues, and is not some artefact of the measurement and coding system. Examining the figures reported in Chapters 4 and 9 and mapping them onto what we know about histories of these policy domains show that most of the trends—the rise of different topics or their decline—are traceable to changes in policy that accounts of British politics and public policy have also documented. Even if these patterns are not obvious, it is possible to establish what they are by exploring the content of the speeches and the laws, or examining reasons for the changes in budgetary spending. In this way, not only do we replicate existing accounts of British politics and policy, we identify some patterns that are novel or at least are not so well known. With this scrutiny of the data, other analysts can be confident that we are measuring what we say we do.

In saying that we have represented the policy agenda of British politics and government since 1945, we need to be careful what we mean by this. We are not claiming that we have described the kind of intervention a policy is promoting, such as a particular law on standards in education or the restriction of immigration; nor do we ascertain what tools government used at particular points in time, such as taxation or regulation; nor do we do know the extent to which a measure in the Speech from the Throne or Act of Parliament is controversial or ideological—such as whether it introduces market mechanisms or promotes state intervention. Other measures can get at these attributes (see Bartle *et al.* 2010; Budge *et al.* 2001; Laver *et al.* 2002; McDonald and Budge 2005), which could be combined with the data on the policy agenda. The policy agenda does not constitute such things and should not be confused with them. In that sense, we are focused on a particular dimension of policy-making (see Hay and Farrall 2011, p. 44), the policy topics, which is the decision to be interested in health or crime as distinct features of activity, which measures to what extent the effort of government is focused on particular kinds of public problems. Thus, the changes we observe are about the prioritisation of issues. It is our claim, however, that the unique features of the Policy Agendas Project coding system and data allow us to provide a new lens for studying British politics and policy that would not be possible if we had included changes to the left and right.

We also emphasise that we are not tracing the whole of the decision-making agenda. There are other venues for decision-making in British government, such as for delegated legislation (Page 2001), budget speeches (Hakhverdian 2010), parliamentary debates and questions (Bertelli and Dolan 2009; John and Bevan 2012), and even venues that have not been studied yet, such as Cabinet minutes (when they become available for scrutiny under the 30-year rule), departmental documents and Select Committee reports. These venues have their own policy agendas that no doubt have distinct trends from those examined here. Nonetheless, we argue that the Speech from the Throne, the primary legislation passed in Parliament and budgetary spending are key components of decision-making—the core policy agenda of British government for each year. They are probably more important than other venues, especially given the power of the executive in Britain in the period since 1945. And it is the nature of executive prioritisation in the unique institutional environment of British politics that we wish to understand.

To get a sense of how key decision-makers approach policy-making, we reviewed different understandings about change in British politics and policy as set out by the leading scholars on British politics. These writers use the distinctive features of the British political system—the comparative lack of veto players, the control of government by a single party and the way in which power is delegated from Parliament to the Prime Minister and Cabinet—to make generalisations about the pace and character of policy-making. Broadly, there are two schools of thinking about these institutions, which draw radically different conclusions. One emphasises stasis and the stability of decision-making, while the other finds instability and protean policy-making. These approaches make inferences about the nature of Britain's governing institutions and are well founded in research. There is evidence for both propositions in case studies and some quantitative analysis. However, most studies tend to oversimplify these trends, partly because they do not use data that comprehensively cover all policy domains. Our data permit examination of these propositions more thoroughly than before.

Most existing studies of British politics and policy do not encompass the way in which decision-makers are alert to the current balance of problems and seek to craft a strategy to respond to them. Political leaders want to pursue a policy agenda that responds to rapid changes in the pressures facing them, which allows them to promote their priorities. They seek to find and seize opportunities at certain points in time. In short, we expect some periods of stability, but also bursts of change and adaption. In this way, our approach has some similarities with punctuated equilibrium as developed by Baumgartner and Jones (1993, 2009). Our perspective is distinctive, however, as becomes apparent in the empirical analysis presented in the book. In Chapter 1, after reviewing three major theories of agenda setting—incrementalism, the issue attention cycle and punctuated equilibrium—we set out a new approach we call focused adaptation, which is designed to elucidate the change points in the policy agenda and which we test in this book. Focused adaptation is rooted in a re-election-seeking government that has institutional levers for attending to policy domains. It posits a landscape of policy problems that concern voters that government searches to identify its characteristics, a search which includes information about mass and elite views of policy priorities. Given the fruits of its search, government allocates attention to reflect what it has learned. Search and adaptation continues in an iterative manner, and populates the policy agenda with topics as it proceeds. We think the classic approaches do not fully resolve the question of when and why does the policy agenda change or stay stable, which is the perennial question that every student of public policy asks.

So what do we find? The main finding is that the agenda of British politics and government is not stable. There are large changes in policy prioritisation during the post-war period, some of which are dramatic. The claim that there is stable issue processing or that there is a strict hierarchy of policy issues, which reflects the way in which certain policy topics are embedded in the routines and power structures of the central state, does not hold, at least with the policy agenda. We show that the topics a previous generation of political scientists deemed very important, or even essential for the management of the state and its constituencies, have dropped off the decision-making agenda or have been relegated in their importance. Consider defence, which was integral to the functioning of the state and the role of Britain in the world; but successive governments have decreased their attention to it. Similarly, territorial management, which is about the state and its relations to other territories, has also declined in prominence. Agriculture, which represented the interests of a key constituent and pressure group, a classic case study for the research on lobbying and policy communities (Grant 1995; Smith 1990, 1992), has fallen out of fashion.

The policy agenda of British government now embraces new topics, such as civil rights, which have emerged from a very low level of salience during the 1950s and 1960s to be an important aspect of policy-making. Law and crime did not overly preoccupy governments in the decades following the Second World War, but since the 1990s has leapt up the policy agenda. The same holds for health. Other topics tend to rise and fall on the agenda as the challenges facing the state change, such as relating to the economy or to demographic change. The significance of these changes in the policy agenda should not be understated. They are not empty rhetorical speeches and tactical presentations of government activity to deal with the problems of the day. Policy priorities have real costs in the form of credible commitments to policies, the amount of resources committed to the bureaucratic machinery of government, taking up time in Parliament and committing real levels of public spending. The changes in the policy agenda across each of the institutional venues impose costs and benefits for the government of the day, and fundamentally affect the amount of benefits that members of the policy communities around each topic receive.

In this way, we seek to challenge the conclusions of earlier scholars of public policy who argued that policy was stable for long periods of time because of the way in which interest groups locked in policy-making. The idea that policy always moves incrementally or tends back to equilibrium as implied by the work of Richardson and Jordan (1979), and of Heclo and Wildavsky (1974), does not appear to be the case, although issue attention cycles appear to be present in a variety of policy topics. Most of all, the claim of those who examined British policy-making over time, such as Rose and Davies (1993), who stated that policy programmes are set in place for many years to come—inherited and hard to alter—is not sustained here. This finding applies as much to budgets as it does to speeches and laws.

In some ways our findings are consistent with those of Baumgartner and Jones in the US: that periods of policy stability are followed by feedback and rapid change. Indeed, it is possible to find examples from our data on the policy agenda that conform to the expectations of punctuated equilibrium. If we examine the topic of government operations, plotted in Figure 4.4, there does appear to be nearly two decades of stability until the 1990s followed by rapid change in attention under New Labour. So too with law and crime, which rapidly gained the attention of policy-makers in the 1990s. Not all the changes across the policy agenda conform to this pattern, however. Consider the macroeconomy, for example, where there are gradual shifts in attention excepting a few issue attention cycles when attention rose and then fell away the year after. Even though the policy agenda for health in Figure 4.6 contains large leaps, it is possible to observe a gradual rise in attention over the period since the 1980s. Education is quite similar in that respect. In fact, for many policy topics there has been a gradual shift in priorities as parties have become alert to those issues, and governments have altered their portfolios of policies in response.

In the language of public policy scholarship, this is consistent with incrementalism, which can encompass change over time through gradual adjustments (Lindblom 1979), sometimes called disjointed incrementalism. The policy agenda for some other topics seems to be at a stable level with occasional bursts of activity, such as is the case for the environment, energy, banking and science (space, telecommunications and communications), which is consistent with the issue attention model. Indeed, Downs (1972) used the environment as the main example for his analysis. Visual inspection of the graphs in Chapter 4 shows how few policy topics conform to the punctuated model, at least in its pure form, where there is a long period of stability interrupted by a large break. What is striking is the diverse pattern of shifts in attention and the different trends and fluctuations that occur, and how trade-offs between issues are managed. This is because of the particular pressures and problems of each sector that generate pressures and change throughout the whole agenda; and it also reflects an approach by policy-makers who seek to anticipate and plan for such changes rather than simply react to them.

The reality is that neither too much nor too little attention is allocated to a particular topic. In this sense, the picture of constrained policy-making in the classic accounts of British public policy is not supported, but neither is the more recent focus on unconstrained leaps and lurches in policy that has increasingly appeared in the literature (Butler et al. 1994; Dunleavy 1995). In fact, all policy topics exhibit elements of stability and change that reflect the exigencies of external factors and the strategies through which government manages those pressures. With such competing considerations at work, it is entirely plausible that the executive, when guiding the ship of state, generates variations in attention that are observable across the policy agenda (Bertelli and John n.d). These strategies of managing the wider environment lead to structural changes in the agenda, where decision-makers adapt to the changing circumstances they face by shifting the level of attention to a new path.

This is the pattern of focused adaptation, where there are certain points in time when a change in direction becomes desirable and policy-makers push it through. We contrast this to the process of incrementalism where there are step-by-step changes, to the issue attention cycle where changes nearly return to equilibrium and to punctuated equilibrium where there are large leaps in attention that persist. Though there are some random walks as in energy policy, some issue attention cycles, and some genuine punctuations in the policy agenda, most of the change points are in fact elements of the focused adaptation process, which is about how policy can go in a new direction in a way that is planned and strategic.

To understand policy change in Britain, we need to read or re-read the works of previous generation of scholars who understood the strategic approach of Britain's ruling elite to coping with the problems of governing. Examples include Bulpitt's (1986, 1988) notion of statecraft, Birch's

(1964) account of responsible government and Dunsire's (Dunsire 1986, 1993) cybernetic approach, which is about managing a complex system with feedback. When seen in these ways, the trends in the policy agenda are a function of a strategy to manage risk to maintain the programme of government and the interests of the state. Such considerations have inspired another book project that considers a policy attention marketplace in which governments invest in policies to achieve returns that have electoral consequences (Bertelli and John n.d).

The implication of the findings of this book is that scholars of public policy could reconsider or adapt the framework and methods of punctuated equilibrium. This is not because the approach is wrong, or that there are not some policy changes that conform to this pattern. Tests on the distribution of policy changes are valuable and produce important insights about the extent to which changes in the series are distributed evenly or exhibit disproportionately sudden shifts. We have conducted tests for the normality of our data on changes in the policy agenda and each venue is leptokurtic, as the punctuated equilibrium model suggests. Moreover, the hierarchy of kurtosis scores for agenda venues is as expected, with venues subject to greater institutional friction, such as budgets, exhibiting a greater frequency of large shifts in attention, compared with speeches and laws.

There are limits to what can be generalised from this kind of analysis in that the large average leaps in the policy agenda may be short-run bursts of attention that then die down. To enhance the measurement of policy punctuations, we develop a typology of different kinds of large changes in public policy that are capable of distinguishing between changes in attention, and isolating about half of them as major changes in policy, which we ascertain by an examination of the historical record. Our conclusion is that—on its own—the aggregate method does not comprehensively capture the variability and complexity of policy change. The method of Baumgartner and Jones can be complemented by other means of interrogating the data on the policy agenda. In fact there is no substitute for examining the policy agenda for each topic and discovering the underlying details of the changes in attention therein. In some ways, this brings the study of public policy full circle to the approach that Baumgartner and Jones were reacting against when developing punctuated equilibrium for contemporary decision-making.

In addition, we enlist a statistical method for analysing the policy agendas data, change point analysis, which is suited to identifying the timing of shifts in the process generating the policy agenda. We argue in Chapter 1 that such changes are the result of a search-and-revise process undertaken by governments called focused adaptation. This statistical analysis is not dependent on the identification of a single large shift, although some policy punctuations are, of course, identified as structural changes. Change points are a way of demarking one era from another, such as a shift in government operations in 1996 which presaged New Labour's preoccupation with the topic in its constitutional reforms, or the shift in acts on crime in the same year which represented the starting point of the unusually active period of legislation on crime under New Labour. For budgets, the change points identify important break points, such as the changes in spending for defence in 1990 or in social welfare in 1996.

These change points often reflect the presence of particular problems or pressures in each topic, such as the end of the Cold War that affected the defence budget in 1990. They also reflect partisan concerns, such as the emphases that particular governments place upon topics, such as New Labour's reforming programme. We find that partisanship is a theme behind some movements in the policy agenda, and one that partly explains their shape and the change points. In contrast to some accounts of party preferences in policy (e.g. Alesina *et al.* 1997; Castles 1982), we find it less important in accounting for the level of attention across the topics, the occurrence of policy punctuations or of change points. This finding conforms to comparative research on the impact of parties on policy agendas (Mortensen *et al.* 2011) and to our own (John *et al.* n. d.). There are eleven punctuations in the speech in election years when one would expect a leap in attention, but this is not different from other periods during a Parliament. Structural breaks do not coincide with election years either.

More generally, the impact of a new party taking power can be evidence of a particular approach to reform. The best example of this is the record of New Labour, which brought a particular approach to policy-making by emphasising new issues, such as social welfare and constitutional reform, and paying greater attention to health and education in a programme of government. New Labour emerged from the shift of the policy agenda that had started to take shape in the 1990s and was less a government wishing to stress traditional Labour-owned issues than it was a government that sought to combine some of those new issues to create a novel and modernising programme of polices which would sustain it in power. The result is that it paid more attention to labour issues, and less to international affairs and defence. This makes it the most distinctive government in its policy agenda for the post-war period.

In spite of the distinctiveness of New Labour's approach to government, it was one that emerged more as a consequence of long-running changes in the policy agenda and the opportunities it presented for political parties to manage, rather than the imposition of a particular approach to policy-making at the point of election. In our data on the content of the policy agenda, we observe that changes in the environment of British policy-making structured the choices it made. Many of the opportunities that New Labour grasped were already happening in the 1990s under the government of John Major, such as the rise in attention to crime in the speeches. The decline in the attention to the economy and foreign policy gave policy-makers the opportunity to attend to other issues. What distinguishes New Labour is that it understood this and pushed it further than perhaps another government would have done. It thus represents a good example of focused adaptation. At the end of the New Labour period, this opportunity receded as government became preoccupied once again with the economy.

As well as partisan considerations, the policy choices of governments are affected by the institutional context within which they operate. In Chapter 2, we find it hard to infer the impact of the institutional structure of British government on the style of policy-making. The same description of British institutions as unitary, lacking veto players and with control of government by single disciplined parties can generate both stability as these governments lock in change to ensure the basic hierarchy of issues remains in place, or instability as untrammelled governments generate policy changes, the lurches in attention envisaged in the punctuated equilibrium model. In this book we suggest that both accounts are not supported. However, at the same time it might be consistent with the trends in our data that some of the same institutional contours have changed, such as the increased complexity of policy-making, the openness of government, the speed of information processing in the media, the numbers of interest groups, the different levels of decision-making at the EU-level and in regional government, what may be described as reflecting the movement from government to governance (Rhodes 1997). This may have influenced the numbers of issues on the policy agenda and the speed with which policy changes, probably slowing it down as the discretion of the central executive is thought to fall.

The picture of change over time is mixed. In terms of the tendency to large shifts in the agenda, there is no pattern. If we consider the numbers of punctuations, we find a clustering in the 1950s, not the usual period that political scientists and historians consider important.

For the policy punctuations in the speeches there is an even pattern of change across the decades. Change point analysis again finds the 1950s to be prominent, with a decline in the 1960s and 1970s, and fresh volatility in the 1990s. What appears to be happening is neither greater stability nor instability but cycles as the policy agenda moves ahead and policy-makers respond to the emergence of new sets of problems.

Some of the changes in British politics may, indeed, alter policy-making, in particular, the decline of party unity and the increase in parliamentary rebellions (Cowley 2002; Cowley and Stuart 2012). It may be the case that changes in British politics will make it harder for governments to stick to policy programmes and reduce the power of the central executive, which has been responsible for the changes in the policy agenda we observe over the post-war period. The constitutional changes introduced by New Labour have effectively created new veto players in British politics, such as an independent judiciary and constitutionally entrenched devolved governments. These changes build on the pooling of sovereignty with the institutions of the EU that has grown since 1973, which constrain executive choice. However, even in the period since 2010, much of the traditional framework of decision-making is still in place, with the Coalition Agreement taking the place of the single-party manifesto, and where party discipline ensures the implementation of that agreement, at least in the main. Speeches from the Throne continue even if given at a different time of the year; laws get passed even if they are amended more often, and the budget cycle continues in spite of reversals. In that sense, the management of the policy agenda remains much the same for the time being, displaying some of the key features of the British executive. As the twenty-first century proceeds, we expect the policy agenda to continue to display many of the same trends and patterns that we observe in the years since 1945.

Notes

Preface and Acknowledgements

1. http://www.britishpoliticalspeech.org/speech-archive.htm?speech=202. Note the judicious or clever use of the word 'main'.

1 The Policy Agenda and British Politics

1. This claim is very similar to the common agency theory of special interest politics if one repeats the static implications to generate dynamic predictions. See Grossman and Helpman (2001); Bertelli and Lynn (2004).
2. For much of the period they take place in November or early December. But one is needed straight after a general election, which is often in early May, making a June speech a common occurrence, and then there is an 18-month gap until the next one. Occasionally, there are two speeches in a year, such as the two elections and speeches of 1974, and some special sessions and speeches, as in 1947. Since 2010, the coalition government has broken with tradition: it had one speech in June 2010 and then waited until June 2012 until the next one, timings that reflect the fixed-term Parliament.
3. The Cabinet used to make minor amendments to the speech, such as when it discussed the speech on 23 October 1973, recommending adjustments in the light of fast-moving events in the Middle East and to ensure that housing reforms were not pre-empted (Cabinet Minutes, 23 October 1973, item 2).
4. Because of the ancient method of production, it takes about a week for the ink to dry on the vellum. Otherwise, changes to the content could be made up to the day of the speech itself.

2 Policy-Making and British Politics

1. See Bulpitt (1986), Marsh (1995), Kerr (2001) and the review by Hay (2007). A discussion of different periodisations of the Thatcher government appears in Hay and Farrall (2011).

3 Measuring the Policy Agenda: Policy, Public and Media in Britain

1. The data are stored in the UK Data Archive at Essex. The catalogue record created for the data collection can be viewed at the following URL: http://www.esds.ac.uk/findingData/snDescription.asp?sn=6974& key=/&flag=true.
2. http://www.policyagendas.org/page/datasets-codebooks#codebook.

3. See http://www.comparativeagendas.info for more details, including a list of projects from each country and further website links.
4. The majority of these modifications of the coding system for the UK occur at the sub-topic level, which is not used for the analyses presented in this book. These include the addition of a sub-topic relating to fisheries (under the agriculture major topic) and a sub-topic for the monarchy entitled The Monarchy, Royal Family Issues and British Nobility. There are two changes that affect allocation to the major topics where we allocate terrorism to defence and immigration under civil rights. The complete details of these changes are included in the topic codebook available on the project website (www.policyagendas.org.uk) as well as in the online appendix to the book. Users of the dataset are free to make new combinations of the sub-topics as they see fit and the recording of the data allows this.
5. In addition, the project coded Prime Minister's Questions (PMQs) 1997–2008, but they were not used for this book, but see Bevan and John (n.d).
6. Krippendorff (2004, p. 241) indicates that an alpha of 0.8 and above might be used as a guideline (see also Mikhaylov *et al.* 2012, p. 85), which approximates to 85 per cent inter-coder agreement (for two coders using a 19 topic coding framework). This guideline must, however, 'be related to the validity requirements imposed on the research results' (Krippendorff 2004, p. 242), and in our case does not mean that the reliability of the final data is coded at a level of accuracy of 80 per cent better than chance. Instead, the level of data reliability is further enhanced through systematic cross-checks and recodes by the project leaders. As well as checking those cases where there were disagreements between coders, additional cases were also checked to ensure there were no systematic misclassifications (as systematic error poses a greater concern than random error). This process means that the final level of data reliability is well above 95 per cent, and the availability of the data means that the coding can be replicated and validated by other researchers. The full details of the coded materials are reported on the project website, www.policyagendas.org.uk.
7. For the public opinion chapter we use calendar year data due to the use of exogenous variables that have this time period.
8. This average becomes 59.8 if the 1948 special short session that was focused on the passage of what later became the 1949 Parliament Act is excluded from this calculation.
9. In rare cases, Henry VIII clauses in Acts of Parliament allow for the amending of acts directly through statutory instruments. These clauses are generally quite controversial.
10. With one notable exception, the MIP/MII categories do not match a single major topic code. The Ipsos-MORI MII data includes a category that refers to 'defence, foreign affairs and international terrorism'. Whereas defence and terrorism are coded under major topic 16 (Defence), foreign affairs is covered by major topic 19 (International Affairs). Because MII responses cannot be disaggregated, this MII category is coded under major topic 16. As a consequence, the MII series for major topic 19 consists of responses about Europe but does not include responses about foreign affairs. In some circumstances, then, it may be necessary to merge these defence and international affairs MIP/MII series. In this book we do not aggregate these topics in order to make the analysis of public opinion consistent with other agendas.

11. Because the final year of Gallup MIP data is incomplete and cannot be reliably imputed it has been excluded from the series (it therefore runs from 1960 to 2000).
12. For a more detailed exposition and methodological analysis of the relationship between Gallup's MIP and Ipsos-MORI's MII measures, see the work of Jennings and Wlezien (2011).
13. While a set transition point makes some sense, to establish the clear change in responses across all issues in the transition year means that other analyses sensitive to change in the transition year can be affected. Therefore, multiple points must be tested in order to confirm the robustness of the results. It is important to reiterate that these are, however, different series and that the use of a break point must be accounted for in the model or graphical analysis in order to account for the differences between the MIP and MII series.
14. The decision to sample this specific day of the week was designed to calibrate the timing of data on the media agenda with data on PMQs, which was held on Wednesdays after 1997, the period for which the UK Policy Agendas Project collected data on PMQs.
15. The use of headlines instead of the complete text of newspaper stories was a practical decision based on available resources and the complexity of the data-collection process. However, an in-depth pilot comparing the coding of complete stories versus headlines alone showed that in more than 90 per cent of cases the major topic codes assigned matched when coding the complete stories or headlines alone. The majority of disagreements between these two techniques occurred in non-policy topics such as arts, history, culture and entertainment (28) or sports and recreation (29) where more ambiguous headlines were often used.
16. Several major topic codes such as weather (26), fire (27) and human-interest stories (34) were added to the codebook to cover all the non-policy-related stories covered by the media. These additions follow the strategy employed by the US Policy Agendas Project's *New York Times Index* dataset.
17. A break in this dataset occurred from December 1978 to November 1979 due to striking and this break is discussed in detail in the subsection below.
18. 'News' stories included before the first full page of 'News' in the paper are also included in the dataset, leading to a slight over-sampling in this period occurring largely at random based on the amount of other front-page attention.
19. The shutdown of *The Times* was not unique with the paper itself reporting on the striking and shutdowns of numerous other papers up until its own shutdown.

4 Change and Stability in Executive and Legislative Agendas

1. 'Under this Government, Britain will not return to the boom and bust of the past', Pre-Budget Report, 9 November 1999, and similar statements in the pre-budget report of 8 November 2000, and budget statements of 21 March 2000, 7 March 2001, 22 March 2006 and 21 March 2007.
2. There are private providers in primary and secondary education, with independent (non-state) schools making up around 10 per cent of

pupils in the sector. Universities in Britain are largely state-funded, however.
3. Official state visits of the monarch are reported in the Speech from the Throne. On average, one or two visits are mentioned in the executive section per speech. This consistent number of mentions means that state visits do not affect the variance of attention to international affairs.
4. These are coded as relating to the administration of devolved government both because they are required by the differentiated legal systems of the countries and to avoid double-counting of legislation of issues when the primary purpose of the legislation was to replicate the same policy measure that had already been put in place in the UK Parliament in Westminster.
5. These results are for proportions of attention, but the results are normally much the same with unbounded raw measures. Nonetheless, the same point applies: that if attention falls for one topic, this gives an opportunity to increase attention to another.

5 Policy Punctuations

1. Kurtosis is the fourth moment around the mean (where variance and skew are the second and third moments). This is a measure of the relative 'peakedness' of a given distribution.
2. Note that for the Speech from the Throne and Acts of UK Parliament, cases in which attention to a particular topic remains stable at zero are treated as missing to avoid over-inflation of the kurtosis scores (which could lead to false acceptance of theoretical hypotheses) due to empirical redundancy of some topic codes under certain circumstances.
3. Friction conveys the extent to which the institutional rules make it easy or difficult for decisions to be made, such as by having veto players, for example. In this case, it is assumed the greater difficulty of getting policy through the legislature as opposed to a speech amounts to more friction. Greater friction causes a more punctuated pattern of policy change because there is an overreaction to periods when policy is slowly moving. There is, however, not likely to be that much friction in the UK legislature because of largely unified party voting, which is in contrast to other political systems.
4. The later part of this chapter draws from John and Bevan (2012).
5. This is calculated as: $Y = [(X_t - X_{t-1})/X_{t-1}] \times 100$.
6. The coding system, of course, plays a role in the creation of procedural punctuations. For example, in the case of the UK Policy Agendas Project both education and the arts end up in the same category, leading to several procedural punctuations focused on minor changes to educational and arts policy. Other procedural punctuations have less to do with the coding system though and more to do with attention to similar, but unrelated policy. For example, refinements to the mental health system and to the system for treating tuberculosis are both clearly health issues and it is government or events that caused the two issues to collide producing a procedural punctuation as attention to both issues clearly follow different causal processes.
7. This is calculated as: $Y = [(X_t/Z_t) - (X_{t-1}/Z_{t-1})]/(X_t/Z_t) \times 100$.

8. Using other cut-off points can logically change the results. For example, lower thresholds such as a cut-off of 150 per cent leads to a greater number of both procedural and low-salience punctuations, but no additional high-salience punctuations. A lower threshold is therefore inappropriate. Higher cut-offs such as 300 per cent lead to similar decreases in all three types of punctuations. Combined, these alternative cut-offs suggest that 200 per cent is an appropriate and consistent cut-off point.
9. The identification of procedural policy punctuations was completed through a qualitative analysis of the acts that comprise each one. When unrelated policy areas within major topics were found, with no single policy area large enough to be recognised as a punctuation in its own right, it was classified as procedural. No procedural punctuations occur when more than four acts were passed on a major topic.

6 Structural Shifts in British Political Attention

1. Our approach to treating change points is Bayesian (Barry and Hartigan 1993; Erdman and Emerson 2007, 2008; see also Western and Kleykamp 2004).
2. We consider structural shifts at least one year into our series so that we do not base changes solely on data that overwhelm our prior selections.
3. Two elections were held in 1974. We estimated the probability of a change point in each legislative session beginning with the Speech from the Throne as a separate unit of time. The indicated change point is in association with the Parliament opened on 12 March 1974.
4. 19 November 1967.

7 Public Opinion and the Policy Agenda

1. Note that the MII portion of our measure of public attention to defence in Figure 7.1 also includes MII responses relating to foreign affairs, which cannot be disaggregated (for the period 1980–2008). The MII portion of public attention to international affairs in Figure 7.3 therefore only includes MII responses on Europe (1980–2008). After the Gallup MIP data ends in 2000, most public attention to foreign affairs is therefore incorporated in the defence topic.
2. The Pearson correlation between public opinion and the executive agenda for macroeconomics is 0.69 ($p \leq 0.001$), civil rights and immigration 0.39 ($p \leq 0.01$), health 0.58 ($p \leq 0.001$), labour and employment 0.34 ($p \leq 0.05$), education 0.41 ($p \leq 0.01$), environment 0.51 ($p \leq 0.001$), law and crime 0.52 ($p \leq 0.001$), public lands and territorial issues 0.25 ($p \leq 0.10$), agriculture −0.29 ($p \leq 0.05$) and foreign trade −0.30 ($p \leq 0.05$).
3. The Pearson correlation between public opinion and the legislative agenda on health is 0.43 ($p \leq 0.01$), law and crime 0.30 ($p \leq 0.05$), public lands and territorial issues 0.42 ($p \leq 0.01$), agriculture −0.30 ($p \leq 0.05$), foreign trade −0.36 ($p \leq 0.05$) and welfare −0.32 ($p \leq 0.05$).
4. The Pearson correlation between public opinion and budgetary spending on health is 0.67 ($p \leq 0.001$), education 0.41 ($p \leq 0.01$), environment 0.40 ($p \leq 0.01$), law and crime 0.72 ($p \leq 0.001$), macroeconomic issues −0.34

($p \leq 0.05$), agriculture −0.32 ($p \leq 0.05$), welfare −0.33 ($p \leq 0.05$) and housing −0.25 ($p \leq 0.10$).
5. The Pearson correlation between public opinion and the media agenda on macroeconomics is 0.70 ($p \leq 0.001$), civil rights and immigration 0.61 ($p \leq 0.001$), health 0.55 ($p \leq 0.001$), agriculture 0.45 ($p \leq 0.01$), education 0.53 ($p \leq 0.001$), environment 0.60 ($p \leq 0.001$), transportation 0.74 ($p \leq 0.001$), law and crime 0.74 ($p \leq 0.001$), housing 0.50 ($p \leq 0.001$), foreign trade −0.34 ($p \leq 0.05$), defence −0.34 ($p \leq 0.05$) and international affairs −0.52 ($p \leq 0.001$).
6. It is not possible to examine the public agenda for all years because of the large amount of zeros in the data on the MIP (because the public agenda tends to be focused on a smaller number of issues, so issues can remain off the agenda for a long period of time), so some series are estimated over slightly shorter periods of time.

8 The Media

1. Namely defence, foreign trade, and international affairs and foreign aid.
2. See Table A8.1 in the Appendix 8A for a complete list of major topic codes used in the media dataset.
3. To account for this, a binary variable indicating if the UK, through its citizens or government, was directly involved in a story (coded 0) or not (coded 1) was created with the default assumption being that a story involved the UK (coded 0).

9 Budgets and Policy Implementation

1. Governments often fund unforeseen military commitments from the Contingencies Fund that do not appear in the functional spending figures.

References

Addison, P. (1982) *The Road to 1945* (London: Quartet Books).
Adler, E. S. (2002) 'New issues, new members: committee composition and the transformation of issue agenda on the House banking and public works committees' in F. Baumgartner and B. Jones (eds.) *Policy Dynamics* (Chicago, IL: Chicago University Press).
Adler, E. S. and J. Wilkerson (2013) *Congress and the Politics of Problem Solving* (Cambridge: Cambridge University Press).
Alesina, A., N. Roubini and G. Cohen (1997) *Political Cycles and the Macroeconomy* (Cambridge, MA: MIT Press).
Alexandrova, P., M. Carammia and A. Timmermans (2012) 'Policy punctuations and issue diversity on the European Council agenda', *Policy Studies Journal*, 40, 69–88.
Allan, T. (1994) *Law, Liberty, and Justice: The Legal Foundations of British Constitutionalism* (Oxford: Clarendon).
Andrews, D. and W. Ploberger (1994) 'Optimal tests when a nuisance parameter is present only under the alternative', *Econometrica*, 62, 1383–1414.
Annesley, C. (2001) 'New Labour and welfare' in S. Ludlam and M. Smith (eds.) *New Labour in Government* (Basingstoke: Macmillan).
Annesley, C., I. Engeli and F. Gains (2012) 'Gendering executive attention: the impact of women's representation', *Perspectives on Europe*, 42, 33–40.
Bachrach, P. and M. Baratz (1962) 'Two faces of power', *American Political Science Review*, 56, 947–952.
Bacon, R. and W. Eltis (1976) *Britain's Economic Problem: Too Few Producers* (London: Macmillan).
Bai, J. and P. Perron (2003) 'Computation and analysis of multiple structural change models', *Journal of Applied Econometrics*, 18, 1–22.
Bailey, J. and R. J. O'Connor (1975) 'Operationalizing incrementalism: measuring the muddles', *Public Administration Review*, 35, 60–66.
Balchin, P. (2002) *Housing Policy: An Introduction* (London: Routledge).
Baldock, J., N. Manning and S. Vickerstaff (2007) *Social Policy* (Oxford: Oxford University Press).
Baldwin, T., R. Ford and S. Tendler (2002) 'Blair "nationalises" police over muggings', *The Times*, 3 July: 1.
Ball, S. (1990) *Politics and Policy Making in Education: Explorations in Policy Sociology* (London: Routledge).
Bara, J. (2005) 'A question of trust: implementing party manifestos', *Parliamentary Affairs*, 58, 585–599.
Barry, D. and J. A. Hartigan (1993) 'A Bayesian analysis for change point problems', *Journal of the American Statistical Association*, 88, 309–319.
Bartle, J., S. Dellepiane-Avellaneda and J. Stimson (2010) 'The moving centre: preferences for government activity in Britain, 1950-2005', *British Journal of Political Science*, 41, 259–285.

Baumgartner, F. (2006) 'Punctuated equilibrium theory and environmental policy' in R. Repetto (ed.) *Punctuated Equilibrium and the Dynamics of US Environmental Policy* (New Haven, CT: Yale University Press).

Baumgartner, F., C. Breunig, C. Green-Pedersen, B. Jones, P. Mortensen, M. Nuytemans and S. Walgrave (2009a) 'Punctuated equilibrium in comparative perspective', *American Journal of Political Science*, 53, 603–620.

Baumgartner, F., S. Brouard and E. Grossman (2009b) 'Agenda-setting dynamics in France: revisiting the partisan hypothesis', *French Politics*, 7, 75–95.

Baumgartner, F. and J. Gold (2002) 'The changing agenda of Congress and the Supreme Court' in F. Baumgartner and B. Jones (eds.) *Policy Dynamics* (Chicago, IL: Chicago University Press).

Baumgartner, F., C. Green-Pedersen and B. Jones (2006) 'Comparative studies of policy agendas', *Journal of European Public Policy*, 13, 959–974.

Baumgartner, F. and B. Jones (1993) *Agendas and Instability in American Politics*, 1st edn (Chicago, IL: University of Chicago Press).

Baumgartner, F. and B. Jones (2002) *Policy Dynamics* (Chicago, IL: Chicago University Press).

Baumgartner, F. and B. Jones (2009) *Agendas and Instability in American Politics*, 2nd edn (Chicago, IL: University of Chicago Press).

Baumgartner, F., B. Jones and M. MacLeod (1998) 'Lessons from the trenches: quality, reliability, and usability in a new data source', *The Political Methodologist*, 8, 1–11.

Baumgartner, F., B. Jones and M. MacLeod (2000) 'The evolution of legislative jurisdictions', *Journal of Politics*, 62, 221–249.

Baumgartner, F., B. Jones and J. Wilkerson (2011) 'Comparative studies of policy dynamics', *Comparative Political Studies*, 44, 947–972.

Beer, S. (1965) *Modern British Politics* (London: Faber & Faber).

Behr, R. and S. Iyengar (1985) 'Television news, real-world cues, and changes in the public agenda', *Public Opinion Quarterly*, 49, 38–57.

Benn, T. (1980) *Arguments for Socialism* (London: Penguin Books).

Bennett, W., R. Lawrence and S. Livingston (2007) *When the Press Fails: Political Power and the News Media from Iraq to Katrina* (Chicago, IL: University of Chicago Press.)

Berlinski, S., T. Dewan, K. Dowding and G. Subrahmanyam (2009) 'Choosing, moving and resigning in the UK' in K. Dowding (ed.) *The Selection of Ministers in Europe: Hiring and Firing* (London: Routledge).

Berry, W. (1990) 'The confusing case of budgetary incrementalism: too many meanings for a single concept', *Journal of Politics*, 52, 167–196.

Bertelli, A. and R. Dolan (2009) 'The demand and supply of Parliamentary policy advocacy: evidence from UK health policy 1997–2005', *Government and Opposition* 44, 219–243.

Bertelli, A. and P. John (n.d.) *Public Policy Investment: A New Theory of British Statecraft*, forthcoming with Oxford University Press.

Bertelli, A. and P. John (2013) 'Public policy investment: risk and return in British politics', *British Journal of Political Science*, forthcoming.

Bertelli, A. and L. Lynn (2004) 'Policymaking in the parallelogram of forces: common agency and human service provision', *Policy Studies Journal*, 32, 28–29.

Bertelli, A. M. (2008) 'Credible governance? Transparency, political control, the personal vote and British quangos', *Political Studies*, 56, 807–829.

References 217

Bevan, G., H. Copeman, J. Penin and R. Rosser (1980) *Health Care Priorities and Management* (London: Croom Helm).
Bevan, G. and C. Hood (2006) 'What's measured is what matters: targets and gaming in the English public health system', *Public Administration*, 84, 517–538.
Bevan, S. and W. Jennings (2010) 'The opinion-responsiveness of government agendas: public opinion, institutions, and agendas in the United Kingdom 1945–2009', paper presented at the *American Political Science Association Conference*, Washington, DC, 3 September 2010.
Bevan, S. and P. John (n.d.) 'Policy representation by party leaders and followers in UK Prime Minister's Questions', unpublished paper, http://papers.ssrn.com/sol3/papers.cfm?abstract_id=2039356.
Bevan, S., P. John and W. Jennings (2011) 'Keeping party programmes on track: the transmission of the policy agendas of executive speeches to legislative outputs in the United Kingdom', *European Political Science Review*, 3, 395–417.
Bevir, M. (2008) 'The Westminster model, governance and judicial reform', *Parliamentary Affairs*, 61, 559–577.
Bevir, M. and R. Rhodes (2003) *Interpreting British Governance* (London: Routledge).
Birkland, T. (1997) *After Disaster: Agenda Setting, Public Policy, and Focusing Events* (Washington, DC: Georgetown University Press).
Birch, A. H. (1964) *Representative and Responsible Government* (London: George Allen and Unwin).
Boydstun, A. (n.d.) *Politics, Media, and Agenda-Setting: How Policy Issues Make the News* (under contract, University of Chicago Press).
Bräuninger, T. and M. Debus (2009) 'Legislative agenda-setting in parliamentary democracies', *European Journal of Political Research*, 48, 804–839.
Braybrooke, D. and C. Lindblom (1963) *A Strategy of Decision* (New York: The Free Press).
Breeman, G., D. Lowery, C. Poppelaars, S. Resodihardjo, A. Timmermans and J. de Vries (2009) 'Political attention in a coalition system: analyzing Queen's Speeches in the Netherlands 1945–2007', *Acta Politica*, 44, 1–27.
Breunig, C. (2006) 'The more things change, the more stay the same: a comparative analysis of budget punctuations', *Journal of European Public Policy*, 13, 1069–1085.
Breunig, C. and C. Koski (2006) 'Punctuated equilibria and budgets in the American States', *Policy Studies Journal*, 34, 363–379.
Breunig, C. and C. Koski (2012) 'The tortoise or the hare? Incrementalism, punctuations, and their consequences', *Policy Studies Journal*, 40, 45–68.
Brock, M. (1973) *The Great Reform Act* (London: Hutchinson Press).
Budge, I. and D. Farlie (1983) *Explaining and Predicting Elections: Issue Effects and Party Strategies in Twenty-Three Democracies* (London: Allen and Unwin).
Budge, I., H-D. Klingerman, A. Volkers, J. Bara and E. Tanenbaum (2001) *Mapping Policy Preferences I (1945–1998)* (Oxford: Oxford University Press).
Bullock, A. (1967) *The Life and Times of Ernest Bevin Volume Two: Minister of Labour 1940–45* (London: Heineman).
Bulpitt, J. (1983) *Territory and Power in the United Kingdom: An Interpretation.* (Manchester: Manchester University Press).
Bulpitt, J. (1986) 'The discipline of the new democracy: Mrs Thatcher's domestic statecraft', *Political Studies*, 34, 19–39.

Bulpitt, J. (1988) 'Rational politicians and conservative statecraft in the open polity' in P. Byrd (ed.) *British Foreign Policy under Thatcher* (Oxford: Philip Allan).

Bulpitt, J. and P. Burnham (1999) 'Operation Robot and the British political economy in the early-1950s: the politics of market strategies', *Contemporary British History*, 13, 1–31.

Burch, M. and I. Holliday (1996) *The British Cabinet System* (Hemel Hempstead: Prentice Hall).

Busenberg, G. (2004) 'Wildfire management in the United States: the evolution of a policy failure', *Review of Policy Research*, 21, 145–156.

Butler, D., A. Adonis and T. Travers. (1994) *Failure in British Government: The Politics of the Poll Tax* (Oxford: Oxford University Press).

Butler, D. and D. Stokes (1974) *Political Change in Britain: The Evolution of Electoral Choice* (London: Macmillan).

Button, J. (1978) *Black Violence: Political Impact of the 1960s Riots* (Princeton, NJ: Princeton University Press).

Campbell, J. (1993) *Edward Heath* (London: Jonathan Cape).

Carmines, E. and J. Stimson (1989) *Issue Evolution: Race and the Transformation of American Politics* (Princeton, NJ: Princeton University Press).

Carpenter, D. (1996) 'Adaptive signal processing, hierarchy, and budgetary control in federal regulation', *The American Political Science Review*, 90, 283–302.

Cashore, B. and M. Howlett (2007) 'Punctuating which equilibrium? Understanding thermostatic policy dynamics in Pacific Northwest forestry', *American Journal of Political Science*, 51, 532–551.

Castles, F. (ed.) (1982) *The Impact of Political Parties: Politics and Policies in Capitalist Democratic States* (London and Beverly Hills, CA: Sage).

Cerny, P. and M. Evans (2004) 'Globalization and policy under New Labour', *Policy Studies*, 25, 51–65.

Chaqués-Bonafont, L. and A. Palau (2011) 'Assessing the responsiveness of Spanish policymakers to the priorities of their citizens', *West European Politics*, 34, 706–730.

Chapman, C. (ed.) (2009) *Radical Reforms: Perspectives on an Era of Educational Change* (London: Routledge).

Chong, T. (1995) 'Partial parameter consistency in a misspecified structural change model', *Economics Letters*, 49, 351–357.

Chow, G. (1960) 'Tests of equality between sets of coefficients in two linear regressions', *Econometrica*, 28, 591–605.

Clark, T. and A. Dilnot (2002) *Long-Term Trends in British Taxation and Spending* (London: Institute for Fiscal Studies).

Clarke, P. (2004), *Hope and Glory Britain 1900–2000* (London: Penguin).

Cobb, R. W. and C. D. Elder (1983) *Participation in American Politics: The Dynamics of Agenda-Building*, 2nd edn (Boston, MA: Allyn & Bacon).

Cohen, J. (1995) 'Presidential rhetoric and the public agenda', *American Journal of Political Science*, 39, 87–107.

Cole, A. and P. John (2001) *Local Governance in England and France* (London: Routledge).

Cowley, P. (2002) *Revolts and Rebellions: Parliamentary Voting under Blair* (London: Politico's).

Cowley, P. and M. Stuart (2012) 'A coalition with two wobbly wings: backbench dissent in the House of Commons', *Political Insight*, 3, 8–11.

Cox, G. (1987) *The Efficient Secret: The Cabinet and the Development of Political Parties in Victorian England* (Cambridge: Cambridge University Press).
Crawford, R., C. Emmerson and G. Tetlow (2009) *A Survey of Public Spending in the UK* (London: Institute for Fiscal Studies).
Crenson, M. (1971) *The Un-Politics of Air Pollution: A Study of Non-Decisionmaking in the Cities* (Baltimore, MD and London: The Johns Hopkins Press; Toronto, ON: Copp Clark).
Crewe, I., B. Särlvik and J. Alt (1977) 'Partisan dealignment in Britain 1964–1974', *British Journal of Political Science*, 7, 129–190.
Dahl, R. and C. Lindblom (1953) *Politics, Economics, and Welfare* (Chicago, IL: University of Chicago Press).
Darwin, J. (1987) 'The end of empire', *Contemporary British History*, 1, 51–55.
Darwin, J. (1988) *Britain and Decolonisation: The Retreat from Empire in the Post-War World* (Basingstoke: Macmillan).
Davis, O., M. Dempster and A. Wildavsky (1966) 'A theory of the budget process', *American Political Science Review*, 60, 529–547.
Davis, O., M. Dempster and A. Wildavsky (1974) 'Toward a predictive theory of government expenditure: U.S. Domestic Appropriations', *British Journal of Political Science*, 4, 419–452.
Deakin, N. and R. Parry (2000) *The Treasury and Social Policy* (Basingstoke: Palgrave).
DeLeon, P. (1999) 'The stages approach to the policy process: what has it done? Where is it going?' in P. Sabatier (ed.) *Theories of the Policy Process*, 1st edn (Boulder, CO: Westview Press).
Department of Employment and Productivity (1969) *In Place of Strife: A Policy for Industrial Relations* (London: HMSO).
Dicey, A. (1917) *Lectures on the Relation Between Law and Public Opinion in England During the Nineteenth Century* (LF ed.). http://oll.libertyfund.org/?option=com_staticxt&staticfile=show.php%3Ftitle=2119&Itemid=27.
Donoughue, B. (2005) *Downing Street Diary With Harold Wilson in No. 10* (London: Jonathan Cape).
Dorey, P. (2006) *The Labour Governments, 1964–1970* (London: Routledge).
Downs, A. (1972) 'Up and down with ecology: the "issue-attention cycle"', *The Public Interest*, 28, 38–50.
Driver, S. and L. Martell (2006) *New Labour* (Cambridge: Polity).
Dudley, G. and J. Richardson (2000) *Why Does Policy Change? Lessons from British Transport Policy, 1945–99* (London: Routledge).
Dunleavy, P. (1981) *The Politics of Mass Housing in Britain, 1945–1975: A Study of Corporate Power and Professional Influence in the Welfare State* (Oxford: Oxford University Press).
Dunleavy, P. (1995) 'Policy disasters: explaining the UK's record', *Public Policy and Administration*, 10, 52–70.
Dunleavy, P. (2006) 'The Westminster model and the distinctiveness of British Politics' in P. Dunleavy, R. Heffernan, P. Cowley and C. Hay (eds.) *Developments in British Politics*, 8 (Basingstoke: Macmillan).
Dunleavy, P. and R. Rhodes (1990) 'Core executive studies in Britain', *Public Administration*, 68, 3–28.
Dunsire, A. (1986) 'A cybernetic view of guidance, control and evaluation in the public sector' in F-X. Kaufmann, G. Majone, V. Ostrom and W. Wirth (eds.)

Guidance, Control and Evaluation in the Public Sector: The Bielefeld Interdisciplinary Project (New York: Walter de Gruyter).
Dunsire, A. (1993) 'Modes of governance' in Jan Kooiman (ed) *Modern Governance. New Government–Society Interactions* (London: Sage): 21–34.
Entman, R. (1989) 'How the media affect what people think: an information processing approach', *The Journal of Politics*, 51, 347–370.
Erdman, C. and J. Emerson (2007) 'bcp: An R Package for performing a Bayesian analysis of change point problems', *Journal of Statistical Software*, 23, 1–13.
Erdman, C. and J. Emerson (2008) 'A fast Bayesian change point analysis for the segmentation of microarray data', *Bioinformatics*, 24, 2143–2148.
Etzioni, A. (1967) 'Mixed-scanning: a "third" approach to decision-making', *Public Administration Review*, 27, 385–392.
Ewing, K. (2009) 'Judiciary' in M. Flinders, A. Gamble, C. Hay and M. Kenny (eds.) *The Oxford Handbook of British Politics* (Oxford: Oxford University Press).
Farrall, S. and W. Jennings (2012) 'Policy feedback and the criminal justice agenda: an analysis of the economy, crime rates, politics and public opinion in post-war Britain', *Contemporary British History*, 26, 467–488.
Featherstone, K. (2009) 'Europeanization' in M. Flinders, A. Gamble, C. Hay and M. Kenny (eds.) *The Oxford Handbook of British Politics* (Oxford: Oxford University Press).
Feeley, T. (2002) 'The multiple goals of science and technology policy' in F. Baumgartner and B. Jones (eds.) *Policy Dynamics* (Chicago, IL: Chicago University Press).
Fielding, S. (2003) *The Labour Governments 1964–1970: Labour and Cultural Change* (Manchester: Manchester University Press).
Finer, S. (1975) 'Introduction: adversary politics and electoral reform' in S. E. Finer (ed.) *Adversary Politics and Electoral Reform* (London: Anthony Wigram).
Flinders, M. (2008) *Delegated Governance and the British State: Walking Without Order* (Oxford: Oxford University Press).
Flinders, M. (2009) 'Delegation' in M. Flinders, A. Gamble, C. Hay and M. Kenny (eds.) *The Oxford Handbook of British Politics* (Oxford: Oxford University Press).
Foster, C. (2005) *British Government in Crisis, or, the Third English Revolution* (Oxford: Hart).
Freeman, J. (1955) *The Political Process: Executive–Bureau–Legislative Committee Relations* (Garden City, NY: Doubleday & Company).
Fry, G. (1983) 'Succession of government in the post-colonial states of the South Pacific: new support for constitutionalism?', *Politics*, 18, 48–60.
Gallup. (2001). *Gallup Political and Economic Index, Monthly Reports 1959 to 2001* (London: Gallup Organisation).
Gamble, A. (1988) *The Free Economy and the Strong State: The Politics of Thatcherism* (Basingstoke: Macmillan).
Gandy, O. (1982) *Beyond Agenda Setting: Information Subsidies and Public Policy* (Norwood, NJ: Ablex Publishers).
Garrett, G. (1998) *Partisan Politics in the Global Economy* (New York and Cambridge: Cambridge University Press).
Gaventa, J. (1980) *Power and Powerlessness: Quiescence and Rebellion in an Appalachian Valley* (Urbana, IL: University of Illinois Press).

Geweke, J. (1992) 'Evaluating the accuracy of sampling-based approaches to calculating posterior moments' in J. Bernado, J. Berger, A. Dawid and A. Smith (eds.) *Bayesian Statistics*, 4 (Oxford: Clarendon Press).
Gist, J. (1982) ' "Stability" and "competition" in budget theory', *American Political Science Review*, 76, 859–872.
Glennerster, H. (2000) *British Social Policy Since 1945* (Oxford: Blackwell).
Goodin, R. E. (1982) 'Discounting discounting', *Journal of Public Policy*, 2, 53–71.
Grant, W. (1995) *Pressure Groups, Politics and Democracy in Britain* (Brighton: Harvester Wheatsheaf).
Gray, A., W. Jenkins and B. Segsworth (2000) *Budgeting, Auditing, Evaluating: Functions and Integration in Seven Governments* (New Brunswick, NJ: Transaction Publishers).
Greener, I. (2008) *Healthcare in the UK: Understanding Continuity and Change* (Bristol: Policy Press).
Green-Pedersen, C. and J. Wilkerson (2006) 'How agenda-setting attributes shape politics: basic dilemmas, problem attention and health politics developments in Denmark and the US', *Journal of European Public Policy*, 13, 1039–1052.
Grossman, G. and E. Helpman (2001) *Special Interest Politics* (Cambridge, MA and London: MIT Press).
Hakhverdian, A. (2010) 'Political representation and its mechanisms: a dynamic left-right approach for the United Kingdom, 1976–2006', *British Journal of Political Science*, 40, 835–856.
Hall, S. (1980) 'Popular democratic vs. authoritarian populism' in A. Hunt (ed.) *Marxism and Democracy* (London: Lawrence and Wishart).
Hann, A. (ed.) (2007) *Health Policy and Politics* (Aldershot: Ashgate).
Hansen, B. (1997) 'Inference in TAR models', *Studies in Nonlinear Dynamics and Econometrics*, 2, 1–14.
Hansen, B. (2001) 'The new econometrics of structural change: dating breaks in US labor productivity', *Journal of Economic Perspectives*, 15, 117–128.
Hardin, J. (2002) 'Multiple topics, multiple targets, multiple goals, and multiple decision-makers: Congressional considerations of comprehensive health care reform' in F. Baumgartner and B. Jones (eds.) *Policy Dynamics* (Chicago, IL: Chicago University Press).
Harrison, B. (1999) 'The rise, fall and rise of political consensus in Britain since 1940', *History*, 184, 301–324.
Hay, C. (1999) *The Political Economy of New Labour: Labouring under False Pretences?* (Manchester: Manchester University Press).
Hay, C. (2007) 'Whatever happened to Thatcherism', *Political Studies Review*, 5, 183–201.
Hay, C. (2010) 'Chronicles of a death foretold: the winter of discontent and construction of the crisis of British Keynesianism', *Parliamentary Affairs*, 63, 446–470.
Hay, C. and S. Farrall (2011) 'Establishing the ontological status of Thatcherism by gauging its "periodisability": towards a "cascade theory" of public policy radicalism', *British Journal of Politics and International Relations*, 13, 439–458.
Hazell, R. (2010) 'Conclusion: where will the Westminster model end up?' in R. Hazell (ed.) *Constitutional Futures Revisited: Britain's Constitution to 2020* (Basingstoke: Palgrave).

Heath, A., R. Jowell and J. Curtice (2001) *The Rise of New Labour Party Policies and Voter Choices* (Oxford: Oxford University Press).
Heclo, H. and A. Wildavsky (1974) *The Private Government of Public Money: Community and Policy Inside British Politics* (London: Macmillan).
Heidelberger, P. and P. D. Welch (1983) 'Simulation run length control in the presence of an initial transient', *Operations Research*, 31, 1109–1144.
Hennessy, P. (2007) *Having It So Good: Britain in the 1950s* (London: Penguin).
Herman, V. (1974) 'What governments say and what they do: analysis of post-war Queen's speeches', *Parliamentary Affairs*, 28, 22–30.
Hobolt, S. and R. Klemmensen (2005) 'Responsive government? Public opinion and government policy preferences in Britain and Denmark', *Political Studies*, 53, 379–402.
Hobolt, S. and R. Klemmensen (2008) 'Government responsiveness and political competition in comparative perspective', *Comparative Political Studies*, 41, 309–337.
Hofferbert, R. and I. Budge (1992) 'The party mandate and the Westminster model: election programmes and government spending in Britain, 1948–85', *British Journal of Political Science*, 22, 151–182.
Hogg, Q. (1976) 'Elective dictatorship', *The Listener*, 21 October 1976, 496–500.
Hogwood, B. (1992) *Trends in British Public Policy: Do Governments Make Any Difference?* (Milton Keynes: Open University Press).
Holmes, M. (1985) *The Labour Government, 1974–79* (London: Macmillan).
Hood, C. (1983) *The Tools of Government* (London: Macmillan).
Hood, C. and H. Margetts (2007) *The Tools of Government in the Digital Age* (Basingstoke: Macmillan).
House of Commons Library (2009) *Parliamentary Trends: Statistics About Parliament*, Research Paper 09/69 (London: House of Commons Library).
Howlett, M and A. Migone (2011) 'Charles Lindblom is alive and well and living in punctuated equilibrium land', *Politics and Society*, 30, 53–62.
Hudson, J. (1994) 'Granger causality, rational expectations and aversion to unemployment and inflation', *Public Choice*, 80, 9–21.
Hunt, V. (2002) 'The multiple and changing goals of immigration reform: a comparison of House and Senate activity, 1947–1993' in F. Baumgartner and B. Jones (eds.) *Policy Dynamics* (Chicago, IL: Chicago University Press).
Imbeau, L. M., F. Pétry and M. Lamari (2001) 'Left-right party ideology and government policies: a meta-analysis', *European Journal of Political Research* 40, 1–29.
Ipsos MORI (9 March 2005) 'Voting intention by newspaper readership'. Retrieved 16 September 2011 from, http://www.ipsos-mori.com/research publications/researcharchive/755/Voting-Intention-by-Newspaper-Readership .aspx.
Iyengar, S. (1991) *Is Anyone Responsible? How Television Frames Political Issues* (Chicago, IL: University of Chicago Press).
Iyengar, S. and D. Kinder (2010) *News That Matters: Television and American Opinion*, Updated edn (Chicago, IL: University of Chicago Press).
Jacoby, W. (2000) 'Issue framing and public opinion on government spending', *American Journal of Political Science*, 44, 750–767.
Jasperson, A., D. Shah, M. Watts, R. Faber and D. Fan (1998) 'Framing and the public agenda: media effects on the importance of the Federal budget deficit', *Political Communication*, 15, 205–224.

Jennings, W. (2009) 'The public thermostat, political responsiveness and error-correction: border control and asylum in Britain, 1994–2007', *British Journal of Political Science*, 39, 847–870.
Jennings, W. (2010) 'Bureaucratic performance and control in British politics: asylum policy 1994–2007', *British Journal of Politics and International Relations*, 12, 539–568.
Jennings, W., S. Bevan and P. John (2011a) 'The agenda of British government: the Speech from the Throne, 1911–2008', *Political Studies*, 59, 74–98.
Jennings, W., S. Bevan, A. Timmermans, G. Breeman, S. Brouard, L. Chaqués Bonafont, C. Green-Pedersen, P. John, P. Mortensen and A. Palau (2011b) 'The effects of core functions of government on the diversity of executive agendas', *Comparative Political Studies*, 44, 1001–1030.
Jennings, W. and P. John (2009) 'The dynamics of political attention: public opinion and the Queen's Speech in the United Kingdom', *American Journal of Political Science*, 53, 838–854.
Jennings, W. and C. Wlezien (2011) 'Distinguishing between most important problems and issues?', *Public Opinion Quarterly*, 75, 545–555.
Jensen, C. (2009) 'Policy punctuations in mature welfare states', *Journal of Public Policy*, 29, 287–303.
John, P. (2006a) 'Explaining policy change: the impact of the media, public opinion and political violence on urban budgets in England', *Journal of European Public Policy*, 13, 1053–1068.
John, P. (2006b) 'The policy agendas project: a review', *Journal of European Public Policy*, 13, 975–986.
John, P. (2011) *Making Policy Work* (London: Routledge).
John, P. (2012) *Analyzing Public Policy*, 2nd edn (London: Routledge).
John, P. and S. Bevan (2012) 'What are policy punctuations? Large changes in the legislative agenda of the UK Government 1911–2008', *Policy Studies Journal*, 40, 89–108.
John, P., S. Bevan and W. Jennings (n.d.) 'Party politics and the policy agenda: the case of the United Kingdom' in C. Green-Pederson and S. Walgrave (eds.) *Policy Agenda-Setting Theory: From Policy Theory to a Theory of Politics*, forthcoming.
John, P., S. Bevan and W. Jennings (2011) 'The policy-opinion link and institutional change: the legislative agenda of the UK and Scottish Parliaments', *Journal of European Public Policy*, 18, 1052–1068.
John, P. and W. Jennings (2010) 'Punctuations and turning points in British politics: the policy agenda of the Queen's speech', *British Journal of Political Science*, 40, 561–586.
John, P. and H. Margetts (2003) 'Policy punctuations in the UK: fluctuations and equilibria in central government expenditure since 1951', *Public Administration*, 81, 411–432.
John, P. and H. Margetts (2009) 'The latent support for the extreme right in British politics', *West European Politics*, 32, 496–513.
Johnson, N. (1975) *In Search of the Constitution* (London: Anthony Wigram).
Jones, B. (1995) *Reconceiving Decision-Making in Democratic Politics: Attention, Choice, and Public Policy*, 1st edn (Chicago, IL: University of Chicago Press).
Jones, B. (1999) 'Bounded rationality', *Annual Review of Political Science*, 2: 297–321.
Jones, B. (2001) *Politics and the Architecture of Choice* (Chicago, IL: University of Chicago Press).

Jones, B. and F. Baumgartner (2004) 'Representation and agenda setting', *Policy Studies Journal*, 32, 1–24.
Jones, B. and F. Baumgartner (2005a) *The Politics of Attention: How Government Prioritizes Problems* (Chicago, IL: University of Chicago Press).
Jones, B. and F. Baumgartner (2005b) 'A model of choice for public policy', *Journal of Public Administration Research and Theory*, 15, 325–351.
Jones, B., F. Baumgartner, F. C. Breunig, C. Wlezien, S. Soroka, M. Foucault, A. François, C. Green-Pedersen, C. Koski, P. John, P. Mortensen, F. Varone and S. Walgrave (2009a) 'A general empirical law of public budgets: a comparative analysis', *American Journal of Political Science*, 53, 855–873.
Jones, B., F. Baumgartner and J. True (1998) 'Policy punctuations: US Budget Authority, 1947–1995', *Journal of Politics*, 60, 1–33.
Jones, B., F. Baumgartner and J. True (2002) 'Policy macropunctuations: how the US budget evolved', discussion paper for conference, *Budgetary Policy Change: Measures and Models*, Oxford, 8–9 March 2002.
Jones, B., H. Larsen-Price and J. Wilkerson (2009b) 'Representation and American Governing Institutions', *Journal of Politics*, 71, 277–290.
Jones, B., T. Sulkin and H. Larsen (2003) 'Policy punctuations in American political institutions', *American Political Science Review*, 97, 151–169.
Jones, B., J. True and F. Baumgartner (1997), 'Does incrementalism stem from political consensus or from institutional gridlock?', *American Journal of Political Science*, 41, 1319–1339.
Jones, H. (1996) 'A bloodless counter-revolution: the Conservative Party and the defence of inequality 1945–51' in H. Jones and H. Kandiah (eds.) *The Myth of Consensus* (Basingtoke: Macmillan).
Jones, H. and H. Kandiah (eds.) (1996) *The Myth of Consensus* (Basingtoke: Macmillan).
Jordan, A., R. Wurzel and A. Zito (2003) *New Instruments of Environmental Governance? National Experiences and Prospects* (London: Frank Cass & Co. Ltd.).
Judge, D. (1993) *The Parliamentary State* (London: Sage).
Judge, D. (2005) *Political Institutions in the United Kingdom* (Oxford: Oxford University Press).
Kavanagh, D. (1989) *Consensus Politics from Attlee to Thatcher* (London: Institute of Contemporary British History).
Kelly, S. (2002) *The Myth of Mr. Butskell: The Politics of British Economic Policy, 1950–1955* (Aldershot: Ashgate).
Keman, H. (2006) 'Parties and government: features of governing in representative democracies' in R. Katz and W. Crotty (eds.) *Handbook of Party Politics* (London and Thousand Oaks, CA: Sage).
Kerr, P. (2001) *Postwar British Politics: From Conflict to Consensus* (London: Routledge).
King, A. (1976) 'Modes of executive–legislative relations: Great Britain, France, and West Germany', *Legislative Studies Quarterly*, 1, 11–36.
King, A. (2007) *The British Constitution* (Oxford: Oxford University Press).
King, A. and R. Wybrow (eds.) (2001) *British Political Opinion, 1937–2000: The Gallup Polls* (London: Politico's Publishing).
Kingdon, J. (1995) *Agendas, Alternatives, and Public Policies*, 2nd edn (New York: Longman).
Klein, R. (2010) *The New Politics of the NHS: From Creation to Reinvention*, 6th edn (Oxford: Radcliffe).

Kleykamp, M. (2004) 'A Bayesian change point model for historical time series analysis', *Political Analysis*, 12, 354–374.
Kollman, K., J. Miller and S. Page (1992) 'Adaptive parties and spatial elections', *American Political Science Review*, 86, 929–937.
Kollman, K., J. Miller and S. Page (1998) 'Political parties and electoral landscapes', *British Journal of Political Science*, 28, 139–158.
Krippendorff, K. (2004) *Content Analysis: An Introduction to Its Methodology*, 2nd edn (Thousand Oaks, CA: Sage).
Krutz, G. (2002) 'Omnibus legislation: an institutional reaction to the rise of new issues' in F. Baumgartner and B. Jones (eds.) *Policy Dynamics* (Chicago, IL: Chicago University Press).
Lasswell, H. (1956) *The Decision Process* (College Park, MD: University of Maryland Press).
Laver, M., K. Benoit and J. Garry (2003) 'Extracting policy positions from political tests using words as data', *American Political Science Review*, 97, 311–331.
Layton-Henry, Z. (1984) *The Politics of Race in Britain* (London: Allen and Unwin).
Lijphart, A. (1999) *Patterns of Democracy: Government Forms and Performance in Thirty-Six Countries* (New Haven, CT: Yale University Press).
Lindblom, C. (1959) 'The science of muddling through', *Public Administration Review*, 19, 78–88.
Lindblom, C. (1975) *The Policy-Making Process* (Englewood Cliffs, NJ and London: Prentice-Hall).
Lindblom, C. (1977), *Politics and Markets: The World's Political Economic. Systems* (New York: Basic Books).
Lindblom, C. (1979) 'Still muddling, not yet through', *Public Administration Review*, 39, 517–526.
Lukes, S. (1974) *Power: A Radical View* (London: Macmillan).
MacLeod, M. (2002) 'The logic of positive feedback: telecommunications policy through the creation, maintenance, and destruction of a regulated monopoly' in F. Baumgartner and B. Jones (eds.) *Policy Dynamics* (Chicago, IL: Chicago University Press).
Majone, G. (1989) *Evidence, Argument, & Persuasion in the Policy Process* (New Haven, CT: Yale University Press).
Manza, J. and F. Cook (2002) 'A democratic polity? Three views of policy responsiveness to public opinion in the United States', *American Politics Research*, 30, 630–667.
Marquand, D. (1981) 'Club government: the crisis of the Labour Party in national perspective', *Government & Opposition*, 16, 19–36.
Marquand, D. (1988) *The Unprincipled Society* (London: Cape).
Marsh, D. (1995) 'Explaining "Thatcherite" policies: beyond uni-dimensional explanation', *Political Studies*, 43, 595–613.
Marsh, D. and R. Rhodes (1992a) *Implementing Thatcherite Policies: Audit of an Era* (Buckingham: Open University Press).
Marsh, D. and R. Rhodes (1992b) *Policy Networks in British Government* (Oxford: Clarendon Press).
Marshall, G. (1984) *Constitutional Conventions: The Rules and Forms of Political Accountability* (Oxford: Oxford University Press).
Marwick, A. (1968) *Britain in the Century of War: War, Peace and Social Change 1900–1967* (Boston, MA: Little, Brown and Company).

226 References

Mayhew, D. (1991) *Divided We Govern* (New Haven, CT: Yale University Press).
Mazmanian, D. and P. Sabatier (1983) *Implementation and Public Policy* (Glenview, IL: Scott Foresman).
McCombs, M. (2004) *Setting the Agenda: The Mass Media and Public Agenda* (Malden, MA: Blackwell).
McCombs, M. and D. Shaw (1972) 'The agenda–setting function of mass media', *Public Opinion Quarterly*, 36, 176–187.
McDonald, M. and I. Budge (2005) *Elections, Parties, Democracy: Conferring the Median Mandate* (Oxford: Oxford University Press)
McKenzie, R. (1955) *British Political Parties: The Distribution of Power within the Conservative and Labour Parties* (London: W. Heinemann).
McLean, I. (2010) *What's Wrong with the British Constitution?* (Oxford: Oxford University Press).
Middlemas, K. (1979) *Politics in Industrial Society* (London: André Deutch).
Midtbø, T. (1999) 'The impact of parties, economic growth, and public sector expansion: a comparison of long-term dynamics in the Scandinavian and Anglo-American democracies', *European Journal of Political Research*, 35, 199–223.
Mikhaylov, S., M. Laver and K. Benoit (2012) 'Coder reliability and misclassification in the human coding of party manifestos', *Political Analysis*, 20, 78–91.
Miliband, R. (1991) *Parliamentary Socialism: A Study of the Politics of Labour* (London: Allen and Unwin).
Mintrom, M. and P. Norman (2009) 'Policy entrepreneurship and policy change', *Policy Studies Journal*, 37, 649–667.
Moran, M. (1977) *The Politics of Industrial Relations: The Origins, Life, and Death of the 1971 Industrial Relations Act* (London: Macmillan).
Moran, M. (2001a) 'Not steering but drowning: policy catastrophes and the regulatory state', *Political Quarterly*, 72, 414–427.
Moran, M. (2001b) 'The rise of the regulatory state in Britain', *Parliamentary Affairs*, 54, 19–34.
Moran, M. (2002) 'Understanding the regulatory state', *British Journal of Political Science*, 32, 391–413.
Moran, M. (2003) *The British Regulatory State: High Modernism and Hyper-Innovation* (Oxford: Oxford University Press).
Moran, M. (2009) *Business, Politics, and Society: An Anglo-American Comparison* (Oxford: Oxford University Press).
Mortensen, P. (2005) 'Policy punctuations in Danish local budgeting', *Public Administration*, 83, 931–950.
Mortensen, P., C. Green-Pedersen, G. Breeman, L. Chaqués-Bonafont, W. Jennings, P. John, A. Palau and A. Timmermans (2011) 'Comparing government agendas: executive speeches in the Netherlands, United Kingdom, and Denmark', *Comparative Political Studies*, 44, 973–1000.
Namenwirth, J. and R. Weber (1987) *Dynamics of Culture* (London: Allen & Unwin).
Natchez, P. and I. Bupp (1973) 'Policy and priority in the budgetary process', *American Political Science Review*, 67, 951–963.
Neustadt, R. (1969) 'White House and Whitehall' in A. King (ed.) *The British Prime Minister* (London: Macmillan).

North, D. (1990) *Institutions, Institutional Change and Economic Performance* (Cambridge: Cambridge University Press).

Norton, P. (2005) *Parliament in British Politics* (Basingstoke: Palgrave).

Norton, P. (2011) *The British Polity*, 5th edn (Boston, MA: Longman).

Olshen, A. and E. Venkatraman (2004) 'Circular binary segmentation for the analysis of array-based DNA copy number data', *Biostatistics*, 5, 557–572.

Owen, N. (1996) 'Decolonisation and postwar consensus' in H. Jones and H. Kandiah (eds.) *The Myth of Consensus* (Basingtoke: Macmillan).

Padgett, J. (1980) 'Bounded rationality in budgetary research', *The American Political Science Review*, 74, 354–372.

Padgett, J. (1981) 'Hierarchy and ecological control in federal budgetary decision making', *American Journal of Sociology*, 87, 75–129.

Page, E. (2001) *Governing by Numbers: Delegated Legislation and Everyday Policy Making* (Oxford: Hart Publishing).

Page, E. (2003) 'The civil servant as legislator: law making in British administration', *Public Administration*, 81, 651–679.

Parsons, W. (1995) *Public Policy* (Brighton: Edward Elgar).

Peters, B. and B. Hogwood (1985) 'In search of the issue attention cycle', *The Journal of Politics*, 47, 238–253.

Petrocik, J. (1996) 'Issue ownership in presidential elections, with a 1980 case study', *American Journal of Political Science*, 40, 825–850.

Pierson, C. (2004) *Politics in Time: History, Institutions, and Social Analysis* (Princeton, NJ: Princeton University Press).

Pimlott, B., D. Kavanagh and P. Morris (1989) 'Is the "post-war consensus" a myth?', *Contemporary Record*, 2, 12–15.

Pralle, S. (2003) 'Venue shopping, political strategy, and policy change: the internationalization of Canadian forestry advocacy', *Journal of Public Policy*, 23, 233–260.

Pressman, J. and A. Wildavsky (1973) *Implementation: How Great Expectations in Washington Are Dashed in Oakland* (Berkeley, CA: University of California Press).

Prindle, D. (2006) 'Stephen Jay Gould as a political theorist', *Politics and the Life Sciences*, 25, 2–14.

Prindle, D. (2012) 'Importing concepts from biology into political science: the case of punctuated equilibrium', *Policy Studies Journal*, 40, 21–44.

Pugh, M. (2002) *The Making of Modern British Politics*, 3rd edn (Oxford: Basil Blackwell).

Quandt, R. (1960) 'Tests of the hypothesis that a linear regression obeys two separate regimes', *Journal of the American Statistical Association*, 55, 324–330.

Quinn, K., B. Monroe, M. Colaresi, M. Crespin and D. Radev (2010) 'How to analyze political attention with minimal assumptions and costs', *American Journal of Political Science*, 54, 209–228.

Ranson, S. (1989) 'Education reform' in J. Stewart and G. Stoker (eds.) *The Future of Local Government* (London: Macmillan).

Rawnsley, A. (2000) *Servants of the People: The Inside Story of New Labour* (London: Hamish Hamilton).

Rawnsley, A. (2010) *The End of the Party: The Rise and Fall of New Labour* (London: Penguin).

Repetto, R. (ed.) (2006) *Punctuated Equilibrium and the Dynamics of U.S. Environmental Policy* (New Haven, CT: Yale University Press).

Resodihardjo, S. (2009) *Crisis and Change in the British and Dutch Prison Services: Understanding Crisis-Reform Processes* (Farnham: Ashgate).

Rhodes, R. (1988) *Beyond Westminster and Whitehall: The Sub-central Governments of Britain* (London: Unwin Hyman).

Rhodes, R. (1997) *Understanding Governance: Policy Networks, Governance, Reflexivity, and Accountability* (Milton Keynes: Open University Press).

Richards, D. and M. Smith (2002) *Governance and Public Policy in the United Kingdom* (Oxford: Oxford University Press).

Richardson, J. and A. Jordan (1979) *Governing under Pressure: The Policy Process in a Post-parliamentary Democracy* (Oxford: Robertson).

Robertson, D. (1976) *A Theory of Party Competition* (London: John Wiley & Sons).

Robinson, S., F. Caver, K. Meier and L. O'Toole (2007) 'Explaining policy punctuations: bureaucratization and budget change', *American Journal of Political Science*, 51, 140–150.

Rollings, N. (1996) 'Butskellism, the postwar consensus and the managed economy' in H. Jones and H. Kandiah (eds.) *The Myth of Consensus* (Basingtoke: Macmillan).

Rose, R. (1974) *The Problem of Party Government* (New York: Free Press).

Rose, R. (1980) *Do Parties Make a Difference* (London: Chatham House).

Rose, R. and P. Davies (1994) *Inheritance in Public Policy: Change Without Choice in Britain* (New Haven, CT: Yale University Press).

Russell, M. (2010) 'A stronger second chamber? Assessing the impact of House of Lords reform in 1999 and the lessons for bicameralism', *Political Studies*, 58, 866–885.

Saalfeld, T. (2003) 'The United Kingdom: still a single "chain of command"? The hollowing out of the "Westminster model"' in K. Strøm, W. Müller and T. Bergman (eds.) *Delegation and Accountability in Parliamentary Democracies* (Oxford: Oxford University Press).

Sabatier, P. (1986) 'Top-down and bottom-up approaches to implementation research: a critical analysis and suggested synthesis', *Journal of Public Policy*, 6, 21–48.

Sabatier, P. and H. Jenkins-Smith (eds.) (1993) *Policy Change and Learning: An Advocacy Coalition Approach* (Boulder, CO: Westview).

Sachs, J., R. Cooper and S. Fischer (1981) 'The current account and macroeconomic adjustment in the 1970s', *Brookings Papers on Economic Activity*, 1981, 201–282.

Sanders, D. (1990) *Losing an Empire, Finding a Role: British Foreign Policy Since 1945* (Basingstoke: Macmillan).

Saran, R. (1973) *Policy-making in Secondary Education: A Case Study* (Oxford: Clarendon).

Schattschneider, E. E. (1960) *The Semisovereign People: A Realist's View of Democracy in America* (Chicago, IL: Holt, Rinehart and Winston).

Schmidt, M. (1996) 'When parties matter: a review of the possibilities and limits of partisan influence on public policy', *European Journal of Political Research*, 30, 155–183.

Schulman, P. (1975) 'Non-incremental policy making: notes toward an alternative paradigm', *American Political Science Review*, 69, 1354–1370.

Schulman, P. (1980) *Large-scale Policymaking* (New York: Elsevier North Holland).

Seldon, A. (1981) *Churchill's Indian Summer* (London: Hodder and Stoughton).
Seldon, A. (1994) 'Consensus: a debate too long', *Parliamentary Affairs*, 47, 501–514.
Sheingate, A. (2006) 'Promotion versus precaution: the evolution of biotechnology policy in the United States', *British Journal of Political Science*, 36, 243–268.
Shepsle, K. (1979) 'Institutional arrangements and equilibrium in multidimensional voting models', *American Journal of Political Science*, 23, 27–59.
Simon, H. (1955) 'A behavioral model of rational choice', *The Quarterly Journal of Economics*, 69, 99–118.
Smith, B. (1976) *Policy-Making in British Government* (Oxford: Martin Robertson and Co. Ltd.).
Smith, M. (1990) *The Politics of Agricultural Support in Britain: The Development of the Agricultural Policy Community* (Aldershot: Dartmouth Publishing Company Limited).
Smith, M. (1992) 'The agricultural policy community: maintaining a close relationship' in R. Rhodes and D. Marsh (eds.) *Policy Networks in British Government* (Oxford: Clarendon Press).
Smith, M. (1999) *The Core Executive in Britain* (Basingstoke: Macmillan).
Smith, S. and M. Smith (1988) 'Analytical background: approaches to the study of foreign policy' in M. Smith, S. Smith and B. White (eds.) *British Foreign Policy* (London: Unwin Hyman).
Soroka, S. (2006) 'Good news and bad news: asymmetric responses to economic information', *Journal of Politics*, 68, 372–385.
Soroka, S. and C. Wlezien (2005) 'Opinion–policy dynamics: public preferences and public expenditure in the United Kingdom', *British Journal of Political Science*, 35, 665–689.
Soroka, S. and C. Wlezien (2010) *Degrees of Democracy: Politics, Public Opinion, and Policy* (Cambridge: Cambridge University Press).
Soroka, S., C. Wlezien and I. McLean (2006) 'Public expenditures in the UK: how measures matter', *Journal of the Royal Statistical Society A*, 169, 255–271.
Stone, D. (1989) 'Causal stories and the formation of policy agendas', *Political Science Quarterly*, 104, 281–300.
Streeck, W. and K. Thelen (eds.) (2005) *Beyond Continuity: Institutional Change in Advanced Political Economies* (Oxford: Oxford University Press).
Studlar, D. (1978) 'Policy voting in Britain: the colored immigration issue in the 1964, 1966, and 1970 general elections', *The American Political Science Review*, 72, 46–64.
Sulkin, T. (2005) *Issue Politics in Congress* (Cambridge: Cambridge University Press).
Swank, D. (2002) *Global Capital, Political Institutions, and Policy Change in Developed Welfare States* (Cambridge: Cambridge University Press).
Talbert, J. and M. Potoski (2002) 'The changing public agenda over the postwar period' in F. Baumgartner and B. Jones (eds.) *Policy Dynamics* (Chicago, IL: Chicago University Press).
Thain, C. and M. Wright (1995) *The Treasury and Whitehall* (Oxford: Clarenden Press).
Thane, P. (2000) 'Labour and welfare' in D. Tanner, P. Thane and N. Tiratsoo (eds.) *Labour's First Century* (Cambridge: Cambridge University Press).

Theodoulou, S. and C. Kofinis (2004) *The Art of the Game: Understanding American Public Policy Making* (Belmont, CA: Wadsworth/Thomson Learning).
Tomlinson, J. (2009) 'After decline?', *Contemporary British History*, 23, 395–406.
Toynbee, P. and D. Walker (2010) *The Verdict: Did Labour Change Britain?* (London: Granta).
True, J. (2002) 'The changing focus of national security policy' in F. Baumgartner and B. Jones (eds.) *Policy Dynamics* (Chicago, IL: Chicago University Press).
True, J., B. Jones and F. Baumgartner (1999) 'Punctuated equilibrium theory: explaining stability and change in policymaking' in P. Sabatier (ed.) *Theories of the Policy Process* (Boulder, CO: Westview Press).
Tsebelis, G. (1995) 'Decision making in political systems: veto players in presidentialism, parliamentarism, multicameralism and multipartyism', *British Journal of Political Science*, 25, 289–325.
Tsebelis, G. (2002) *Veto Players: How Political Institutions Work* (Princeton: Princeton University Press).
Volkens, A. (2002) *Manifesto Coding Instructions. Discussion Paper FS III 02-201* (Berlin: WZB).
Walgrave, S. and M. Nuytemans (2009) 'Friction and party manifesto change in 25 countries, 1945-98', *American Journal of Political Science*, 53, 190–206.
Walgrave, S. and F. Varone, (2008) 'Punctuated equilibrium and agenda-setting: bringing parties back in: policy change after the Dutroux crisis in Belgium', *Governance*, 21, 365–395.
Walker, J. (1977) 'Setting the agenda in the U.S. senate: a theory of problem selection', *British Journal of Political Science*, 7, 423–445.
Weakliem, D. (2003) 'Public opinion research and political sociology', *Research in Political Sociology*, 12, 49–80.
Western, B. and M. Kleykamp (2004) 'A Bayesian change point model for historical time series analysis', *Political Analysis*, 12, 354–374.
Whitehead, P. (1985), *The Writing on the Wall* (London: Michael Joseph/Channel 4).
Wildavsky, A. (1984) *The Politics of the Budgetary Process*, 4th edn (Boston, MA: Little Brown).
Wilkerson, J., T. Feeley, N. Schiereck and C. Sue (2002) 'Using bills to trace attention in Congress: policy windows in health care legislation' in F. Baumgartner and B. Jones (eds.) *Policy Dynamics* (Chicago, IL: Chicago University Press).
Wilson, D. (1994) 'The Westminster model in comparative perspective' in I. Budge and D. McKay (eds.) *Developing Democracy. Comparative Research in Honour of J F P Blondel* (London: Sage Publications).
Wlezien, C. (2005) 'On the salience of political issues: the problem with "Most Important Problem"', *Electoral Studies*, 24, 555–579.
Wlezien, C. and S. Soroka (2007) 'The relationship between public opinion and policy' in R. Dalton and H-D. Klingemann (eds.) *The Oxford Handbook of Political Behavior* (Oxford: Oxford University Press).
Workman, S., B. Jones and A. Jochym (2009) 'Information processing and policy dynamics', *Policy Studies Journal*, 37, 75–92.
Youris, T. (ed.) (1990) *Implementation in Public Policy* (Aldershot: Dartmouth).

Author Index

Addison, P., 27–8
Adler, S., 4, 43
Alesina, A., 5, 206
Alexandrova, P., 10
Allan, T., 27
Allison, K., xii
Andrews, D., 115
Annesley, C., 67, 177
Atlee, C., 64

Bachrach, R., 29
Bacon, R., 30
Bai, J., 115
Bailey, J., 6
Baldock, J., 73
Baldwin, T., 165
Ball, S., 71
Bara, J., 168
Baratz, M., 29
Barry, D., 116, 126–9, 213
Bartle, J., 34, 200
Baumgartner, F., xii, 3, 8, 9, 10, 36, 40–3, 54, 94–5, 97, 99, 112, 115, 125, 131, 140, 147, 153, 157, 166, 170, 201, 203, 205
Baybrooke, D., 5
Beer, S., 14
Behr, R., 153
Benn, T., 25
Bennett, W., 153
Berlinski, S., 17
Berry, W., 6
Bertelli, A., xi, 4, 5, 16, 200, 204–5
Bevan, S., xi, 29, 96, 140, 146, 149, 194, 200, 210
Bevin, E., 28
Bevir, M., 14
Binding, K., xii
bin Sadat, W., xii
Birch, A. H., 24, 26, 205

Birkland, T., 4, 153, 166
Blair, T., x, 31, 35, 56, 71, 72, 121, 177, 185, 198
Boydstun, A., 52, 157
Bradbury, J., xii
Bräuninger, T., 3
Breeman, G., 18
Breunig, C., 9
Brock, M., 24
Brown, G., 35, 58, 101, 121
Budge, I., 5, 6, 88, 170, 181, 200
Bullock, A., 28
Bulpitt, J., 29, 34, 39, 60, 118, 204–5, 209
Bupp, I., 6
Burch, M., 15
Burnham, P., 118
Busenberg, G., 10
Butler, D., 36, 137, 204
Butler, R., 27
Button, J., 5

Cairney, P., xii
Callaghan, J., 71
Campbell, J., 119, 193
Carmines, E., 157
Carpenter, D., 9, 12
Cashore, B., 10
Castles, F., 5, 6, 206
Cerny, P., 16
Chapman, C., 71
Chaqués-Bonafont, L., xii, 140
Chester, H., xii
Chong, T., 115
Chow, G., 115
Churchill, W., 28
Clark, T., 193
Clarke, P., 30, 111
Cobb, R. W., 5, 130, 153, 166
Cohen, J., 18

Author Index

Cole, A., 71
Cook, F., 140
Copeland, P., xii
Cowley, P., 16, 48, 208
Cox, G., 15, 33
Crawford, R., 174, 194–5
Crenson, M., 29
Crewe, I., 34

Dahl, R., 5
Darwin, J., 28
Davies, P., 26, 36, 170, 197, 203
Davis, O., 5, 9
Deakin, N., 169
Debus, M., 3
DeLeon, P., 14
Dicey, A., 27, 131
Dilnot, A., 193
Dolan, A., 200
Dorey, P., 31, 72
Downs, A., 4, 7, 79, 131, 157, 204
Driver, S., 35
Dudley, G., 118
Dunleavy, P., 14–16, 28, 36, 204
Dunsire, A., 205

Eden, A., 31
Elder, C. D., 5, 130, 153, 166
Eltis, W., 30
Emerson, J., 126–7, 213
Erdman, C., 126–7, 213
Etzioni, A., 7
Evans, M., 16
Ewing, K., 16

Fairlie, D., 88, 181
Farrall, S., 120, 135, 184, 200, 209
Featherstone, K., 16
Feeley, T., 43
Fielding, S., 31, 118
Finer, S., 33, 38
Flinders, M., 16
Foster, C., 16
Freeman, J., 2
Fry, G., 123

Gaitskell, H., 27
Gamble, A., 34
Gandy, O., 153

Garrett, G., 5
Gaventa, J., 29
Geweke, J., 127
Gist, J., 6
Glennerster, H., 27–8
Gold, J., 43
Goodin, R. E., 6
Gorbachev, M., 92
Grant, W., xii, 202
Gray, A., 172
Greener, L., 69, 194
Green-Pederson, C., xii, 135, 185
Grossman, G., 209

Hakhverdian, A., 60, 200
Hall, S., 34
Halpin, D., xii
Hann, A., 70
Hansen, B., 115
Hardin, J., 43
Harrison, B., 28
Hartigan, J. A., 116, 126–9, 213
Hay, C., 34–5, 40, 120, 200, 209
Hazell, R., 16, 32
Heath, E., 30, 35
Heclo, H., 14, 26, 169, 197, 203
Heidelberger, P., 127
Helpman, E., 209
Hennessy, P., 28
Herman, V., 19, 168
Hobolt, S., 18
Hofferbert, R., 5–6, 170
Hogg, Q., 33
Hogwood, B., 8
Holliday, I., 15
Holmes, M., 31, 123
Hood, C., 18, 69
Howard, M., 68, 124
Howlett, M., 9, 10
Hudson, J., 131
Hughes, C., xii
Hunt, V., 43

Imbeau, L. M., 5
Ipsos-MORI, 52
Iyengar, S., 153

Jacoby, W., 153
Jasperson, A., 153

Author Index

Jenkins-Smith, H., 6
Jennings, W., xi, 19, 39, 51, 56, 87, 93, 95, 100, 119–20, 121, 131, 135, 138, 140, 146, 149, 183, 184, 190, 198, 211
Jensen, C., 9
John, P., xi, 4–5, 9, 14, 18, 36, 39, 41, 67, 71, 95–6, 100, 119–20, 121, 130–1, 140, 146, 170, 183, 190, 198, 200, 204–6, 210
Johnson, N., 16
Jones, B., 3, 6, 8–10, 27–8, 36, 40–3, 54, 94–5, 97, 99, 112, 115, 125, 131, 140, 147, 153, 157, 166, 170, 190–1, 201, 203, 205
Jordan, A., 2, 26, 79, 111, 203
Judge, D., xii, 15–16

Kandiah, H., 28
Kavanagh, D., 28
Kelly, S., 28
Keman, H., 5
Kerr, P., 34, 39, 209
Kinder, D., 153
King, A., 15–16, 50, 133
Kingdon, J. W., 1, 5, 8, 17, 131
Klein, R., 70
Klemmensen, R., 18
Kleykamp, M., 116, 213
Kofinis, C., 168
Kollman, K., 12
Koski, C., 9
Krippendorff, K., 210
Krutz, G., 43

Lasswell, H., 14
Laver, M., 200
Layton-Henry, Z., 123
Lijphart, A., 14, 34
Lindblom, C., 5–6, 29, 203
Liu, H., xii
Lovenduski, J., xii
Lukes, S., 29

MacLeod, M., 43
Majone, G., 5
Major, J., 58, 207
Manza, J., 140

Margetts, H., xi, 10, 18, 36, 39, 121, 170, 190
Marquand, D., 32
Marsh, D., 2, 34, 39, 169, 209
Marshall, G., 13, 25
Martell, L., 35
Marwick, A., 28
Mason, D., xii
Mayhew, D., 105
Mazmanian, D., 169
McCombs, M. E., 131, 153, 166
McCormick, K., xii
McDonald, M., 5, 170, 200
McKenzie, R. T., 24
McLean, I., 14–15, 17, 36
Middlemas, K., 27–9
Midtbø, T., 5
Migone, A., 9
Mikhaylov, S., 210
Miliband, R., 29
Mintrom, M., 5
Moran, M., 30, 32
Mortensen, P., 10, 18, 206
Mortimore, R., 50

Namenwirth, J., 19
Natchez, P., 6
Neustadt, R., 14
Norman, P., 5
North, D., 23–4
Norton, P., 15, 33
Nuytemans, M., 10

O'Connor, R. J., 6
Olshen, A., 115
Owen, N., 28

Padgett, J., 9, 12
Page, E., 4, 20, 48
Palau, A., 140
Parry, R., 169
Parsons, W., 7
Perri 6, xii
Perron, P., 115
Peters, B., 8
Petrocik, J., 88
Pettitt, R., xii
Pierson, C., 24
Pile, A., xii

Author Index

Pimlott, B., 28
Ploberger, W., 115
Potoski, M., 43
Powell, E., 137
Pralle, S., 10
Pressman, J., 168–9
Prindle, D., 10
Pugh, M., 27
Purcell, T., xii

Quandt, R., 115
Quinn, K., 44

Ranson, S., 71
Rawnsley, A., 35
Reilly-Cooper, R., xii
Repetto, R., 10
Resodijardjo, S., 10
Rhodes, R., 2, 14–15, 32, 39, 169, 207
Richards, D., 2, 15
Richardson, J., 2, 26, 111, 118, 203
Robertson, D., 5
Robinson, S., 10
Rollings, N., 28
Rose, R., 15, 26, 33, 36, 170, 197, 203
Russell, M., 16

Saalfeld, T., 14, 17
Sabater, A., xii
Sabatier, P., 6, 169
Sachs, J., 119
Sanders, D., 60
Saran, R., 71
Schattschneider, E. E., 5, 29
Schmidt, M., 5
Schulman, P., 6
Seldon, A., 27–8
Shaw, D., 131, 153, 166
Sheingate, A., 43
Shepsle, K., 3, 154
Simon, H., 12
Smith, B., 14, 130, 168
Smith, J., 185
Smith, M., 2, 15, 61, 202
Smith, S., 61
Soroka, S., 49, 51, 65, 140, 70, 190

Stimson, J., 157
Stokes, D., 137
Stone, D., 5
Streeck, W., 24
Stuart, M., 48, 208
Studlar, D., 137
Sulkin, T., 43
Swank, D., 5

Talbert, J., 43
Thain, P., 26, 169
Thane, P., 31, 108
Thatcher, M., 31, 34, 39, 56, 88, 137, 198
Theelen, K., 24
Theodoulou, S., 168
Timmermans, A., xii
Tomlinson, J., 30
Toynbee, P., 35
True, J., 8–10, 43, 95
Tsebelis, G., 33

Varone, F., xii, 10
Venkatraman, E., 115

Walgrave, S., xi, 10
Walker, D., 35
Walker, J. L., 5
Weakliem, D., 140
Weber, R., 19
Welch, P. D., 127
Western, B., 116, 213
Whitehead, P., 30
Wildavsky, A., 5, 14, 26, 168–9, 172, 197, 203
Wilkerson, J., 4, 43, 135, 185
Wilson, D., 14
Wilson, H., 25, 62, 72, 123
Wlezien, C., 51, 65, 131, 140, 170, 211
Workman, S., 9
Wright, M., 26, 169
Wybrow, R., 50, 133

Youris, T., 168

Zhong, Y., xii

Subject Index

Acts of Parliament, 41, 47–8, 55
  definition and coding, 21
adaptive signal processing, 9
adversarial politics, 33
advocacy coalition, 6
Afghanistan, 65, 133, 151, 163, 174, 183
Agendas and Instability in US Politics, 41–2
agriculture, 2, 42, 50, 55, 79, 92, 94, 166
  in Acts of Parliament, 57, 82–4
  budgets, 171, 180–1, 196–7
  change points: Acts of Parliament, 122; budgets, 192; media, 164; public opinion, 150; Speech from the Throne, 117–18
  major topic codes, 167
  media, 157–60
  policy agenda, 189
  public opinion, 141, 148–9
  punctuations, 103, 107, 110
  in Speech from the Throne, 57, 82–4
Al-Queda, 163
art(s)
  major topic codes, 167
  punctuations, 108

Bank of England, 30, 35
banking, 42, 93, 203–4
  in Acts of Parliament, 88–9, 103
  major topic codes, 167
  media, 154
  in Speech from the Throne, 88–9, 100–1
  see also commerce
banking industry, punctuations, 108
BH (Barry and Hartigan) approach, 126–9
Blue Book, 49–50
Bosnia, 174

Britain's Economic Problem: Too Few Producers, 30
British Academy, xi
British Political Opinion, 1937–2000, 50
budgetary expenditure, definition and coding, 48
business and commerce
  in Acts of Parliament, 89
  in Speech from the Throne, 89
  see also commerce
Business and Legislation Committee, 18
Butskellism, 27

Cabinet Office, Economic and Domestic Affairs Secretariat, 18
Central Government Supply Estimates (Budget Year-Following Year): Main Supply Estimates, 171
Central Statistical Office, 49
Chernobyl, 140
Child Support, Pensions and Social Security Act 2000, 75
church, major topic codes, 167
civil rights, 42, 55, 92, 202
  in Acts of Parliament, 86–7, 103–4
  budgets, 171
  change points: Acts of Parliament, 121–4; media, 164; Speech from the Throne, 117
  major topic codes, 167
  media, 158, 160
  public opinion, 141, 148
  punctuations, 94, 100, 104, 107, 110
  in Speech from the Throne, 86–7, 100–1
  see also immigration
civil rights, minority issues, immigration and civil liberties
  in Acts of Parliament, 86–7
  in Speech from the Throne, 86–7
  see also civil rights; immigration
club government, 32

236 Subject Index

Cold War, 92, 108, 133, 163, 165, 174, 195–6, 206
commerce, 42
  in Acts of Parliament, 57, 88–9
  budgets, 171
  change points: Acts of Parliament, 122; budgets, 192; media, 164; public opinion, 150; Speech from the Throne, 117
  major topic codes, 167
  media, 154, 158, 160
  public opinion, 141; *see also* banking
  punctuations, 101, 107, 110
  in Speech from the Throne, 57, 88–9
community development, planning and housing
  in Acts of Parliament, 75–7; *see also* housing
  in Speech from the Throne, 75–7, 101
Company Securities (Insider Dealing) Act 1985, 89
Comparative Agendas Project, xi, 44–5
Comprehensive Spending Review, 171
Conciliation and Arbitration Service, 46
Congress, Policy Agendas Project, 43
Congressional Quarterly, 43
conservatism hypothesis, 25–6, 33, 37
Cotton (Centralised Buying) Act 1947, 84
crime, punctuations, 2, 107, 110
  see also law and crime
Cuban Missle Crisis, 133

Daily Telgraph, The, 51–2
death, major topic codes, 167
defence, 21, 42, 45, 50, 56, 92
  in Acts of Parliament, 57, 62–5, 69, 103, 143
  budgets, 171, 173–4, 196–7
  change points: Acts of Parliament, 122; budgets, 192, 195; media, 164; public opinion, 150; Speech from the Throne, 117
  major topic codes, 167
  media, 157, 158, 159, 160–3
  policy agenda, 183–4

public opinion, 132–3, 141, 150
punctuations, 100, 102–3, 107–8
in Speech from the Throne, 57, 62–5, 69, 143
Democracies, 34
Department of Employment and Productivity, 109–10
Diceyan tradition, 15
disability benefits, punctuations, 108
domestic commerce
  in Speech from the Throne, 101
  see also commerce
Donovan Commission, 30

economic emphasis hypothesis, 29–31
economy, 18, 28–9, 35, 39, 42–3, 56, 92, 202–3
  in Acts of Parliament, 57–60, 62, 104
  budgets, 171–3, 181
  change points, 117–18, 122–3, 124–5; Acts of Parliament, 122; budgets, 191–3, 195; media, 164–5; Speech from the Throne, 117
  major topic codes, 167
  media, 158, 160–3
  policy agenda, 182–3
  public opinion, 133–4, 141, 150
  punctuations, 94, 103–4
  in Speech from the Throne, 57–60, 62, 73
  see also macroeconomics
education, x, 17, 21, 26, 28, 30, 35, 42, 50, 55
  in Acts of Parliament, 57–9, 71–3, 75, 101–2, 103
  budgets, 171, 176–7, 196
  change points: Acts of Parliament, 121–2, 126; budgets, 192; media, 164; public opinion, 150; Speech from the Throne, 117
  major topic codes, 167
  media, 158, 160
  policy agenda, 186
  public opinion, 135, 141, 144, 146, 148–9, 150
  punctuations, 107–9

in Speech from the Throne, 57–9, 71–3, 75, 100–2, 142–4, 146
Education (Handicapped Children) Act 1970, 109
elective dictatorship, 33
Employment Protection Act, 194
energy, 42, 92
  in Acts of Parliament, 57, 84–6, 103
  budgets, 171
  change points: Acts of Parliament, 122; budgets, 192; media, 164; public opinion, 150; Speech from the Throne, 117
  major topic codes, 167
  media, 158, 160
  public opinion, 138–41, 148
  punctuations, 107, 110
  in Speech from the Throne, 57, 84–6, 100, 102
environment, 42–3, 56
  in Acts of Parliament, 57, 78–80, 83–4, 93, 104
  budgets, 171, 179
  change points: Acts of Parliament, 122; budgets, 192; media, 164; public opinion, 150; Speech from the Throne, 117
  major topic codes, 167
  media, 158, 160
  public opinion, 138–40, 148
  punctuations, 100, 102–4, 107–8, 110
  in Speech from the Throne, 57, 78–80, 83–4, 93, 100, 102
Environmental Protection Act 1990, 79, 124
European Convention on Human Rights, 15, 35
European Economic Community, 32
European Science Foundation, xi

Falkland Islands, 3, 31
Falklands War, 102, 132, 163, 174, 183
Family Income Supplements Act 1970, 74
family issues
  in Acts of Parliament, 67–8
  in Speech from the Throne, 67–8

finance, in Speech from the Throne, 101
Financial Times, The, 157
fire, major topic codes, 167
focused adaptation, 10–13, 21, 201–2, 204
focused adaptation hypothesis, 38–40
foreign affairs, 29, 93
  in Acts of Parliament, 57
  budgets, 171
  change points: Acts of Parliament, 122; budgets, 192; media, 164; public opinion, 150; Speech from the Throne, 117
  major topic codes, 167
  media, 158–61
  public opinion, 132–4, 141–2, 150–1; *see also* international affairs
  punctuations, 107
  in Speech from the Throne, 57
foreign affairs emphasis hypothesis, 31
foreign trade, 92
  in Acts of Parliament, 90–1
  change points, 119, 123
  in Speech from the Throne, 90–1
  see also trade
Forestry (Sale of Land) (Scotland) Act 1963, 82

Gallup, 46, 50, 211, 213
Gallup Political and Economic Index, 50
General Agreement on Tariffs and Trade (GATT), 90–1
Geneva Conference, 65
Governing Under Pressure, 26
government operations, 42, 56, 93
  in Acts of Parliament, 57, 65–6, 103
  budgets, 171, 181, 196
  change points: Acts of Parliament, 120–2; budgets, 192; media, 164; public opinion, 150; Speech from the Throne, 117–18
  major topic codes, 167
  media, 158–60
  public opinion, 141
  punctuations, 108, 110

in Speech from the Throne, 57, 65–6, 100, 102
Great Reform Act of 1832, 24
Green Party, 79, 124
Gulf War, 132–3, 163, 165, 183
see also Persian Gulf War

health, x, 18, 21, 25, 28, 35, 42–4, 50
 in Acts of Parliament, 57, 69–71
 budgets, 171, 174–6, 196
 change points: Acts of Parliament, 122; budgets, 192, 194–5; media, 164; Speech from the Throne, 117
 major topic codes, 167
 media, 158, 160
 policy agenda, 185
 public opinion, 135–6, 141, 148, 150–1
 punctuations, 108, 110
 in Speech from the Throne, 57, 69–71, 100–1, 143–4, 146
health care, Policy Agendas Project, 43
high-salience punctuations, 112
housing, 26–8, 42, 50
 in Acts of Parliament, 57, 145–6
 budgets, 171, 178–9, 181, 196–7
 change points: Acts of Parliament, 122; budgets, 192–4; media, 164; public opinion, 150; Speech from the Throne, 117
 major topic codes, 167
 media, 158, 160
 policy agenda, 187–8
 public opinion, 141, 148, 150
 punctuations, 107–8, 110
 in Speech from the Throne, 57, 100, 142, 145–6
 see also community development, planning and housing
Housing Finance Act 1972, 151, 193
human interest, major topic codes, 167

immigration, 42–3, 86–7
 in Acts of Parliament, 104, 146
 Policy Agendas Project, 43
 public opinion, 135–8, 148
 punctuations, 109

in Speech from the Throne, 101, 146
 see also civil rights
Immigration Act 1971, 123
incrementalism, 5–7, 38, 203–4
 criticism of, 6
 disjointed, 203–4
Industrial Development Act, 59
Industrial Re-organisation Corporation, 59
In Place of Strife, 109–10
institutions, 14, 23–7, 30, 37, 40, 207
interest groups, 2, 25–6, 32, 37, 40
international affairs, 37, 42, 56
 in Acts of Parliament, 61–2, 103–4, 143
 in Speech from the Throne, 61–2, 102, 143
 see also foreign affairs
Ipsos-MORI, 50
Iraq, 174
Iraq War, 31, 65, 133, 151, 162–3, 166, 183
Iron and Steel Act, 59
issue attention cycle, 7–8
issue monopolies, 8

Keynesian, 28, 34–5
King's Speech, 19–20
 see also Speech from the Throne
Korean War, 64, 150, 174
Kosovo, 65, 151, 163, 174
Kuwait, 174

labour and employment, 42, 54
 in Acts of Parliament, 57, 87–8, 103
 budgets, 171, 196
 change points: Acts of Parliament, 122; budgets, 192; media, 164–5; public opinion, 150; Speech from the Throne, 117
 major topic codes, 167
 media, 158, 160, 162
 public opinion, 138, 141, 150–1
 punctuations, 107, 110
 in Speech from the Throne, 57, 87–8, 100–1
labour unions, 29
 see also trade unions

lands, 42
  in Acts of Parliament, 57, 103
  budgets, 171
  change points: Acts of Parliament, 122; budgets, 192; media, 164; public opinion, 150; Speech from the Throne, 117
  major topic codes, 167
  media, 158, 160
  public opinion, 141, 150
  punctuations, 107
  in Speech from the Throne, 57
  see also territorial issues
law and crime, 42, 45, 56
  in Acts of Parliament, 57, 67–8, 146
  budgets, 171, 174–5, 196
  change points, 117, 121–2; Acts of Parliament, 122; budgets, 192, 194–5; media, 164–5; public opinion, 150; Speech from the Throne, 117
  major topic codes, 167
  media, 158–60
  policy agenda, 184–5
  public opinion, 135–6, 141, 148, 150
  punctuations, 102, 107, 110
  in Speech from the Throne, 57, 67–78, 146–7
  see also crime
Les Trente Glorieuses, 32
Lib-Lab pact of 1977–1978, 48
London School of Economics and Political Science, xi
long boom, 35
low- and high-salience punctuations, 105–6
low-salience punctuactions, 112
  see also punctuated equilibrium

macroeconomics, 42
  in Acts of Parliament, 128, 142
  change points, 129
  public opinion, 142, 148
  in Speech from the Throne, 42, 56–60, 102, 114
  see also economy
media, definition and coding, 51
MII (most important issues), 50–1

minority issues, in Acts of Parliament, 104
MIP (most important problem), 50–1
monetary policy, 30
monopolistic instability, 37
  see also non-monopolistic instability
monopolistic stability, 37
  see also non-monopolistic stability
museums, punctuations, 108

National Health Service (NHS), 50, 69, 151, 185
National Health Service Act 1948, 111
National Science Foundation, 42
national security, 43
National Service (Release of Conscientious Objectors) Act of 1946, 64
National Steel Corporation, 59
neo-pluralist, 29
New Hebrides Act 1983, 123
New Labour, x, 7, 40, 56, 60, 65, 70–1, 73, 75, 77, 93, 100–2, 110–12, 120–1, 123–4, 126, 135, 146, 173, 177–8, 184–5, 198, 203, 206–8
New Towns Act 1946, 76
New York Times, 43, 211
NHS, *see* National Health Service
9/11, 133
1988 Education Reform Act, 72
non-monopolistic instability, 37
non-monopolistic stability, 37
North Atlantic Treaty Organization (NATO), 65
Northern Ireland Assembly Act 1973, 66

Offensive Weapons Act 1996, 68, 124
Office of National Statistics, 49
Office of Population Censuses and Surveys, 49
OPEC, 119
Operation Robot, 118
Options for Change, 195

Pakistan Act 1974, 123
Papua New Guinea, Western Somoa and Nauru (Miscellaneous Provisions) Act 1980, 123

240 Subject Index

parties, major topic codes, 167
pensions, punctuations, 108
Persian Gulf War, 183
    see also Gulf War
planning, change points, 118
pluralism, 32–4
Policy Agendas Project, 41–4, 95, 104, 130, 168, 170, 199
    Congress, 43
    health care, 43
    immigration, 43
    national security, 43
    science and technology, 43
    Supreme Court, 43
    telecommunications, 43
policy elites, 11
policy entrepreneur, 5
policy environment, 11–12
policy landscape, 17
political elites, 27, 30, 39
Politics of Attention, The, 41
Price Commission Act 1977, 123
Prices and Income Act, 59
procedural punctuations, 104–5
public lands and water management (territorial issues)
    in Acts of Parliament, 80–2
    in Speech from the Throne, 80–2
    see also lands
public opinion, definition, 50–1, 131–2
Public Service Vehicles (Travel Concessions) Act 1955, 77
punctuated equilibrium, 8–10, 12, 23, 38–9, 41, 95–7, 131, 205
    negative feedback, 9
    positive feedback, 9
punctuation hypothesis, 32–6
punctuations (policy), 40

Queen's Speech, 19–20, 46
    see also Speech from the Throne

Race Relations Act 1976, 137
regional government, major topic codes, 167
relative power hypothesis, 29
Representation of the People Act 1974, 123
"Rivers of Blood", 137

science, 42–3
    in Acts of Parliament, 89–90, 103–4
    budgets, 171
    change points, media, 164
    major topic codes, 167
    media, 158, 160
    public opinion, 141
    punctuations, 107, 110
    in Speech from the Throne, 89–90
science and technology, Policy Agendas Project, 43
Scottish Nationalist Party, 32
Second World War, 41, 49, 64, 83, 174, 183, 202
serial judgement model, 9
serial processing, 8
Sexual Offences (Conspiracy and Incitement) Act 1996, 68, 124
Single European Act 1986, 79
Social Contract, 193–4
social policy, 68–9
    punctuations, 108
Social Security Pensions Act 1975, 194
social welfare, 42, 50
    in Acts of Parliament, 57, 73–5, 103, 145–6
    budgets, 171, 177–8, 197
    change points: Acts of Parliament, 122, 124; budgets, 192–3; media, 164; public opinion, 150; Speech from the Throne, 117
    major topic codes, 167
    media, 158–60
    policy agenda, 186–7
    public opinion, 141, 148, 150
    punctuations, 107, 110
    in Speech from the Throne, 57, 73–5, 101, 142, 145
Soviet Union, 92
space, in Speech from the Throne, 102
Speech from the Throne, 19–21, 25, 41
    change points, 117
    definition and coding, 45–7
    see also King's Speech or Queen's Speech
sport, major topic codes, 167
stages model, 14

State Earnings Related Pension
    Scheme, The, 194
*Statement on Defence Estimates 1991:
    Britain's Defence for the 1990s*, 195
structural hypothesis, 31–2
Suez crisis, 31, 62, 150
Supplementary Estimates, 171
Supreme Court, Policy Agendas
    Project, 43

Teaching Council (Scotland) Act 1970,
    109
telecommunications, Policy Agendas
    Project, 43
territorial issues
    change points, 123
    public opinion, 150–1
    see also lands
Thatcherism, 40
Times The, 51–2, 109, 154–7, 159, 163,
    165–6, 211
    change to broadsheet, 52
    change to tabloid, 52–3
    union dispute, 53–4
Town and Country Planning Act, 76
trade, 42
    in Acts of Parliament, 57
    budgets, 171
    change points: Acts of Parliament,
        122; budgets, 192; media, 164;
        public opinion, 150; Speech
        from the Throne, 117–18
    major topic codes, 167
    media, 158–60
    public opinion, 141
    in Speech from the Throne, 57
    see also foreign trade
trade unions, 30
    see also labour unions
transport, 42, 50
    in Acts of Parliament, 57, 77–8
    budgets, 171, 179–80
    transport, change points: Acts of
        Parliament, 122; budgets, 192;
        media, 164; public opinion,
        150; Speech from the Throne,
        117–18
    major topic codes, 167

media, 158, 160
policy agenda, 187–9
public opinion, 141–8
punctuations, 107, 110
in Speech from the Throne, 57,
    77–8, 100, 102
Transort Act 1980, 77–8
Trustee Savings Bank, 89

UK *Blue Book*, 49–50
    see also *Blue Book*
UK Economic and Social Research
    Council, xi
UK Policy Agendas Project, 45, 154–7,
    165, 212
    see also Policy Agendas Project
UK Policy Agendas Project Datasets, 46
Ulster Workers Council Strike of 1974,
    66
University of Manchester, xi
University of Southern California,
    xi–xii
US Policy Agendas Project, 211
    see also Policy Agendas Project

veto players, 33, 36
Vietnam, 62, 133, 150

War Damage (Valuations Appeals) Act
    of 1945, 64
weather, major topic codes, 167
welfare
    in Acts of Parliament, 103
    in Speech from the Throne, 100
    see also social welfare
Welsh National Opera Company Act
    1970, 109
Westminster model, 14, 16, 24
Westminster system, 48, 191
Whitehall, 27
Winter of Discontent, 34, 138–40
World in Action, 137
World Trade Center, 166
World Trade Organization (WTO),
    90–1

Yugoslavia, 133